HOW *to* STAND APART @ WORK

Judith Bowman, an author and internationally recognized authority on etiquette and international protocol, has written the definitive book for those wishing to hone their people skills, achieve excellence and advance in their profession. Reading and incorporating the treasure trove of pearls and wisdom that Judith imparts will allow anyone to adroitly and confidently navigate all the challenges in a myriad of business and day to day interpersonal interactions. I'm confident that the reader who follows the instructions clearly laid out, often with true stories embedded that convey powerful messages, will cruise with confidence and earn the trust and respect of many a potential business partner. Kudos to Judith for sharing her knowledge in this timely book.

—**Sanjiv Chopra**, M.B.B.S., M.A.C.P., Professor of Medicine,
Faculty Dean for Continuing Education, Harvard Medical School
Senior Consultant in Hepatology, Beth Israel Deaconess Medical Center, Boston, MA

This book has been crying out to be written. Good education and skills are necessary, but most corporations and civil society organizations also now strongly evaluate personal qualities of would-be recruits during job interviews. In this book Judith Bowman has penned detailed tips on how to improve personal qualities and effectiveness in dealing with people in the workplace. Managers at various levels will find the book useful to improve their own effectiveness, as well as for on-the-job training for their staff.

—**Mahabub Hossain**, Executive Director, BRAC

This book is like having a "Google for Graciousness." I love the format! *How to Stand Apart @ Work* is a must-read for anyone from an early careerist to an accomplished executive and I regret I did not have such a resource years ago! Despite having broken through the glass ceiling, I perhaps would not have had as many shards to contend with had I know some of the things Ms. Bowman points out. I will be gifting this book to lots of young ladies and a few of my colleagues….and know it will be a treasured resource for me as well.

—**Lynn Nicholas**, FACHE | President & CEO, Massachusetts Hospital Association

One never knows where life will take them whether they are fresh out of college or as a mature adult. Today the number of different experiences and the variety of social situations that we find ourselves in is endless and diverse. Because not everyone is raised knowing how to respond to every situation either in business, socially, or with regard to international travel. *How to Stand Apart @Work…Transforming Fine to Fabulous* is a must-read for social intelligence and a positive outcome in business and in life. I never could have imagined that I would have been exposed to so many different situations in my life including military and government protocol, entertaining and hosting prominent guests both national and international, and traveling to many foreign countries for business and social reasons. Judith Bowman shares her own personal experiences and combines them with her "Fine to Fabulous" etiquette to provide a wonderful guide that is useful for people of all ages who strive to be successful while treating others with respect."

—**Kati Machtley**, Director of The Women's Summit, Bryant University

How to Stand Apart @ Work is a "must read" on what makes for effective people skills in business. This is a book with immediate payoffs: thoughtful principles, authentic illustrations, and a well-honed set of tools to improve interpersonal skills. Bowman's top tips are sharp, practical, and masterful.

—**Philip L. Quaglieri** PhD, College of Management, University of Massachusetts Boston

It is with great pleasure that I am writing to recommend Judith Bowman, the President and Founder of Protocol Consultants International.

I became acquainted with Ms. Bowman when my company, Copyright Clearance Center, secured her to lead a "Professional Presence" executive etiquette seminar for my sales and business development staff earlier this year. I believed that my group of more than 40 customer-facing sales and account representatives could greatly benefit from the training and coaching for which her expertise is well-known. Throughout the planning process, the event itself, and in follow-up correspondence, I found Ms. Bowman to be thoughtful, authoritative and effective.

Since Ms. Bowman led our group in executive etiquette training I am pleased to share that I have both heard and seen results of the communication lessons taught so thoroughly that day. By utilizing role playing exercises and group discussions, my staff was able to review existing skills while obtaining new techniques for becoming prepared, polished and confident. Finally, we made copies of Ms. Bowman's book *Don't Take the Last Donut: New Rules of Business Etiquette* available to staff. This has been a highly sought-after resource and has been well-used as a refresher for what was learned.

If you have any additional questions, please do not hesitate to contact me directly.

—**Miles McNamee**, Vice President of Licensing and
Business Development, Copyright.com

The luxury hospitality industry demands that our associates present themselves as confident professionals who engage with others in a refined manner. We brought Judy Bowman onboard as part of our Team Member Health & Wellness Festival to provide just the right mix of information, fun, and focus in assisting our staff to recognize the nuances that define superior communication and relationship building skills. Participants commented that the workshop was "incredible," "excellent," and "gave me so much knowledge."

Judy is passionate about her work and was a delight to collaborate with when preplanning the program. She is also very engaging when presenting her material working to give you and your team an edge in advancing forward!

—**Pat Ciavola**, Director, Recruitment & Staff Development,
The Breakers, Palm Beach, FL

On May 5, 2010 Judith Bowman brought her outstanding energy to Management Grand Rounds at Children's Hospital. She covered the basics of Professional Presence, Networking, and Interpersonal Communications in an interactive session delivered in a direct, powerful and meaningful way. People walked away with a clearer sense of how they can take even the smallest steps to enhance their Personal and Professional Presence. I highly recommend Ms. Bowman's services to any organization seeking to maximize its impact on consumers, colleagues, and the competition.

—**Amy Weinberg**, Administrative Director, Children's Hospital, Boston, MA

"Judith was an inspirational speaker that educated the attendees on tips n' tricks that she has amassed throughout her career. Everyone left the conference with at least 1-2 tips from her that we took away to incorporate into our lives."

"This session was absolutely wonderful. I could have watched and listened to Judith all day. I truly enjoyed it from a professional and personal perspective. She is one of the best presenters I have ever seen. And so practical. I loved it and will use it."

"Judy had great content — she was funny, informative, and covered ground that we always think we know, but are afraid to ask."

"She was great! Such a fun topic and presentation style. It was nice that she so strongly discusses and teaches those small details no one ever tells you that you should know!"

"Very interactive, which is wonderful. She is very effective at getting the point across. And her knowledge and content are actually very needed in the world as a whole."

"Very fun session — great take aways!"

"Exceptional!"

—Comments by Attendees at New England Hospital Association, Executive Women in Healthcare Conference, from Kirsten L. Singleton, CAE, Sr. Director, Center for Education and Professional Development, Massachusetts Hospital Association, Burlington, MA 01803

Judy, I wanted to write you to let you know how beneficial your training has been to our department. Our sales desk is often required to attend special events with our clientele. At these events it is critical to our success as a firm that they represent the company professionally. Your program has helped us achieve that goal. You have helped us coach and train our people on how to effectively host a dinner, provide proper introductions, dress for success and how to handle delicate situations in a professional manner. I believe your training carries over into all aspects of our interaction with people. I have found that I personally use much of the knowledge I gained from your program in my personal life as well. I am truly pleased with your program and I would recommend it to anyone. I wish you continued success,

—**William Dron**, National Sales Manager, Inside Sales, John Hancock Funds, LLC, Boston, MA

All too often, as individuals endeavor to distinguish themselves as professionals, they overlook the huge impact that character and behavioral traits such as etiquette, manners, appearance, and civility play. More than we care to admit, it is such nuances that frequently determine who gets the job or who wins the business. I finally found a firm, Judy Bowman and Protocol Consultants International, who not only understand their importance, but can help you and your team elevate their game by raising their awareness of the "do's and don'ts" in professional as well as social settings.

—**Allen J. Williamson,** Managing Director, National Sales Director, CIMA | Rydex|SGI,

HOW*to* STAND APART @WORK

Transforming **Fine** *to* **Fabulous**

JUDITH BOWMAN

NEW YORK

HOW *to* STAND APART @ WORK
Transforming **Fine** *to* **Fabulous**

Published in New York, New York, by Morgan James Publishing. Morgan James and The Entrepreneurial Publisher are trademarks of Morgan James, LLC. www.MorganJamesPublishing.com

The Morgan James Speakers Group can bring authors to your live event. For more information or to book an event visit The Morgan James Speakers Group at www.TheMorganJamesSpeakersGroup.com.

BitLit
FOR ALL THE BOOKS YOU OWN

FREE eBook edition for your
existing eReader with purchase

_____
PRINT NAME ABOVE

For more information,
instructions, restrictions, and
to register your copy, go to
www.bitlit.ca/readers/register
or use your QR Reader to scan
the barcode:

ISBN 978-1-61448-687-9 paperback
ISBN 978-1-61448-856-9 hard cover
ISBN 978-1-61448-688-6 eBook
ISBN 978-1-61448-689-3 audio
Library of Congress Control Number:
2013945572

Cover Design by:
Rachel Lopez
www.r2cdesign.com

Interior Design by:
Bonnie Bushman
bonnie@caboodlegraphics.com

In an effort to support local communities, raise awareness and funds, Morgan James Publishing donates a percentage of all book sales for the life of each book to Habitat for Humanity Peninsula and Greater Williamsburg.

Get involved today, visit
www.MorganJamesBuilds.com.

Habitat
for Humanity®
Peninsula and
Greater Williamsburg
Building Partner

DEDICATION
Inspired by Matthew R. Schiffman

STORY

Many years ago, a well-respected national sales manager in the Financial Services industry recognized the need for *Professional Presence/*Business Etiquette services in his very established and robust financial services firm brimming with talent, and contacted us. Matt Schiffman was that national sales manager and the first person in the Financial Services world to identify this need, and introduce our *Professional Presence/*Business Etiquette services to that arena. Matt became a loyal client and ardent advocate for our message and as a result this industry quickly became a strong niche market for Protocol Consultants International.

Matt and I would check in from time to time and one day I was compelled to ask, "Matt, how do you do it? You are always so high energy, positive and gracious to everyone. People clearly respect and love you and respond so positively to you. (Plus, you always look so well put together...) How do you do it?"

To which Mr. Schiffman replied, "You know, Judy, I work hard. I travel a lot and I'm away from home. I miss my wife and my girls, and there are times I don't really like my job, however, whenever anyone asks, 'Matt, how are you doing?' regardless of how I really may be feeling... do you know what I always say?"

"What is that, Matt?" I asked.

To which he replied in his *je ne sais quoi*, indubitably charismatic manner, "I'm **fabulous**!"

Hearing that word and the way Matt said this was, in effect, an edict, and took on a life all its own. I wanted to be **fabulous**! ... and we espouse the notion that, regardless of how any of us really may be feeling, we should all endeavor to be *fabulous*.

Finding ways to transform **fine** to **fabulous** is the underlying precept of this book.

Table of Contents

ACKNOWLEDGEMENTS

I am thankful to the good people at Morgan James publishing including David Hancock, Dave and Cindy Sauer, Lyza Poulin, and the entire Morgan James Family for embracing our message early on. It has been a wonderful experience and a joy working with each of you.

Denise Yuspeh Hidalgo, Editor-*Extraordinaire*, a true professional, a gift. Thank you for treating this book as if it were your own and helping make this a reality for me; when we literally say the same word at the same time, it's all good!

Thank you to Ellen Neuborne who helped me draft the first version of this manuscript.

My mother Jeanne, who was there for me at every turn, for helping me laugh even in the face of greatest challenge and for always being there for me. Thank you for grooming me and inspiring me to be the woman I am today. We all love the way you shamelessly boast about all your children's accomplishments throughout all of *Skaneateles (!)* and beyond... Thank you for believing in me and for your love and encouragement Thank you for all your "pearls" of wisdom which I try to "wear" every day.

My beloved son Bowman... you remain the light of my life.

My husband Jay, the love of my life.

Aunt Helen, for your love and support, confidence and very special gift of friendship.

My brothers, Peter, Stephen and Ronnie, whose real-life tales provide me with great stories here and in life... my sister Kim who thought of the book cover design... my talented nieces and nephews Sarsfield, Honor and Cormac Bowman... my wonderful cousin Kevin "The Doctor"... and dear Shane Hopkins for providing me with great material... for this book and for my next, which will be a reality "tell all" manuscript!

John Maihos, my esteemed General Manager, whose loyalty, friendship and invaluable business help and advice I continue to honor. Thank you for being in my life.

Simba-Helen, Dallas, Sierra (puppies), South, Savvy (kitties), Three's, Cody, U.S.S. Laffey and Ballerina (horses), my "furry family" — I could not have written this book without you.

My dear friends Kate Murray, Nancy O'Sullivan, Catherine Gerson, Kim Prager, Ann Marie Ryan, Lynn Pivik, Catherine Blake, Jean Citarella and finally, Ms. Jacqueline for helping me through the many years and supporting me through the book writing process… and it is a process.

Thanks also to my professional colleagues and friends, Hal Lord (Asia expert), Richard Whiteley (expert on being "fully present"), Dana Mosher (men's attire) and Kaylie LaGrange (graphics — and graphics model!).

There is definitely a long list of people to thank in developing, editing, and producing this book. I sincerely hope that their work (and mine) will be of value to those of us who wish to Stand Apart @ Work™ and make the transformation from **fine** to **fabulous**!

INTRODUCTION

Interpersonal communication skills are central to the fabric of our society and quickly becoming a lost art. In today's fast-paced frenetic world, timeless people skills are not being taught and as a result, next generation leaders are massively disadvantaged. We acknowledge the opportunity at hand to restore the valuable people skills necessary to succeed in our global business climate today. While most of us may know how to behave in a way that is considered "*fine*," very few know how to truly be "*fabulous*!" Consider this book as your guide on How to Stand Apart @ Work™ with an arsenal of *fabulous* skills.

Interestingly, employers seek out and eagerly hire those who have the "it" factor and clients retain/engage those they like and *trust*. Given the high-ranking quotient for interpersonal relationships and people skills together with the call for *leadership* these days, it is not only ironic but ill-fated that many in the workplace are uninformed about basic rules governing etiquette and protocol, or even how to execute a proper handshake. Today's young adults are ambitious and educated, however, they need more than just book knowledge and technical know-how to advance. In an economy where downsizing and mergers and acquisitions are rampant, mental flexibility and alertness are required as companies hire and keep only the best of class. Therefore, those chosen and remaining need to be confident knowing that everything said and done is completely within acceptable codes of conduct and professional behavior.

The world today needs leaders. *How to Stand Apart @ Work*™ outlines specific ways to achieve leadership distinction and exude quiet confidence through *nuances*. Nuances are explicit, detailed and deliberate, however, they are intended to come across as subtle and understated, which occurs after practice. The little things get noticed — and others particularly notice when they are missing. These little things have the power to make or break relationships because they (or their absence) can make others feel exceedingly special (or slighted) which is (either) a *fabulous* (or poor) reflection on you. An effective leader is able to motivate others by demonstrating respectful gestures and using basic people skills. In so doing, important tasks are accomplished and everyone gets elevated, recognized, energized!

Doing a good job today isn't good enough and being an effective leader requires extra effort... and we are all overtaxed as it is. However, being **fabulous** is energizing and infectious and is both a lubricant and a stimulant. Moreover, it is also a showcase for work performance and competency. **Fabulous** becomes a state of mind, a form of *being* and a great way to be! Being **fabulous** holds the competitive edge and is the secret weapon of very successful people. This way "to be" is not an end or a substitute for accomplishments and expertise — it's that extra "it" factor we exude that transforms something ordinary into something extraordinary, delightfully unexpected, special.

No one is born knowing anything. We maintain that once we *know* "the difference" we can make a difference for mankind. *How to Stand Apart @ Work*™ showcases everyday business situations and illustrates how to leverage them as stand-alone opportunities to acknowledge we know "the difference," while demonstrating the ultimate respect toward others. As a result, *trust* is inspired, critical business relationships blossom, careers advance.

How to Stand Apart @ Work™ provides present and "Next Generation" leaders with the essential people skills and confidence to know how to:

- Present themselves with *confidence.*
- Interact effectively with *people* (not just IT devices).
- "Be a man/woman well-met."

This book emphasizes that the way we conduct ourselves every day, and the way we treat others, is noticed and judged. When we demonstrate more respect, listen more attentively, communicate more effectively, we are more resilient and flexible in a world where others notice. While we may live in the moment we must not lose sight of the fact that in order to be fully effective we need to be fully *present* in the moment with other people.

We must also meet with people in the medium of their choice. When our clients and colleagues are "e-people" we need to become proficient in the use of their chosen portal — even though these days that medium may change and transform rapidly. Where are pagers and fax machines today? What happened to MySpace? Blackberries? Instant Messaging? ... and now there are even articles that "Texting is Dead"!!! Regardless of how quickly the format or medium may change, there are protocols to "behaving" online, just as there are in person. We should always endeavor to comport ourselves with thoughtfulness of others and awareness of our own presentation to the world, with the goal of being perceived as our "best selves" in the business arena. If we pay attention to dressing appropriately and using good table manners in order to *stand apart* in person, we should give equal consideration to our online appearance... invest the time (or hire a professional) to help you write (and proof!!) your résumé, develop or review your LinkedIn or other online professional profile, design your business cards, etc. ... and think carefully before uploading any old video to YouTube, posting wild photos or status updates on Facebook, vulgar (or poorly edited) writing in your blog, etc.

While it is important to stay current and take advantage of all the current technological devices and apps and software, it continues to be vitally important to know how to interact effectively and *connect* with other people via social media, texting, etc. In fact, most of the same basic rules of etiquette and protocol apply online as they do in real life; they are just easier for people to ignore, overlook or forget. Current HR professionals note that many people do not utilize current technology to their benefit: they check their cell phones during an interview (!), send inappropriate informal texts (or IMs) rather than respond by telephone (or email or personal note), neglect to check their online résumé or emails for typos and bad grammar, post racy photos or vulgar texts on open social media sites — and generally behave in ways they never would in person, or if they bothered to reflect and consider consequences. Again, this is all *learned* behavior, and if we take the time, make the effort, practice, and prepare, we can truly be a "Man/Woman well met" in person or online.

Imagine combining the brilliant technological advances of today with timeless people skills, and consider the potential of future generations. The core of this book revolves around hallmarks of respect and consideration. Therefore, whether you are entering, re-entering or transitioning in the world of business or, just want to get ahead, this book provides specific ways to achieve leadership distinction. And, despite today's extremely competitive global business climate, it is actually easier than ever to *stand apart*, simply by practicing these small nuances because so few people do these days!

My Story: Personal

I grew up in Syracuse, New York, in a family of five children, and we were your typical American family. Our parents instilled in us what we all considered to be "basic manners" from a young age. My father was self-taught and self-made. He had an unquenchable appetite to learn and exhibit that he knew "the difference," and my father shared what he learned with all of us. He instilled in us the importance of being "ladies" and "gentlemen." Doing things right was important to him: "Are my white socks showing?" was one familiar quip. We were brought up with the philosophy, "To whom much is given, much is expected," and frequently heard the word "*Contribute.*" The family dinner hour was an institution in our home and we were expected to come to the table prepared to *contribute* to table talk conversation — whether this was something we learned that day in school, something we were reading, etc.

When my parents invited their friends to our home, their friends often brought their children. We were told to "Play with their children… and interact! Make them feel glad they came to our home!" (This was an order, of sorts.) I used to dread going to others' homes with my parents because their kids would ignore us. (Apparently, they never got the same order that we did!) We felt very awkward and couldn't wait to leave.

When my parents entertained we were expected to be the quintessential junior hosts/ hostesses and we were encouraged to make others feel welcomed and comfortable while guests in our home. We were taught how to shake hands, and the importance of giving a "good handshake." We were told to "look into their eyes!" We were also taught to keep an eye on guests' glasses and offer to *freshen* as needed. We were trained to take guests' coats and would bring these to a designated room where my sister Kim and I would play "dress up" with the (fur) coats… we got caught a few times!

I was aware at an early age that treating others in this very respectful manner not only made them feel comfortable in our home it also reflected well on us and made us feel special, as well. We were taught how to set and clear the table which I did nearly every night. I still fold napkins in a way my mother taught us and I still enjoy cleverly inserting utensils into the pouch. Other countless "basics" became ingrained in us such as, "serrated edges (face) IN, gentlemen stand," etc.

In addition, we were trained how to answer the telephone, i.e. (a greeting) — "Good afternoon! Bowman residence, Judy speaking!" My mother said, "Make people feel glad they called!" We were taught to say, "May I tell my Mother who is calling for her, please?" for example… and this one: "My parents are *resting* now, may I take a message or ask you to call back *later*?"

I also used to love to play "secretary" (admin today!) for my father. I enthusiastically and fearlessly placed long distance calls at the age of seven, "Credit card call please!" My father received many compliments on his efficient "secretary" which also made me feel good. Little did I know this early training would serve as a valuable foundation for me later in life!

My Story: Professional

I entered the business world in the mid-1970's (without getting specific about the year!) and my first real job was as a Concierge at the Hyatt Regency Cambridge… the second U.S. version of the European Concierge, the first being Atlanta. I quickly advanced to Concierge Director, helped open the Regency Club Level and wrote the "Concierge Training and Information Manual" wherein, interestingly, I was inspired to speak of the importance of projecting *positive* Energy, Enthusiasm, Sincerity and Style and being professional. I emphasized treating each other — back of the house staff and RCL VIP's — with the same level of respect and dignity. In this capacity I earned a full appreciation that we needed each other to make it all happen, make a positive impression on guests, and acquire repeat business — always the goal. These tenets of my first training manual remain the premise of our *Professional Presence* programs today, as well as my book/s *Don't Take the Last Donut* and this, *How to Stand Apart @ Work.*™

Bringing it All Together:

I also sold intangibles such as travel, corporate travel incentive award programs, hotel room sales, booth space, etc., and in my sales capacity I would wine and dine professionals at all levels — *"lunch"* was very big then and I could not help but notice others' manners. The way some would hold their glasses, i.e., with all five fingers (the "death grip") or grasp utensils ("the banjo grip") was noted. I saw the president of ABC company and the

GM of XYZ company doing this and thought, "*They* are holding their knife and fork like THAT?! Perhaps they have forgotten *how* and need to be reminded... or maybe they don't know how and need to be taught." I further thought silently to myself, "There is a need!" — to teach, to remind people, to reinforce the basics of (dining) etiquette because if I noticed, others surely noticed, and their (lack of) attention to good manners was not serving them well. In fact, the high esteem that I had held essentially from "go" by virtue of their title, notoriety or business success placed silent high expectations which were not met. Oddly enough, this only served to empower *me* (!) — which is another tenet of this book.

After I brought my son Bowman into the world, I started The Etiquette School of Boston in 1993, teaching the basics of etiquette and dining to children, teens and young adults. Because I had never spoken in front of large gatherings, I thought I would christen myself into the world of public speaking with children, make all my mistakes and work my way into the corporate world. Unbeknownst to me, in one of my classes, there was a "young adult" who happened to be a reporter. She ended up writing a story with the caption, "Woman Makes Living Teaching Manners to Children." The article landed on the front page and sold out.

As an indirect result of this article I ended up writing a weekly etiquette column for the Pulitzer prize-winning Eagle Tribune publishing company for ten years. And, as a direct result of the article I received several calls from Fortune 500 senior executives, as well as the General Manager of The Country Club of Brookline, the oldest country club in the country, essentially asking if I could do the same type programs for their senior level managers as I was conducting for children.

I was not yet prepared to "go corporate." However, if anyone ever asks if we can do X, do we ever say no? We say, "Yes, of course!" and figure the rest out, agreed? Well, I said "Yes, of course!"... and my first corporate class was conducted on national television. CBS sent a film crew in from New York, we filmed at Wentworth College and I was very happy when my first corporate class was a *fait accompli!*

Of particular note was my first conversation with David Chag, then and present General Manager of The Country Club, whose support and friendship I honor to this day. When Mr. Chag called, I must confess, I was a bit surprised as I had attended a wedding there recently at his beautiful club and told him this, adding, "At the risk of shooting myself in the foot..." something to the effect of "I would simply expect that the staff at The Country Club would be totally up to par... in fact, over the top in terms of performance, professional conduct and correct behavior." I will never forget Mr. Chag's instant response, "Precisely why I am calling, Judy... because other people *expect* us to be and it is my job to make sure we *are*."

We all have a responsibility to ensure that those who represent our organizations are equipped not only with academic knowledge and technical expertise, but that they also possess critical interpersonal communication skills necessary to lead, motivate and advance in our global business environment today.

How to Stand Apart @ Work™ reveals those things I was taught at a young age, as well as those I have learned from you through our classes and your questions over many years. Please know that I have made every *faux pas* and gaffe, and I hope that you will learn from my missteps and let this information serve to empower you to continue to help you project total *confidence* to outclass the competition, lead, motivate and advance.

Given that others naturally gravitate toward *positive* people, it is my greatest hope that the core of *How to Stand Apart @ Work* is embraced by all generations around the globe, and that as a result the world will be a better place.

Technical Notes: Reference Format

This book is format-friendly to address today's fast-paced, on-demand ethos — "I want the information fast — get in/get out" mentality. You will find many subheads that highlight specific issues and make it easy to locate key concepts. There will be some repetition if you read through the book from cover to cover, since so many topics overlap. Where appropriate, we have provided references to other locations in the book where similar topics are discussed in more depth.

Chapter Organization

The chapters are in (rough) chronological order as to when activities take place. The sequential order carries through each chapter so that topics covered are not from most important to least important, but from the advance preparation through the event to follow-up afterwards. Obviously, the chronological order is not precise, since every event is unique, and some items may or may not occur in order, however, this is the general organizing principle throughout this manuscript.

Grammar Notes

This book follows the modern convention of mis-matching number and using "they/ their" to refer to a singular subject, rather than the clumsier "he/she," "him/her," "his/hers" formulation, e.g., "Identify the client and fulfill their need," or "Ask your connector if you may use their name." (The grammatically correct sentence in these cases, of course, would be "Identify the client and fulfill his/her need," or "Ask your connector if you may use his/her name." This would then have to be continued throughout the rest of the section, which can be intrusive to the reader.)

There is no consensus on the best way to move on from the historical use of the male-biased "he/him/his" only. Other options are to use only plural versions ("Identify the clients and fulfill their needs") or to randomly use "he/him/his" in some sentences/paragraphs and "she/her/hers" in others, which can be distracting and confusing. My editor and I have decided to mis-match number, and wanted to point this out so that any grammar sticklers are aware that this was a conscious decision, making the work easier to read for most people, despite the incorrect structure.

CHAPTER 1

Fabulous @ Networking

We Are *Always* Networking

The days of working for the same company for 30 years and retiring with a gold watch are now history! Statistics show that the average person today will hold between five and fifteen (!) jobs in a lifetime, as opposed to (formerly) one, suggesting that the position you hold presently is probably not one you will have forever... or even in five years. You will likely move into a new position, or even pursue a different career direction, and can anticipate doing so multiple times throughout your career.

Question. Do you believe you will find your (next) position, the one you *really* want, through an internet job site or from an ad in your local community newspaper?

Answer. Most agree that you will find your next position, the one you really want, *through other people* — the people you know (including others you will come to know) and the people they know.

Question. How do we meet more people and expand our network of connections — other than through social media?

Answer. Through networking!

*Herein, we make the assumption that most people are aware of the necessity to access multiple platforms in order to connect with multiple individuals in our now global internet-oriented society. Regardless of business discipline, the fact is that people do business with people they like and *trust*; they need to meet them first. After an initial e-contact, at some point, people want to meet face-to-face, connect handshake to handshake, *mano-a-mano*. The key to establishing genuine relationships and forging them in our business and personal lives is live *networking*.

In this chapter we will focus on how to develop and cultivate interpersonal relationships face-to-face at professional networking venues which is the most effective medium to meet, communicate, and connect. In addition, we will address the delicate issue of networking at social events or leveraging social situations for business gain.

THE SIX DEGREES OF SEPARATION

The Six Degrees of Separation is the theory that anyone on the planet is connected to any other person on the planet through a chain of acquaintances that has no more than five intermediaries. The theory was first proposed in 1929 by the Hungarian writer Frigyes Karinthy in a short story called "Chains" and popularized by the 1990 John Guare play and later movie entitled "Six Degrees of Separation."

Here's how it works: Think of a person you would like to meet or for whom you want to work — someone you do not know yet. Write down the names of six people you (already) know whom (you believe) may know that individual. If they do not know this person directly, when they reach out to six people they know, who they believe may know them or how to get to that person, eventually (in fewer than six steps, or six degrees of separation) you will connect with your target.

Networking is:
- How we meet those we would never otherwise have the *opportunity* to meet.
- The means by which outgoing, successful individuals transition and get ahead.
- How we may find our next (or even very distant) future business opportunity… or even life partner!
- Our *lifeline!*

When You Are the "Mutually Respected Third Party"

When acting as the mutually respected third party and referring people to others:

Fine: Provide their contact information including cell phone and email.

Fabulous: Call your contact in advance (on their behalf) to alert your contact that they will be hearing from this person, and pave the way for a personal introduction.

Fabulous: Share the best time and method to reach that individual, e.g., their preferred time of day, and whether they prefer phone or email, should this information be relevant or known.

For example, knowing someone is a "morning person" and it is best to contact them between 7 and 8 am versus someone is NOT a morning person, and best to contact them after 5, is valuable information and a **fabulous** pearl to share.

Professional Networking Events

While networking events may appear to be *fun* and like a party complete with **fabulous** food, beautiful flowers and perhaps even entertainment, they are, emphatically, <u>not</u>. When you insert yourself into a networking arena, you place yourself on the front line surrounded by fierce competitors. Arm yourself! This chapter provides the armor and ammunition to help fine-tune interpersonal communication skills to help us *stand apart* and handily advance. Smart networking will positively shape our professional futures.

Consider the following purposeful actions to help transform your present networking skills (which are no doubt "just fine") to **fabulous** status. When you follow these specific steps you will optimize your time and investment at any business networking event, and in so doing, show yourself as one who leads and connects while positively shaping your future.

STORY

One of my nephews, Shane, who is particularly attractive, personable and outgoing, was attending a college job fair in Florida. Someone from another booth (Booth X) was watching him interact with others at the job fair. My nephew had never approached Booth X, however, they had been observing him and were so impressed that they approached **_him_**, and ultimately offered him a very lucrative sales position with a generous base, company car, plus, plus, plus. They noticed **_him_**, observed, judged and wanted **_him_**. Receiving a job offer from a company you did not apply to or even approach to is pretty **fabulous**!

Remember, your actions — what you do and say — are always under scrutiny and judged, at times and by those you least suspect. In other words, you never know who is watching or listening (!) and when. Be aware and be prepared!

STORY

When I first started my business, I attended a major networking event which was scheduled for one hour. I did not have time to eat prior to the event, and when I arrived, I looked at the clock on the wall (and at all the fabulous food, which, of course, I could not touch) and went to work. "Hello, I'm JB, President of The Protocol School of Boston," (an earlier name of my firm) introducing myself to person after person, exchanging cards, making/taking personal notes.

In those days I did not know enough to un-encumber, so I also carried a full briefcase (just in case!) ... plus a purse, and a portfolio... and I wore (higher) heels. Despite my encumbrances, I flashed my wide smile, maintained my professional demeanor, expressed genuine interest in others, projected positive energy, enthusiasm and sincerity, and worked that room.

Nearing the end of a very long yet productive hour where I had collected many cards and established more connections, I was now completely ravenous and totally spent. My feet ached, my back and shoulders ached... was it time to go yet? Yes, it's 7:00 — time to go!

Suddenly, a very tall, ominous figure approached me. "Excuse me," the gentleman said. "Who are you?"

"Okay," I said to myself, "One more time, Judy." I looked up, right into his eyes, and proceeded with my pitch. "Of course! Mr. X (referencing his name badge), my name is JB, founder of the Protocol School of Boston..."

He interrupted. "No, I mean who ARE you?"

Moi: "Excuse me?"

Gentleman: "I have been watching you work this room for the past hour and I have never seen anything like it. I don't really care what you do, who you do it for or why you're here. I want to talk to you about doing everything I just saw you do here, for me."

It was then, that I fully understood that others really do notice, observe and judge others.

Change is a Lonely Place to Be

Moving out of your comfort zone and into venues where you know no one can be isolating, even daunting at times. You definitely take a risk by changing-up your game and *modus operandi*. However, the personal and professional rewards are well worth the risk.

STORY

Many years ago, I had an event on my calendar on which I had placed an asterisk, my personal code for "must go," although I had noted neither the type of event nor the fee. That evening, I fought my way through a huge snowstorm, encountered horrific traffic and virtually impossible parking.

Despite all these obstacles, I finally arrived and learned this was an exclusively CEO event with a $500 tariff. In those days, I was accustomed to $65 and $150 events. I could not turn back now — 90% of success is showing up, yes? I had struggled to get there and was not about to let the price of entry stand between the CEOs in the next room et moi. I registered, picked up my name badge, and started to work.

I was in unfamiliar territory and knew only a few people when I arrived. However, I made the conscious decision to stretch out of my comfort zone, and as a result I met so many lovely, accomplished, and truly exceptional individuals.

I was thrilled I had made this effort and felt secure being among "my people!" I would never have met these individuals had I continued to do what I had always done, e.g., attend "the usual" broad-based networking events. Stretching out of my comfort zone and attending an exclusive and new niche market event was an enriching and rewarding experience.

This experience taught me a big lesson in terms of targeted, tactical, strategic marketing as it pertains to networking events: Be selective where you invest your networking time and energy — and reach out of your comfort zone for big results!

STORY

My father, back in the day, was a very successful commercial and industrial real estate broker and developer who came from very humble beginnings. He frequently told me, "In life, always play UP! Surround yourself with those better, brighter, more successful, more accomplished, more driven — because this stimulates and challenges you." In any game (i.e., golf or life), when you play with better players, you learn from them, are stimulated and naturally driven to perform better yourself. I have seen good players (in golf and in life!) play with less driven, less accomplished players, and not perform as well because they lose their competitive edge. Stretch out of your comfort zone, challenge yourself and play UP.

Pre-Networking Activities

Advance work provides business intelligence you can use when meeting others which will propel you skylines beyond your competition.

Fine: R.S.V.P. your acceptance, register and attend.

Fabulous: Yes, certainly R.S.V.P. and register… however, *preparation* prior to any networking event is absolutely essential to ensure peak performance and achieve strong bottom-line results.

You will benefit greatly from the following advance activities. Doing so will reflect positively on you as you will be seen as one "in the know," prepared, professional — **fabulous!**

Fabulous: Request a copy of the guest list — for two reasons:

1. *Review* the names in advance and practice pronouncing them OUT LOUD phonetically, to master proper name pronunciation.

2. *Research* individuals/companies to learn (business and some personal) information you can use in conversation; *Knowledge is Power.* Your advance research shows you as thorough and prepared.

When you are introduced, rather than make inconsequential small talk about the weather or food, reach into your arsenal of pre-networking event research and say (with an engaging smile) "I'm so pleased to meet you (insert perfectly pronounced name of person).

I was very interested to read (yes, you read, you research) the news of your exciting new product launch of XYZ!" (said with enthusiasm and energy). You just popped!

Consider how much more impressive and *memorable* you are to them now. In addition to propelling yourself literally to a different echelon, miles above your competition, you have also instantly transitioned dialogue from random *small talk* to a specific field of limitless substantive talk with the *opportunity* to learn *more information* while advancing the relationship. Pre-research activity positively positions you to pivot and soar to **fabulous** status.

Dressing for a Professional Networking Event

(Please refer to Chapter 5, *Fabulous @ Professional Attire* for more about dressing for professional events.)

- Dress appropriately. Ladies and gentlemen, wear dark colors. When in doubt, know that *Professional Attire* is "never wrong."

Ladies, select a jacket with large pockets — one for incoming and one for outgoing business cards.

Remember, as a representative of the XYZ *brand* and the consummate expert in your field, you want to look and dress the part. The importance of dressing respectfully and appropriately for a business or networking event cannot be overstated.

Eating at Networking Events

"To eat or not to eat?" That is the question!

When you think about it, eating is a fairly indelicate process. Plus, most food served at networking events, for whatever reason, is challenging to eat. Finger food is sticky… shrimp with your fingers? … oysters on a spoon? … etc. What to eat, when to eat, how, where, how much and even *should* we eat are to be considered and present another opportunity to *stand apart.*

Fine: Do a beeline to the bar/buffet table, "dig in" and get comfortable.

Fabulous: Eat something before you go! With all due respect, no one invites us anywhere because they believe we need to be fed! We are invited for one of two reasons:

1. Someone wants to *thank* us for our business/prospective business
2. Someone believes we have something to *contribute*!

We have a *responsibility* to contribute to the overall success of any event to which we have been invited.

Therefore, have a snack *before* you go. Should you choose to eat, consider the consequences, when someone introduces themselves and asks an open-ended question just as you pop something into your mouth:

- They wait… and watch… while you chew… while you swallow… while you dab your mouth with a napkin… and this is *awkward!*
- Crumbs can land on clothes, food can get caught in teeth… and bad breath is real!

Eating before you go eliminates the temptation of eating at the event, allowing you to completely focus on your *raison d'*être*:* meeting and connecting with <u>people</u>, not food.

Exception: If the person with whom you are speaking is eating and invites you to sit with them then, it is fine to take a plate. Of course, avoid difficult to eat foods and messy *hors d'oeuvres* for obvious reasons and select easy to eat foods (i.e., anything on a stick).

During the Event

New connections and business opportunities abound, however, time is limited. Therefore, conducting ourselves judiciously and managing our time is imperative.

Fine: Chat with those you know.

Certainly speak with those you know, however, also:

Fabulous:

- Break out of your comfort zone.
- Connect with those whom you have pre-targeted
- Provide introductions to others

By positioning yourself as a connector, you also position yourself as a resource and a "go to" person! (Not to mention if you make a good connection for someone else, they will want to return the favor.)

Be Open

There will be times when you attend an event with one expectation and stumble upon someone or learn information which diverts you from your initial purpose and completely alters the outcome, yet still provides end-results unimagined. Be "fully present" and open to new experiences, cast some new seeds and see what grows.

STORY

My husband Jay took a ride with a friend who was meeting with a land developer interested in buying a piece of commercial property. My husband and his friend were waiting in the reception area when the friend was called in; Jay remained, flipping through some magazines.

Twenty minutes later, the land developer emerged from the meeting, and cordially greeted my husband. He asked if he could help him with something. Jay explained he was there waiting for his friend. The land developer happened to ask, "What type of business are you in?" My husband told him he was in the thoroughbred horse breeding business. The land developer cordially acknowledged this and started to return to turn away to return to his meeting when he suddenly did an about-face and sat with Jay for almost 30 minutes.

My husband invited the land developer out to the farm. One thing led to another and the land developer ended up buying a race horse from Jay (even though, unfortunately, he never did buy the commercial property from Jay's friend).

This initial brief encounter was actually the beginning of what would become a long-term, mutually rewarding and lucrative business relationship and a beautiful friendship. The land developer became involved, in fact immersed, in the horse business to the point where he now owns one of the premiere breeding farms in Florida today. This chance meeting changed the developer's life by influencing him to expand his interests and build a massive horse breeding farm; it also changed Jay's life, as he developed a new relationship with a great guy and, yes, sold him a lot of horses along the way.

Had my husband not gone along for a ride... had he not been sitting in this reception area... had both gentlemen not been open to the connection... not exuded a friendly persona and expressed an interest in the other's business endeavors and interests... chances are, they would never have met and nothing would have developed. However, both recognized something in each other, seized the moment, embraced the opportunity, and embarked upon an unimagined new journey. Lives were changed and enriched, and new worlds opened.

When we exude a friendly persona and reach out — and the door is open so others can reach back — you just never know what may unfold.

So in addition to being prepared and focused, remember to be open and approachable.

The following are examples of purposeful actions that will further help to optimize your time and positively shape the outcome of any networking event, anywhere in the world.

Name Badges

Wearing a name badge at networking events is virtually required, and for good reason. Knowing and *using* another person's name may seem basic, perhaps even trite — however, the simple act of saying another person's name is often unexpected, will turn heads and get you positively noticed. You endear yourself to another and make a positive impression simply by using their name during the course of your conversation.

Please know emphatically and unequivocally that wearing a name badge is extremely important so others may view, learn, remember and *use* your name. Therefore, where you place your name badge for others to view is significant and can show you as thoughtful, considerate, and aware of *nuances*.

Fine: Wear your name badge on either the right or left side.

Fabulous: Name badges belong on the RIGHT side and should be worn as high as possible on your RIGHT shoulder for others to see!

*Ladies, avoid placing badges on your breasts; and gentlemen, think twice before randomly clipping badges onto your belt buckle or pants pocket — others you meet have little interest in embarking upon this potentially *awkward* reconnaissance mission just to learn your name!

Name Badges for the Speaker

Fine: Speaker, wear a name badge!

Fabulous: It is not necessary to wear a name badge when you are the speaker as everyone knows who you are.

Exception: When speaking at a large conference where every attendee may not know you. In this case, it is appropriate and even considerate for the speaker to wear a name badge to prevent confusion or embarrassment.

Interestingly, even some baseball teams do not have their names on their jerseys when they play at home, because the fans know who they are. The "away" team always wears their names on the back of their shirts.

Briefcases

Briefcases at networking events present another topic to consider.

Fine: Carry your briefcase in your left hand, leaving your right hand free to shake hands.

Fabulous: *Un-encumber.* Leave briefcases in the car if possible, or check briefcases, coats and bags with the coat check; if necessary, ask the bartender or host for assistance.

Ladies' Purses

Ladies: The purse you carry anywhere is significant, as your purse makes a statement about you. Give serious consideration to this accessory, especially at a professional business networking event.

Fine: Carry your big, brand name purse — the one you always bring to the office and to the grocery store.

Fabulous: Consider a chic, small (if at all) *quality*, conservative, understated, over-the-shoulder black purse and forget about it.

Make Your Entrance

Nearly everyone watches the entrance. Know this. *Use* the entrance of a room to your advantage and *stand apart*.

Fine: Do a beeline to the bar/buffet table.

Fabulous:

- Before making your entrance, visit the rest room. Check buttons and zippers, stray hairs, ties (gentlemen), hosiery and lipstick (ladies), etc., and pop a breath mint. Wash and dry your hands thoroughly (clammy hands are the "kiss of death!") You are now ready to rock the room.
- Place name badge high on your RIGHT side.
- Attitude adjustment! Regardless of how you feel, *ACT* as if this is your event, as if YOU are the host and you *OWN* the room. Enter. Step to the side of the door.
- Assume the *Professional Stance.* Keep chin parallel to the floor and assert your good posture.

(See Chapter 7, *Fabulous @ The Presentation*, for illustrations and more information about the *Professional Stance*.)

Your jacket is buttoned — the top two buttoned, the third one open to "vent."

- Pause. Feel the room's energy.
- Visually pan the room.
- Make eye-contact and acknowledge those you know… as well as those you are about to know!

Facial Expression

*Have a pleasant, approachable facial expression

Remember, people are attracted to pleasant, approachable, positive people. Your natural facial expression could, however inadvertently, turn other people away and actually serve as a form of self-sabotage! Be aware of what your *natural* facial expression suggests, and if unsure, ask someone you *trust* to tell you the *truth* about your natural facial expression.

Fine: Be yourself. Your face reflects how you feel inside.

Fabulous: Something as seemingly insignificant as your facial expression has the power to light up a room and draw others toward you — or make others want to turn out the lights and turn away! Even if you are not feeling particularly pleasant, conversational or even confident, endeavor to portray yourself otherwise and present an inviting countenance.

Practice and rehearse in advance: Look in a mirror or at photographs and note your natural facial expression. Does your mouth turn down? Are your eyes closed or shifty? Consciously modify your expression if necessary to project a welcoming visage. Practice turning your lips up into a smile. When you smile, this tells your brain that you are happy and suddenly, you are! (Ref.: *Your Creative Brain*, Shelley Carson, Ph.D.) Make good eye-contact, focusing on the person with whom you are speaking, rather than looking over their shoulder or gazing about the room.

Walking — Your Gait

*Walk purposefully.

The way you stand, carry yourself and even walk is noticed and, however consciously or subconsciously evaluated.

Fine: Meander randomly about the room.

Fabulous: Walk confidently, purposefully throughout the room, even though you may have no particular place to go! "*Walk like a man/woman with a mission!*"

When you walk "with a mission" you will be perceived as a person "well-met," and *perception is reality!*

Your confident, purposeful gait speaks volumes about confident, purposeful *you*. Your senses should be on high alert — however, *enjoy* the journey. When you walk and carry yourself in this confident, authoritative and upbeat manner, you will surely encounter other confident, ambitious individuals whom you might not otherwise meet if you were to merely show up, put in an appearance and just exist and "be" (safe) in your comfort zone.

Approaching Others

The way you approach others is noticed and provides another opportunity to *stand apart*.

Fine: Randomly approach people and hope they will engage; politely interrupting is okay.

Fabulous: Approach others, using the *Professional Stance*. Engage others in conversation at their eye level whenever possible.

For those who are blessed with the gift of height:

Fine: Bend at the neck and look down on the person with whom you are speaking.

Fabulous: Bend at the knee, ever so slightly, and lean IN toward them, so they don't need to crane their neck to look UP at you. Bending and weaving is more conducive to connecting and helps eliminates barriers. We call this the "weave and wend" approach.

Fabulous Tips:

- Purposefully approach singles or groups of three or more. Single individuals will welcome your approach, as will a group of three or more (two individuals are likely engaged in conversation and the third person may be "left out"). *That said, never assume that two people speaking are "happily" engaged; stand alert for opportunity.*
- Walk slowly past twos engaged in close conversation to give them an opportunity to disengage and welcome you to join in.
- Be the initiator: initiate the eye contact, initiate the handshake, initiate your pre-prepared, customized self-introduction and tagline for this event.
- When speaking with others, give them your undivided attention, show respect, be *fully present.*
- Show genuine interest.
- Exude confidence.
- Be *yourself!*

Handshakes and Eye Contact

- Keep thumbs up and out as you prepare to shake hands.
- Lean IN for this all-important handshake. (See Chapter 2, *Fabulous @ Handshaking & Business Cards* for more details about the professional handshake.)
- Make eye-contact for 2–3 seconds (versus a quick glance before you look around the room to see who else you want to meet). This makes them feel acknowledged, special. Bill Clinton is renowned for this technique. However, be careful of going too far; don't stare at them with a fixed gaze, i.e., 9–10 seconds or you will cast an altogether different impression and may even make the other person feel uncomfortable.

Introductions

Introducing Yourself

The way you introduce yourself to others provides another opportunity to *stand apart*. Present yourself to others saying your name slowly and clearly; do not rush to get through this. State your position, business or company affiliation, if appropriate.

Fine: "Hi, I'm Judy."

Fabulous: "Hello, Mr. X! My name is Judith Bowman, founder of PCI."

Follow this with your tagline, customized for this event, e.g.: "We take everyday business situations and show students and professionals at all levels how to leverage these as standalone opportunities to *stand apart* and advance in their careers. We speak specifically to *nuances,* because the *little* things we say and do have the potential to make or derail any relationship. Agreed, Mr. X?"

- When we say another's name (Mr. X), they perk up! That's a fact.

"Hello" is more professional than "Hi" and it is important to say your *first* and *last* name — clearly, slowly and make an association, if necessary. When you introduce yourself to others, your goal is to make them feel you are genuinely pleased to meet them.

State your profession, particularly if different from your passion. Position this to show how your expertise will benefit *them*.

More on Your Tagline

Question. What is a tagline?

Answer. Different people call this different things (elevator pitch, 5-second pitch, one-sentence resume), however, basically, a tagline refers to your name, rank and serial number.

Your tagline is a critical element of your **fabulous** self-introduction. Prepare your tagline in advance and tweak it to connect with this particular group. Taglines may change from venue to venue. For example, if I were attending a generic event with business professionals I would most likely use the tagline mentioned above. However, if I were among a group of food and beverage professionals, I would revise my tagline to be more palatable (pardon the pun) to this group and emphasize our *Dining Savvy* services. With a group preparing to do business overseas I would revise my tagline and emphasize our *International Protocol Awareness* expertise, etc.

*Customize your tagline to show not so much what you do, but how your expertise will benefit them.

STORY

I had the opportunity to meet Mitt Romney when he was Governor of Massachusetts. I had been in contact with his office for a few months discussing a proclamation for "A Day of Civility," which would have been another first for Massachusetts.

When it came my turn to introduce myself and shake the governor's hand, I simply said: "Hello, I'm Judy Bowman," and made the big mistake of assuming Governor Romney would make the association between my name and "A Day of Civility."

Not so! Governor Romney, always the "Gentleman Warrior," was perfectly polite and shook my hand, however, no connection was forged because I failed to be purposeful in my introduction. What I did was "fine" — I said my name and shook the Governor's hand. However, had I said, "Hello, I'm Judith Bowman and I am the 'Day of Civility' lady," this would have made an instant connection, and been **fabulous**.

Please learn from my missteps!

Executing a Proper Business Introduction

Introducing Others

Introductions usually come upon us quickly and when they do we are expected to know names (and proper pronunciation) titles, company names, know whose name to say first — or does it matter? — etc. The ability to execute a flawless business introduction presents another stupendous opportunity to show respect and demonstrate that you absolutely know how! In so doing, you instantly *stand apart* in all positive ways.

Fine: Simply say names and introduce-away.

Fabulous: There is a major difference between a business and a social introduction. A social introduction is based on age/gender; a business introduction is based on rank/status. The following is the protocolically correct way to execute a stellar business introduction anywhere in the world:

Formula for a Business Introduction:

BEGIN by naming the more senior ranked person, and introduce the younger/newer person TO them:

"*Mr./Ms. Senior Executive*, **may I introduce** (the most professional phrasing)... **may I present** (the most formal phrasing)... **may I introduce and present** (the most elegant phrasing) **to YOU** (prepositional phrase)... *Mr./Ms. Junior Executive.*

Mr./Ms. Senior Executive is our new Senior Counsel for the Americas and

Mr./Ms. Junior Executive is our new Vice President of Operations."

Then say something which will serve as a <u>lead-in</u> for future conversation, which has nothing to do with business at hand, i.e. "... and I understand you both enjoy time both on and off the tennis courts." There will be times you may not be able to summon a connection between the two parties, and really need to think on your feet.

STORY

I once introduced two gentlemen at a networking event when I only knew their last names and had not a clue about anything in common on a personal level. I only knew they were both accomplished. And so I used their honorifics and last names and concluded, "...and I understand that you gentlemen are both, clearly, captains of industry!" Both men beamed and the connection was established.

Fabulous Introduction Tips:
- Always say the name of the most important person first.
- In business, this is based on rank/status; socially, this is based on age/gender.
- Match honorifics/first/last names, i.e. "Dr. Nancy Snyderman, may I introduce **TO YOU** Ms. Judy Jones."
- The prepositional phrase "TO YOU" must be intact. If this is reversed, the order of importance is inadvertently inverted (do NOT say "May I introduce **you to**...").
- Identify each person professionally. "Dr. Snyderman is the internationally re-nowned medical health expert for NBC. Ms. Jones is our new Vice President of Operations."
- Then share a non-business related connection.

Positioning Yourself as a Resource
Fine: Introduce yourself to new people.

Fabulous: Introduce yourself to new people AND introduce other people to others. When you do, take the opportunity to *re-introduce* yourself and shake hands. This will help them recall your name and leave another positive impression of you.

Remember to regard this event as if it were *your* event, as if *you* are the host and you *own* the room. Enable connections not just for yourself but for others, as well. Attend this event not just looking for "what's in it for me" but also position yourself as a resource and a connector and help facilitate business connections for others. In so doing, you show yourself as a leader, a force. You also demonstrate respect for your hosts by *contributing* to the success of their event. Moreover, when you make connections for others which result in positive business outcomes, you will be remembered and they will want to do the same for you in the future should the occasion arise.

Personal Information
Sharing personal information presents another point of consideration.

Fabulous: Sharing something of a more personal nature humanizes you and can advance a relationship. However, over-sharing can actually hurt you. Be careful not to share too much personal information (especially not too soon!) during the relationship-building journey.

We already know that certain topics are traditionally taboo. These include family problems, financial concerns, health issues, sexual innuendo, political or religious views, controversial topics, etc. Only share personal information you are comfortable sharing.

Should they tell you about a legal dilemma or start to divulge details of their divorce, think twice before sharing on this level, unless you are so compelled. And even then, be careful. You and you alone can make this call. Should you choose to divulge and "break the rules" for whatever reason, this is entirely your call. Remember, if they divulge too much personal information they may regret having said anything at a later date (the wine may be talking). Discretion is key and the less said, the better. You really don't want to get involved in their health or personal legal matters.

Share lighter personal information (such as spouses' names, children's names/ages, schools, activities). If they mention their daughter's upcoming swim meet, share that your niece is also on the swim team.

Jot this information down when you have a private moment — not in their presence without first asking permission. Asking permission and the gesture of writing this down signals that this information, and they, are important to you; you want to remember. Writing information down is not a slight — it is a compliment. (See *Making Notes* below, in After the Networking Event.)

Engaging and Dis-engaging ... Tactfully

- Initiate and engage in conversation…
- Invest 3-5 minutes (7 maximum) per person and then…
- Move on!

Question. How do we dis-engage *tactfully*, without offending others?

Fine: Say, "I'll be right back." (Saying this when you know you won't does not help engender the *trust* factor.)

Fine: Say, "I am going to freshen my cocktail." (This implies you should offer them one and will therefore be back!)

Fine: Say you are going to "freshen," or go to the "restroom" (*Never: "bathroom"!*) (This also implies you will be back.)

Fabulous: Say, "It has been a pleasure meeting you. Thank you for your time. I have enjoyed our conversation. There are a few other people I see on the other side of the room with whom I would like to connect. Should we miss reconnecting before the end of the event, let's try to find each other within the next few weeks or months or whatever…" — leave this open-ended. Promise nothing! Say what you mean and mean what you say. Remember, you are endeavoring to build *trust*.

Fabulous: Finally, it would be gracious of you to introduce this individual to someone else before you leave so they do not feel abandoned or slighted in any way.

Remembering Names

Remember, most of us are challenged remembering names. When another person approaches us and says their name, we, as professionals should be conditioned to respond in kind, saying our name. In addition, it is good practice to:

- Repeat their name as soon as this is said, and use their name often in conversation.
- Make an association immediately in order to help remember and use their name. (However, see below about the dangers of calling them by the word or phrase used to help remember their name!)
- Use their honorific, "Dr. X, Judge Judy, Chancellor Z."
- Never assume the familiar form of address (i.e., do not call them by their first name).
- Always *ask* how they prefer to be addressed… you need to earn the right to get to the "Jack and Judy" stage.

It is easier to forget rather than make the effort to remember another person's name which is ironic as factually, people like to hear little more than the sound of their own names. As Dale Carnegie says, "Remember that a person's name is to that person the sweetest and most important sound in any language." Whenever we hear our name articulated, we automatically perk up and are drawn to the voice. Therefore, remembering and using another's properly pronounced name is integral to cultivating relationships.

Top Ten Tips Regarding How To Remember Names
Fabulous:

1. Particularly if you have a challenging name, consider offering an association at the outset to help others properly pronounce, remember and use your name.

2. Repeat the name as soon as you hear it and use in conversation. "Susan Flynn. It is a pleasure meeting you, Ms. Susan Flynn. Ms. Flynn,* how do you prefer to be addressed?" They say, after five times of usage you own their name. Hearing you say their name also makes them feel noticed, valued and helps advance the relationship. *Please note: the correct business honorific for women is "Ms." (pronounced: "Mzz") unless they inform you otherwise.*

3. Look at the individual. Concentrate, focus, listen. Really listen to their name and make an association with (i.e.) another Susan you may know… but be careful with associations! (In other words, don't make an embarrassing mental association, such as "Mr. Pink" with "Mr. Pig" because he is chubby or round-faced… you may accidentally call him by the mnemonic rather than the right name!)

4. Repeat their name immediately and use often in conversation. Remember, three times is fine, but after five times of name usage, you own it. This repetition of their name also makes them feel special and helps advance the relationship.

5. Make a visual association — visualize: "Susan" with the sunny or sour disposition, or "Flynn" as in "In like Flynn" or whatever works for the situation.

6. Ask them to pronounce their name again for you.

7. Ask them to make an association. Particularly those with a challenging or unusual first and/or last name.

8. Ask for their card and take advantage of this opportunity to make yet another visual "imprint" of their name and form another mental impression.
9. Ask them to spell their name.
10. Refer to their name badge (obvious).

What To Do When You Forget (or don't have a clue)

Most of us are challenged remembering names perhaps because we are not paying attention or we may be thinking about what we are going to say rather really *listening* in order to learn, remember and use their name.

   Fine: Ignore the other person.

   Fine: Call them "Pal," "Buddy," "Dear," "Honey," or some other moniker. (Never! These are NOT fine.)

   Even if you are not completely 100 percent positive about someone's name, make an effort. How you recover when you forget presents another great opportunity to *stand apart*.

Top Ten Tips If You Forget Someone's Name

1. **Fine**: Say, "What's your name again?"
    Fabulous:
2. Confess! Say, "I am so sorry, I have completely blanked on your name." Said with sincerity, your efforts and this single gesture will be noticed and appreciated. Remember, it is not what you say, rather *how* you say it.
3. Ask the mutually respected third party, "What's the name of the gentleman with the pink tie?" You may then knowingly approach, greet by name and be **fabulous** showing you know their name.
4. The "set-up" — The practice of sending over the "mutually respected third party" to introduce themselves, encouraging your target to respond by saying their name. This tactic is frequently used and highly effective. The person who choreographed this "set-up" may then confidently approach the targeted individual using their name.
5. Introduce yourself. Approach the other person and say your name. In business we should all be conditioned so that when we hear another say their name we respond in kind, saying our name, first and last, slowly and clearly, so this can be understood, remembered and used.
6. Ask them the pointed question, "What is your name, please?" The person should respond saying their first and last name. At which point you might say, "Yes, I knew Flynn, but yes, *Susan Flynn*." Now you have both.
7. Ask them to spell their name. Be careful here... when they say, "J.O.N.E.S." ... Okay! ... "Exactly the way it sounds!" This can happen from time to time. Others understand, and appreciate your effort.
8. Say the name of the person you know and allow the other individual to reveal their name. (This tactic is a bit "tacky," however, works in a pinch.)

9. Ask how they *prefer to be addressed*. This not only gives you their name, it also lets you know how they prefer to be addressed. When they respond, be alert and listen — to learn, remember and use their name.

10. Hasten to help others in distress — divulge your full name promptly if someone seems to be struggling, or share another person's name when it is evident that someone may have forgotten it. This is always appreciated and will help you *stand apart*. (Doing so also makes others more inclined to help you in times of need.)

Business Card Exchange at Networking Events

Business card exchange at networking events is a given. The quality of one's card, where we keep them, the almost ritualistic way in which we present, receive, acknowledge and where we ultimately place cards all present **fabulous** opportunities to demonstrate respect and show we know the difference.

Without a card, we must rely on their good intentions (and for most of us, bad memory). Business cards are an essential tool to have and use. Have one at networking events and use it.

(Please refer to Chapter 2, *Fabulous @ Handshaking & Business Cards* for specific details about business card quality, presentation, and more.)

Making Small Talk and Conversation Skills

Small talk, especially with those you don't know or just met is challenging for most, and truly an art. Initiating conversation is a skill which needs to be practiced and honed in order to help place others at ease and come across as sincere and genuine. Making conversation and small talk presents us all with wonderful opportunities to demonstrate our finely-tuned people skills and *stand apart*.

Fine: Let conversation take its natural course and go with the flow.

Fabulous: Initiate the small talk and conversation topics. Questions beginning with *Who, What, When, Where, Why* and *How* still work! Ask open-ended questions (those that do not end in a "yes" or "no" answer) and make it all about THEM. Get personal. Remember: People love to talk about… *themselves!*

In fact, be prepared to leave a conversation and even the event itself sharing very little about yourself. Actually, this would signal a job "well-done!" Those with whom you have spoken are no doubt singing your praises… i.e., "I just had the best conversation with Judy Jones," when in fact, there was no conversation, there was a monologue. They were taking about themselves!

Remember, the networking event is not an interview, a presentation, or a meeting, where you want to talk about your business and yourself to others in detail. Rather, the networking event is a venue we want to leverage to establish new connections, follow up and forge new relationships.

Fine: "What do you do for a living?" (*Note*: This question implies, "How much $$ do you make?")

Fabulous: "What business are you in?" or "What is your professional field?" (This is less threatening and does not suggest your curiosity regarding their income bracket.)

Fine: "How is business?" (They may not want to talk about work. They may have a sick child at home or be prefer to chat about an exciting upcoming vacation.

Fabulous: Ask, *"How are things?"* (Asking how *things* are leaves the direction/ the conversation "open-ended" and allows them to take the lead by delving into their personal life, i.e., health issues, family, vacation plans — or business news, i.e., "Work has been challenging; however, business is picking up with our new product line." Or, they may choose to keep the topic generic and respond with i.e. *"Things* are fine! Thank you for asking." This leaves the field open for you to take the lead and share something about yourself or your business which may inspire them to offer something in kind to help you connect.)

Voice

Voice is a powerful medium. Much information is conveyed and betrayed through our voice. Therefore, when *we* initiate small talk and conversation, this accomplishes the following:

- Takes the onus off us to speak (first).
- More importantly, affords us the opportunity to hear the other person speak (first) and acquire information.
- Listen — to their tone of voice and inflections. We can hear nervousness, arrogance, boredom, trepidation.
- Listen — to words they use, their vocabulary
- Listen — to their grammar, diction, the way they construct sentences.
- Listen — to their pace. Are they flying in fifth gear or downshifting and deliberate in first gear?

Think about being chameleon-like and adapting to their pace/gear, and even using words they use in order to better relate, connect.

STORY

Howard Stern's dream was to be a radio disc-jockey, despite starting out with a high-pitched, squeaky voice. He practiced and practiced. He failed and fell many times, however, today Howard Stern has defied all ground rules of radio, made his mark and created his own unique identity. With practice and by exaggerating his intonations and inflections, Howard Stern has accentuated his uniqueness and talents and established himself as a trailblazer, an icon of sorts in the radio industry.

After the Networking Event

Concluding
Leaving the event presents another opportunity to *stand apart.*

Fine: You have put in your time. It is okay to duck out and leave on your own.

Fabulous:

- Always thank the host for inviting you and extend your sincere compliments on a great event; be specific.
- Walk your guest to the door. Actually, walk them *outside* the door and perhaps even to their car because, when you think about it, when you leave the vacuum of a room or door to a building, this is when "real talk"… as in the "Meeting after the Meeting!"… begins. Do not miss this *opportunity* to further advance connections. Remember, your goal is to get to "real talk" to advance *trust* and grow relationships. (See Chapter 6, *Fabulous @ The Meeting* for more information about the "Meeting after the Meeting.")

Making Notes

Fine: Make mental notes and hope you will remember everything that everyone shared with you during the course of the event.

Fabulous: Write down that which others have shared immediately after the event while this information is fresh in your mind (names of family members, shared interests, accomplishments, etc.). Reference these topics in subsequent conversations/ correspondence. Doing so demonstrates they made an impression on you, and shows you as a thoughtful person.

Follow-Up

They say "The Fortune is in the Follow-Up."

Fine: Follow up whenever you have the time and get the chance, within a week or so.

Fabulous: Follow up within 24-48 hours at the latest with a quick email, telephone call or a handwritten note. Invite a new contact to join your professional social media network (LinkedIn is more business-oriented).

Caution: A new connection can "go stale" after just a couple of days. Contact new connections soon, while they still remember you — your face, voice and pleasant interaction at the networking event, and how you stood out… because you followed all of these guidelines on how to be **fabulous**!

Social Media Networking

A closing note:

In these technological times, it is popular to use virtual networking tools to connect with like-minded people and promote one's service or business.

My take on virtual networking is this:

Fine: Use social networks to connect and promote yourself and your business.

Fabulous: Use social media networking in combination with face-to-face networking events and personal introductions to achieve maximum results.

Even in today's wired world, people crave real, human connection. Do not let tech toys distract you from making a real connection in the real world. While it is important to be electronically savvy in social media platforms, and to meet your potential contacts on their level — in the medium they prefer — the single most potent platform is to establish real-life, face-to-face connections. This is what ignites *trust*, and remember: people do business with people they *trust*.

Leveraging Social Settings

There was a time when one did not mix business with pleasure. This was actually considered poor form and it was deeply egregious to "talk shop" at a social setting. But times have changed and in today's ever-shifting world the lines between business and social "rules of engagement" have blurred. It is common, wise, even admirable to network and reap business opportunities from social occasions. There are many ways to do this boorishly, and if you do not follow protocol you may run the risk of being tagged a "social climber." In this section I will explore how to ferret out potential new business opportunities astutely obtained from a social setting, and perhaps acquire a few new friends along the way!

Corporate Social Events

While some corporate events may be tagged "social," they are actually intended to be low-key business venues to help advance connections. Such events include company-sponsored outings, industry-sponsored sporting events, charity functions, volunteer outings, office holiday parties, etc. In these situations, it is not only appropriate to discuss business, it would be ill-advised not to.

Some examples:

A Company-Sponsored Outing

Employers today will often host outings for employees, their families and friends. This may be a picnic, a sporting event, some form of retreat or even entertainment, etc. These events are clearly social in nature, providing the opportunity to nurture team spirit and expand connections. It is certainly acceptable, even astute, to have business-related topics surface here.

Fine: Enjoy this time with your team and those you already know.

Fabulous: While it is fine to spend time with your team and those you already know, make the effort to break out of your comfort zone, un-cluster and disperse to meet and mix. Be "fully present" and use this occasion as an opportunity to be seen as one who extends, contributes and connects. Introduce yourself or remind others of who you are. Say your name, where you work, your department, job function. Nurture existing relationships and work to expand your network.

You have to come out of the shadows to show you know how to conduct yourself with confidence and aplomb. When you go out of your way to contribute to the overall success of any company-sponsored event, your actions are positively noticed.

An Industry-Sponsored Sports League

If your company fields a softball team or volleyball squad, these events are certainly great for exercise and team-building, and are also another vehicle to advance business connections. Certainly, you don't want to be too overt or known as the one with business cards falling out of your baseball glove. At the same time, it is reasonable to use these events to get to know people in your industry and access connections. Some of the most meaningful and rewarding business (and even personal) associations start on a level (sports) playing field!

Fundraisers, Charity Events and Volunteer Outings

Coming together for a worthy cause in a neutral environment has ignited around the world. It is increasingly common for employers to sponsor charity events such as walks for hunger, marathons and bike rides, etc. Like the company picnic, corporate-sponsored charity events present another wonderful platform to cultivate existing relationships, expand your network and show yourself as a connector. Business becomes a meaningful by-product of these events.

A Purely Social Setting

I am frequently asked, "Is it acceptable to 'talk shop' or exchange business cards in a purely social setting such as a wedding or an intimate dinner party in someone's home?"

Conducting business or engaging in any form of self-promotion at any purely social setting such as a wedding or an intimate dinner in someone's home is considered taboo, and there are no circumstances under which it is appropriate to exchange *business* cards (especially in the presence of hosts or other guests). However, the judicious individual is able to leverage social settings and connections established here to advance business relationships. As my director of sales at the Interface group used to say, "Reach way down deep inside yourself" to access your **fabulous** artillery and finesse the situation with your keenest, most finely-honed people skills!

Exchanging Contact Information

While all your hard-hitting business instincts clamor to make the overture and offer or request a business card, resist, desist, refrain.

Fabulous: Exchange contact information subtly and quickly via IT device. Quietly programming contact information into an IT device is done, and considered quietly acceptable… but obviously, do *not* use the IT device during the event to make calls, receive or send texts, check your email, browse the web, etc.

STORY

I recently attended a wedding where an individual I met wanted to connect with my husband. The individual asked me for my email address, which he plugged right into his smartphone. The maneuver was subtly yet handily accomplished.

Note: If the social event has a business undercurrent (i.e.) the charity auction or industry softball tournament then yes, business cards may be exchanged freely without concern of any impropriety.

Exchanging Calling Cards at a Social Function.

*Exchanging *calling cards* is infinitely different from exchanging *business cards*, and is completely acceptable at social functions.

Carrying a calling card in addition to your business card, generally speaking, is prudent, because you never know who you may meet when or where, and you do not want to wind up writing your contact information on a cocktail napkin. The mere fact that you have a calling card shows you as up-market, proactive, forward-thinking — not to mention refined.

Today, when so many of us will traverse in and out of companies and continents, the need for connections derived from business-related events and social settings becomes indispensable — something upon which the savvy business professional will capitalize. Doing so will enhance your business reputation as one who is socially astute and well-connected... and you will profit from an opportunity others may miss!

A Wedding, Surprise Party, Housewarming, Graduation etc.

Situation. You have met another guest at any of the above venues and believe you may have some common business synergies you would like to explore.

Fine: You know it is not appropriate, but (quietly) say you would like to follow-up (with them) and offer your card, *sub rosa*. You always carry business cards with you, just in case.

Fabulous: Tact and discretion are absolutely key here. You are this wedding/surprise party/housewarming/graduation for a purpose. Engage your target with something pertaining specifically to the event — which is the reason you are both there. Make the conversation, your curiosity, and excitement all about that event which you are experiencing together. *Look for points of connectivity with the other person through the prism of the event;* never ask for a business card!

Fine: Ask another guest if they know how to contact your target.

Fabulous: Ask your host after the event to connect you. Having your host serve as the conduit further legitimizes you, and will no doubt delight your host knowing they were able to help forge a connection.

OR:

- Tell your target you have enjoyed meeting them and would like to stay in touch. Do not be one of those "hangeron-ers" — *Walk away!* When you do follow-up, mention (i.e.) Stephanie's wedding/Matt's surprise party/Jennifer's housewarming/Brooke's graduation. Remember, it's not about the business, it's about the *connection*!
- Follow-up with a brief personal note, email or text or place a personal telephone call as you deem appropriate; *ask* how they prefer to be contacted.
- Keep initial contact brief and reflective back to the event (the wedding, the one you both attended, where you met, where you shared the fact that you both always cry at weddings, where you enjoyed the beautiful music, admired the imported flowers, laughed the hysterical toasts at the wedding, etc.). *The wedding* is your <u>common denominator</u>.

THEN, explore business interests and underscore "what's in it for them." Determine their receptivity level and proceed accordingly. If not, you'll always have Paris!

Making Conversation

Situation. You met another guest at a friend's house-warming where the hosts proudly displayed unique collectibles from their world travels. Your hosts have opened up their home and their very personal life to you. You are honored to be counted among those present. You are *not* going to bring up the Judy Jones project. You are going to talk about your hosts, their beautiful home, their **fabulous** friends, their amazing collectibles.

Bringing it to the next level

Be strategic:

➢ Take it off the social field and make it compelling.

- Let them know up front *what's in it for them*, i.e., "I'd like to work on your campaign." "I have a few marketing ideas I'd like to share with you."
- *Ask* if you may contact them.
- When you connect, focus on the shared event before you segue into business exploration.

Social savvy is so termed for good reason. Business profit stemming from any purely social event requires finesse, tact and discretion. Social savvy is an *art* and cannot be overstated. Sometimes an impulse-move works as well, but be careful.

En Medias Res

You are in a state of professional transition and people inquire about employment status at social gatherings.

Fine: Evade the question regarding where you are employed (or that you are unemployed or "between jobs") by any means.

Fabulous: Be upbeat and confident. Be prepared to state succinctly your expertise, including what you do, have done, are hoping to do. Confidently articulate what you bring to a new employer or situation.

Fabulous: Have a *calling card* at the ready. You do not want to insult your host by turning their social gathering into your personal job counseling service — at the same time, you do not want to let an opportunity fade. A personal calling card is a great way to make a connection at a social event; you can follow up later for business purposes.

CHAPTER 2

Fabulous @ Handshaking & Business Cards

Wherever you are in the world, professionals will be shaking many hands and exchanging *plus des* business cards. Whether on a plane, at a business meeting, traveling overseas, attending an industry function, or meeting clients at a restaurant, showing you know how to expertly and most respectfully execute these two seemingly perfunctory, yet vitally important actions will definitely help set you apart. Combined with networking skills, being **fabulous** at handshaking and business card etiquette will serve you well in every professional encounter.

Handshaking

Handshaking furnishes important and empowering information about the other person. It is my practice to shake hands with every seminar participant prior to all my programs. I know, after shaking everyone's hand, who is keenly interested, who may be a bit anxious, reticent, etc.

I also make it my practice to ask students and young adults (Gen X and younger), "How many have ever been *taught* how to shake hands?" Interestingly, especially these days, it has become the norm to see NOT ONE hand go up. This is a big problem and should be a major concern to all of us who are trying to prepare and groom our young adults as they come into their own and prepare to enter the world of business. No one is born knowing *anything*. Certainly, no one is born knowing how to shake hands. If they are not being taught, how can we expect our young adults, America's future leaders to *know?*

Origin:

The origin of handshaking dates back to the time of kings and castles. Whenever two knights would approach each other on horseback they would hold up their right arm as a gesture of peace; from this first wave of amity evolved the art of *Handshaking* as we know it today. Although there are different types of handshakes here in the U.S. and in other parts of the world, handshaking is the most common form of greeting in the world today. Remember, whenever we shake hands, we are sending and receiving volumes of powerful, empowering information.

Definition of Handshaking

The dictionary defines handshaking as "The grasping of hands by two people as in greeting or leave-taking." Handshaking is a form of greeting, saying farewell, a sign of a promise or sealing a bargain. Do you remember when the "gentleman's handshake" was not an uncommon way to seal a deal?

You can tell a lot about a person by their handshake. Handshaking provides another opportunity to "be a man/woman well-met." Shake hands like you mean it, like you want to be remembered in all positive ways!

Please consider the following handshakes as the information transmitted will help empower us.

The Correct Handshake

The Number One Rule regarding shaking hands: *whenever you shake hands, always STAND as a sign of respect.*

Connect the "V" of our right hand with the "V" of the other person's right hand — between the thumb and index finger of each hand. Resist the urge to stop at the knuckle. Get IN to the "V" and connect. Pump one to two times.

Steps:

1. Step IN toward the other person.
2. Tilt your head to the side (for warmth).
3. Tuck your left hand behind your back to eliminate the left dangling arm; you don't need it, and it just gets in the way. We refer to this as the *"Presidential Pose."*

Shake hands with authority and conviction. Make excellent eye contact* and offer a warm and sincere smile.

*Be aware that in other parts of the world (i.e., Japan) eye contact is *not* a desired goal… although most Japanese executives are aware of our customs and traditions and are training their business professionals to make eye contact when meeting U.S. executives. In the meantime, U.S. executives are being trained to focus on the knots of their ties when meeting with their Japanese counterparts! Be aware of cross-cultural differences and when in doubt, always ask.

The Fingertip Holder (together with the limp wrist)

The silent message: this person prefers to keep others at a distance. Often, this is an older, reticent individual who is (silently) saying, "I know I must shake hands… let's just do this to get it over with and out of the way."

You then make the determination to either:

1. Honor their preference and keep them at a distance (particularly if this is an older individual or in a more social setting).
2. In business, I urge you to be a bit more aggressive and actually bring the other person into the "V" or *web* of your right hand (see the Correct Handshake above).

The Bone-Crusher

An overly aggressive individual who, however unwittingly, attempts to demoralize their "opponent" is actually over-compensating for their own insecurity or anxiety.

Remember: 94.7% of all adults are a bit nervous or anxious prior to any meeting, networking event, presentation, even a party! Therefore, if you are ever feeling a bit nervous, anxious or insecure, please know you are not alone.

When we shake hands like we mean it we will "be a man/woman well-met" and positively received. There is no need to bone-crush the other person's hand.

The Dominant Handshake

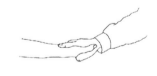

Typically, (some) men will extend their hand in this way to a woman (whom they feel they can control, consciously or subconsciously). They are silently trying to *impose* themselves and *dominate*. Ladies, don't we love this? (NOT!) Do *not* empower this handshake. Quickly and without comment swing *their* right hand upright to the vertical position. Gently yet firmly, with good eye contact (and a twinkle in your eye), flash your infectious smile, and you will be "a person well met" indeed, an individual with whom to be reckoned.

The Double-Handed Handshake (second hand over their forearm or hand)

This handshake is more often used with people you know well, by politicians, or at funerals ("I am so sorry for your loss") and is like a "hand-hug." This is not considered the most professional handshake, however, it is memorable.

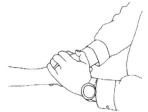

STORY — A HANDSHAKE "EXPERIENCE"

One of the most unforgettable handshakes I have ever had was truly a handshake experience:

I had the pleasure and honor of meeting President Reagan at a private reception at the Waldorf Astoria in New York. My good friend Rick Ahearn was President Reagan's Chief Advance person responsible for arranging all his trips. Rick invited me to a fundraiser and private reception to meet the president and have my picture taken with him. I will never — ever — forget shaking President Reagan's hand.

The President extended to me the double-handed handshake and I will never forget the feeling of his warm padded hands. I felt safe and his hands were so reassuring. This, together with his sparkling eyes looking directly into my soul was an amazing experience; I completely melted.

The On-and-On Handshake

The silent message being conveyed: "So far so good — I know I am doing the right thing. I am initiating the handshake, I have established eye-contact, I am initiating the conversation, but help! Where do I go from here?" You, **fabulous** professional, will take *control* of this awkward yet all-too-familiar situation and offer a firm yet gentle and *reassuring* squeeze, make good eye-contact, and then gently withdraw your hand.

The "Clammy Handshake"

Clammy hands betray your anxiety and are the *"kiss of death!"*

Situation. You look great. You have just finished an amazingly **fabulous** presentation... and you can tell by eye contact and body language that your audience is totally engaged and completely buying IN to your presentation and message, your demeanor and personal style. However, you know, that at the end of your time together you will be shaking hands and yours are dripping!

We suggest eliminating the most remote possibility of any of us being caught with clammy hands ever again.

How: Upon entering the building (for the meeting, the interview, presentation or net-working event) <u>go to the restroom</u>. There, we want to check everything, including dandruff, stray hairs, buttons and zippers. Pop a breath mint. Ladies — make sure your lipstick is not smudged or on your teeth, check for "raccoons" (mascara under the eyes), and carry an extra pair of hosiery, just in case. Gentlemen — straighten your tie, pull up your socks, and you may want to carry an electric razor, just in case.

Then, perform the single most important activity while you are there: *Wash your hands thoroughly with warm water and soap, and dry them thoroughly.* Doing so helps eliminate the body oils which tend to activate dampness and encourage "clammy hands — the kiss of death!"

Running warm water over the veins of your forearms will also help warm you up if hands are cold, or run cold water over your forearms if you are overheated.

Consider brushing your teeth. Sharing breath mints, hair spray, dental floss is not uncommon in restrooms prior to a networking event. Much preparation rightfully goes into our all-important "First Impression," our personal presentation to the world (!) and most basically… our handshake.

International Handshakes

Be aware that in different parts of the world there are different types of handshakes.

France, Germany: One brisk "pump"

Latin American, Arab cultures: A light, lingering handshake; to withdraw your hand too quickly might be misinterpreted as an insult.

Japan: A handshake AND a bow. There are three levels of bow: the 15°, 35° and 50° angles. Each person steps aside to *their* left and will then bow (this prevents butting heads). The more senior the executive, the lower the bow. Meetings should be scheduled "level-to-level," and bows should be bestowed according to rank, status and even age, as age is highly revered in Japan.

Kissing

Kissing is a European tradition, although it is now seen more here in the U.S. today, as we are more of a global culture.

"Air kissing" ("*AHello Dahling!*") is considered an affectation. If you are going to kiss, touch the cheek with your lips or a corner of your lips. If you have this relationship with the other individual, for women, this is an opportunity to endearingly smudge lipstick off the recipient's cheek. Kissing on the mouth is personal and truly reserved to express the most intimate level of expression, reserved for couples socially — no PDA's (Public Displays of Affection) in business. When in doubt: don't do it!

In business, if your relationship suggests a kiss upon greeting or saying farewell, kiss discreetly, i.e., in the lobby or your private office, not the boardroom.

The French are known for two kisses, one on each cheek, starting right to left, as with the handshake.

Italians: Two or even four kisses, alternating cheeks, for a very formal greeting or award recognition.

STORY

When my husband and I visited the Amalfi Coast we were invited to a private performance/award recognition ceremony held by the Italian Ambassador/Director of Tourism. All the mayors of every city in Italy were in attendance on stage, and after each performance, each mayor extended personal congratulations and gave four kisses to each of the performers.

The Germans and Brits are a bit more reserved with kisses, especially in business.

In Spain, kiss twice, and again, start with the right cheek.

The American South: Kissing is common. Read (their) body language and go with it, regardless of how you feel about personal space issues.

Be careful about assuming this level of intimacy too soon in the relationship.

We are global. When first meeting others we need to be on our toes and ready for whatever type of handshake (or other form of greeting) is extended to us.

Eliminating Barriers

Rule: Remove gloves (and if possible, glasses) before shaking hands.

The only person (in the world) permitted to shake hands with gloves ON: The beloved Queen of England!

Fabulous: Eliminate barriers such as gloves, sunglasses and, if you have the ability to wear eyeglasses selectively, take them OFF upon first meeting/greeting another.

Remember, we want nothing to interfere with the warmth we endeavor to establish as we work to build *trust* to grow critical interpersonal relationships.

Fine: Shake hands across the desk.

Fabulous: Come out from behind the barrier of the desk. (If unavoidable, shake hands across the desk, however, acknowledge, "Please excuse the desk.")

Who Should Initiate the Handshake?

Because there are no gender rules in business, whoever initiates the handshake, initiates, acquires and maintains *control* — always our goal. Always try to reach out first.

Shaking Hands and Disabilities

Shaking hands with anyone with a disability requires us to be sensitive. Be aware that someone whose right hand is disabled will usually offer you their left hand in reverse.

Be at the ready and on your toes for whatever type of handshake is offered. Keep a sparkle in your eye, beam your infectious smile and make those you meet feel *acknowledged* and comfortable and you will "be a man/woman well-met." You will be remembered and *stand apart* in all positive ways.

Resisting/Refusing/Ignoring Your Handshake

Situation. You extend your hand to greet another and shake their hand and they walk away or ignore your proffered hand.

Response. Do not take this as a slight. Some may not be thinking, others may be preoccupied and still others may not even be aware! However, in response, professionally, I recommend being a bit more aggressive and actually saying something such as, "I would really like to shake your hand, (use their name)." My experience has been that others feel flattered and are impressed when we are proactive and make this overture.

Handshaking with Those Who are Ill

The handshaking ritual has many rewards and risks, as well. Spreading germs is a common by-product of hand-shakings. Therefore, if you are not well:

- Gesticulate that you are not well (without going into detail). Say: "I am sorry, I would like to shake your hand; however, I am not well and do not want to risk spreading germs." Saying this — without going into morbid detail — is responsible and respectful.

Fine: Carry Kleenex

Fabulous: Carry a cloth handkerchief. This is also a "red flag" that you are not well.

(*International protocol note*: Some societies, notably Japan, consider it extremely unhygienic to use a fabric handkerchief. For utilitarian purposes, only use paper tissues to blow your nose. Do your cultural research! This note is repeated in Chapter 5, *Fabulous @ Professional Attire*.)

Wash your hands after shaking hands, or carry a hand sanitizer. Use this discreetly!

Some Final Notes on Handshaking

- Handshaking is the most common form of greeting in the world today. Even those from countries who historically have bowed or hugged in greeting or farewell now shake hands as well.
- Many young people and even many adults are not comfortable shaking hands. As with anything we do, the more we practice, the more proficient we become. No one is ever too old or too young to start shaking hands, and fabulous professionals should lead by example.
- Those in many Eastern countries, such as China, Japan, the Middle East, India, Pakistan, etc., do not shake hands with members of the *opposite* sex for religious and cultural reasons. Refraining from initiating bodily contact is a show of respect (to the person of the opposite sex). *Note: there is no breach (of protocol) when men shake hands with men and women shake hands with women.*
- Hand-holding, hugging and embracing is common in other cultures and it is not uncommon to do both — handshake and kiss/hug/embrace when meeting

our counterparts — out of respect for them and their culture. We have seen many photographs of President Bush holding hands with foreign dignitaries in the Rose Garden.

Business Cards

The timeless, traditional business card remains an integral part of the business landscape today and when offered expertly, together with a handshake, silently portrays us as the consummate professional. The business card itself is your company's opportunity to establish their "first impression" in the business culture and when used properly the business card will permit us to access and share valuable information about ourselves and our firm/service. Discard any concern that the paper business card may be becoming obsolete in an increasingly paperless world: the traditional business card is *timeless*. The everyday practice of business card exchange is time-honored and presents us with an instant opportunity to *stand apart*.

Consider your business card as your ticket IN. Adhering to traditional rules governing business card protocol demonstrates respect, shows you know "the difference" and will help you *stand apart* and advance. In this section, we will reveal the art of business card protocol from inception to execution.

Note: The Japanese have taught us everything we know about business card exchange. Until very recently, most Japanese worked for the same company their entire lives. Thus, their business card ("*meishi*," which literally translated means "face") represented their "life." Therefore, the quality of the card's paper stock is important, as well as where a business card is kept, how it is presented, received, acknowledged and ultimately placed. Traditional business card protocol and exchange is almost ritualistic.

Paper Stock and Aesthetics

The paper stock you select presents an opportunity to convey silent information pertaining to the quality of your firm/service.

Fine: Make your own card or research low cost online or local printers, and use their standard paper stock.

Fabulous:

- Invest in high quality cards. Use quality stock — as close to 100% cotton/linen as possible, or bamboo is special. A cheap, flimsy or laminated card essentially says you are too! Make sure your card reflects your business brand.
- Have your card professionally set and designed. Include your logo if you have one. Aesthetics are even more important for an entrepreneur or an independent contractor without a recognizable brand.

If someone hands you a cheap, flimsy or laminated business card, you may want to reconsider placing them on your "A" list!

Colors and Font

The colors of our card and even the font we select convey information and present another opportunity to silently make a statement.

Fine: Select whatever colors and font style you personally prefer.

Fabulous: White or ecru is considered the most traditional as well as the most professional color stock. Lettering should be black, blue or gray ink.

Fabulous: Embossed, engraved or raised lettering is recommended.

Color choices are personal, however, many cards sport company colors. Bear in mind that colors in and of themselves hold meaning and subliminally send messages. For example, forest green engenders trust and friendship, blue conveys warmth and trust, lavender is soothing, red says "go!", black is professional, silver suggests a more European influence, gold is elegant, etc.

Use fun colors and graphics if you are in a creative or entertainment business, in the graphics design industry or child daycare business, for example.

Be sure lettering is large enough to read!

Business Card Content

The information printed on your business card is to be considered.

Fine: Place as much information on the card as you are able to fit.

Fabulous: (Protocolically speaking) the *only* information which should appear on the front of a business card is the following:

- Name
- Title
- Company name
- Address
- Email address
- Website
- Telephone/cell phone options
- Fax
- Company logos, cell phone numbers, artwork and photos are discretionary.

Fine: Place marketing information the back of your card.

Fabulous: (Protocolically speaking) the only information that belongs on the back of a business card is the same information which appears on the front of the card, printed in your target country's native language, presented readable side up. (Print any marketing information or support material on a separate flyer or brochure.)

Photographs

Including your picture on your card is an option.

Fine: Have your picture on your card.

Fabulous*:* If you are in an industry where your picture is important for marketing purposes — if you are an actor or model, for example, or in real estate, direct sales, etc. — then it is appropriate to have a photo on your business card.

Artwork
Having artwork on your card is also an option.

Fine: Position artwork anywhere on the card.

Fabulous: Use artwork selectively — unless you are an *artiste* (!)... then make your card a work of (your) art.

Should you choose to use artwork, watermarking is a rich look: superimpose artwork as a translucent design impressed on the paper during manufacture which is visible when the finished paper is held to light. The artwork appears as lightly faded in the background of the card and is very subtle, completely **fabulous**.

Business Card Cases
Business card cases make a statement about you and present another opportunity to *stand apart.*

Fine: Use the complimentary vinyl case provided with the pack of 500, or carry a statement case such as leopard skin, fun bright colors, Swarovski crystal, daisies, pearls, etc.

Fabulous: Invest in a quality case — the case need not be solid gold or silver but *quality.* Leather, tortoise, and pewter are recommended. Be careful with colors again, unless you are in a colorful industry, so to speak, or care to share your sparkling personality in the business arena.

Regarding vinyl card cases, if conducting business in India, for example, where the cow is sacred, then it would be appropriate to use a vinyl case (rather than leather). Also consider metal, tortoise, wood, etc.

Writing on Business Cards
While networking, expect to collect and write on many cards and make brief notations as we meet others. Protocol suggests that we ask before writing on another's business card.

Rule: Never write on another's business card:*
1. In their presence, or
2. Without asking permission, as technically, you are defacing their *life!* (See above, regarding Japanese custom of viewing their business card as their life.)

Situation. Someone is about to share their direct dial, cell phone or home telephone number not listed on their card.

Question. Where to write this information?

Fine: Write this anywhere on their card there is room.

Fabulous: Say, "Would you mind, Mr. X, if I wrote that on the back of your card?" Asking shows you know the protocol, that it is not acceptable to do so, and demonstrates respect.

Making/Taking PERSONAL Notes

While networking, expect to learn and share much information during dialogue.

Fine: Hope to remember everything discussed.

Fabulous: Quickly jot down personal information and key issues after you have spoken. Take a moment and go into the corridor or outside the meeting room, or into the restroom, to write down this information. Writing in their presence suggests they (and their information) are not memorable.

Recording IMPORTANT/BUSINESS Information

Where you record valuable information shared presents another opportunity to *stand apart*.

Fine: Write important information on the back of their card.

Fabulous: Writing "big" information on the back of their small card is not a good idea because it minimizes the importance of the information, possibly even conveying that their data is small or insignificant, hence, insulting. Write important information on a separate sheet of paper from your portfolio and use your quality pen.

Asking a Very Senior Person for their Business Card

Rule: Never ask a very senior executive for their business card.

They won't have one.

Senior Executives do not carry cards unless they are traveling in and among their *ilk*.

Reason: their status suggests you should know how to find this person and follow-up. Therefore, asking very senior executives for their card might be misinterpreted as a slight.

STORY

On many occasions, I have shared the story where I found myself at an event where the president of a major bank in Boston was in attendance. We were introduced (by the mutually respected third party) and the bank president said, "Yes, **Judy!** It is a pleasure meeting you! We have been considering bringing your services in here at the bank. Do you have a card?"

"Of course," I eagerly gave the bank president my card and instinctively added, "and do you have a card, Mr. X?"

Have you ever said something and, as soon as you said it, wished you could reinsert the words back into your mouth? Well, this was one of those times for me! The president looked disapprovingly at me and said, "No, **Ms. Bowman**, I do not." I clearly insulted him by suggesting he was not important enough for me to know how to find him. Or the fact that I asked implied that I did not know the correct protocol here... ergo, what else might I not know? Either way, this was not good.

To this day, I have done a very insignificant amount of business with this bank when I could and should be doing much more... this gentleman is still at the helm!

*Should a very senior person offer you their business card or ask for yours, consider this a great compliment!

Assuming Someone Wants Your Card

Fine: Extend your card automatically whenever you extend your hand for a handshake.
Rule: Never presume anyone wants your card.

Fabulous: Always ask, "May I offer you my card?" or "May I ask for one of your cards?" Asking shows you assume nothing as you endeavor to grow *trust* and cultivate important business relationships.

STORY

Many years ago I attended a business expo and had exchanged many cards at many booths. I came upon one gentleman manning his own booth who unknowingly educated me and forever changed my approach.

After I introduced myself and gave my tagline, I automatically extended my extended my hand to shake hands and offer my card, to which he responded, "I am not here to collect a lot of cards," looking at my name tag adding, "Ms. Bowman. If you want to follow-up with me after the show and send me something, you may do so."

The lesson here: Never assume anyone wants your card; always ASK.

How to Exchange Cards

How to exchange business cards presents another considerable opportunity to *stand apart*.

Fine: Distribute your cards as you would a deck of playing cards; take their cards and tuck them in your wallet for future reference.

Fabulous:

How to Present a Business Card:
- Business cards are not to be treated as a deck of playing cards.
- The most formal method: Use two thumbs, one on either corner, presented readable side UP and facing the recipient.
- The less formal method: One thumb on one corner, again presented readable side UP and facing the recipient.

How to Receive a Card:
- Receive *in kind*, meaning the same way the card was presented. Therefore, if they present their card with both thumbs on either corner, one should receive "in kind" with both of your thumbs on the opposite corners. Should they present their card with one thumb on either top corner, receive "in kind" with one of your thumbs on the opposite corner.

- The almost ritualistic manner of conveying and receiving the much-revered business card is critical in showing, as well as earning respect.

  *Be careful not to cover card information during the exchange, as this conceals one's *life*. (Again, see above for the source of this from Japanese business card protocol.)

- *Acknowledge* the (impressive) *quality* card. Feel it. Caress it. Study the card. Look back at the individual and *acknowledge* their impressive card, title, *life!*

- Place their card some place respectful such as your designated pocket, inside your portfolio, etc. Do not toss, stuff, bend, fold or damage their card in any way; be sure to acknowledge the *life* significance that business card holds and treat the card with near-reverence.

Exchanging Business Cards at Networking Events

Business card exchange at networking events is a given. We expect to exchange many cards, often.

Fine: Keep business cards in your quality business card case and exchange with as many individuals as possible.

Fabulous: When networking, wear attire conducive to business card exchange. Even though we own a *quality* business card holder, using one during a busy networking event where we expect to exchange many cards is often not efficient, because the process of retrieving and opening the case, taking out a card, properly presenting, closing and putting away the case, receiving their cards, etc., can be cumbersome, even awkward.

Ladies: Pre-plan attire to wear a jacket with large pockets — one for incoming and one for out-going business cards, or have a designated area easily accessible such as an outer pocket or purse pouch. Your **fabulous** networking attire arsenal helps ensure a seamless (pun intended) networking experience.

Gentlemen: Keep cards easily accessible such as inside your inner breast pocket, which helps facilitate the smooth transfer and exchange of cards.

Business Card Exchange at a Meeting

The exchange of business cards at a meeting presents another opportunity to show you know "the difference" and *stand apart*.

When to Exchange Cards

Fine: Exchange cards before or after the meeting. (Just be sure to get the cards of all those in attendance.)

Fabulous:

- Exchange business cards *before* the meeting as you introduce yourself to others and shake hands. Subtly, yet strategically, align cards around your portfolio to coincide with seating so that you are able to use cards to access names as you address individuals, thereby keeping you in *control.*

*Note: If a card is presented at the table where only one other person is in attendance, their card is kept on top of your leather case while you talk. If several people are involved in the meeting and you have several *meishi,* position the individual's card holding the highest rank on top of your leather portfolio, with the others strategically aligned beside you on the table.

Presenting Damaged Cards

Situation. You just met someone with whom you would like to exchange cards. However, this is your very last card. The card is marred in some way or has a small stain, or perhaps it is a bit bent from having been kept in your wallet.

Fine: Hand this card out with your apologies, as we do not want to miss an opportunity to connect with this excellent new prospect.

Fabulous: Every card we present to anyone should be pristine. A bent, frayed or damaged card in any way suggests we are, too (so to speak) and should be tossed. Having a damaged card is analogous to having no card at all.

- Apologize and explain you have no cards left; ask for their card.
- Mail them a note on your personal stationery, letting them know how much you enjoyed your encounter and your conversation. Enclose your (quality, pristine) business card along with your note. Be sure to write the note about them, meeting them, your encounter. The card then becomes ancillary. You have reestablished contact, your goal.

*Rule: Never distribute a business card which is bent, frayed or damaged in any way. Damaged cards should be discarded.

STORY

I was conducting a seminar on networking when a gentleman raised his hand, stood, produced his wallet and proceeded to pull out a business card that someone had given him on a train, he explained.

Clearly, this person wanted to be sure they made the connection and had apologized, saying this was their "last card." The gentleman proceeded to unfold the small card which had been folded twice. The card had coffee stains, was frayed and actually looked diseased.

The gentleman did keep the man's card and he certainly will be remembered — however, not for reasons pertaining to conducting future business. The card was kept to show others what <u>never</u> to do, even if it is your "last card!"

Key Takeaways For Business Cards:

1. Select quality stock.
2. Use colors and font style consistent with your business and message.
3. Present and receive "in kind."
4. *Acknowledge* their card!
5. Place cards someplace respectful.
6. If someone would like to give you their (i.e.) direct dial or home phone, write this on the back of their card; *ask first*.
7. Never write on anyone's card in their presence, without first asking permission.
8. Write personal notes *sub rosa*.
9. Never ask a very senior person for their business card. Of course you know how to find them and follow-up.
10. Should a very senior person offer you their business card or ask for yours, consider this a great compliment!
11. Never assume anyone wants your card; always ask.
12. Never give out a damaged or dirty card, even if it is your last one.

The traditional business card continues to be invaluable in its original form, even amidst extraordinary technological advances. Proper use of this timeless business essential will help propel you to **fabulous** status anywhere in the world.

Virtual Cards

Today's digital age unleashes the capability to replicate cards in virtual form.

Fine: Use virtual cards exclusively as they are efficient and cost-effective.

Fabulous: You may *offer* a virtual card to complement, not replace, the paper card. Nothing will ever replace the traditional paper business card, because it is timeless. NOT using a paper card is a missed opportunity; your business card is your ticket IN and a "secret weapon." Draw this from your **fabulous** arsenal of tools and use your time-honored paper card to make a professional statement and *stand apart*.

Calling Cards: Everything Old is New Again

A Bit of History

Calling cards were originally given to the butler in Victorian England when calling on a lady. The caller would place a calling card on a silver tray, which was presented to the lady. The card would be returned and, if the corner was slightly turned down, the lady was not interested in having the visitor pursue her. If the corner was slightly turned up, she was interested.

Calling Cards in Business

Today, calling cards have made a resounding comeback, for social reasons as well as those pertaining to business. Until recently, it was expected that individuals in business would always use their company card when making business connections and reaching out socially.

But life is cyclical and times have changed. In today's turbulent, competitive economic climate, we may expect to change jobs frequently. Individuals in rapidly emerging industries change jobs often and there are many in transition, entering and re-entering the job market, or moving between various fields. When we go on an interview or meet with a potential client or employer, we are promoting *ourselves* — *not* our current company or employer. Therefore, having and using our own calling cards is much more appropriate than using a business card. Those actively engaged in transition, quietly transitioning, and those with a side business and singles should all have calling cards. Scores of individuals are freelancing, consulting, etc., and need cards as a conduit. Having a calling card today is impressive and also speaks to credibility.

Actually, NOT having a personal calling card can compromise one's professional credibility. When someone asks for your card and you have nothing to give them, this does not reflect well on you. Writing your contact information on a cocktail napkin or scrap of paper does not send the **fabulous** message you wish to convey.

Information on Calling Cards

When it comes to creating a calling card, standard guidelines of traditional business cards apply. Our calling card is a reflection of us, therefore, we decide if this is to be quality, elegant, distinctive, fun, playful, ecologically efficient (green), etc., or not. Either way, a calling card should contain the following information only:

- Name
- Telephone
- Email address

Do not provide an actual physical address unless you want to; a post office box address is discretionary.

*If you wish to brand yourself as an "Actor," "Photographer," "Tutor," etc., this may be placed on your calling card, however, this is completely optional, as are photos and artwork.

The calling card should stand alone as your own personal mechanism to use and leverage as you deem appropriate.

*Calling cards are used socially and for subtle business reasons. They are seen more often among the 20-to-40 set. (See Chapter 8, *Fabulous @ The Interview*, for more information on the appropriate use of Calling Cards vs. Business Cards.)

CHAPTER 3

Fabulous @ Telephone Skills

Telephone technology may not be as new and cutting edge as some of the most recent forms of instant communication. However, make no mistake, the telephone offers so many advantages in the business world that this chapter requires three major sub-topics:

1. General Telephone Techniques.
2. Telephone Sales Savvy.
3. Inside Telephone Staff Training (for Receptionists, Operators, and Administrative/ Executive Assistants).

Review the following with Department Heads, Sales Representatives and Administrative Staff, and include in basic company orientation. The result: your business will continue to thrive every time the telephone rings — inbound or outbound! Practice these specific nuances to nurture your **fabulous** phone skills, and you will truly *stand apart* on any professional call.

Introduction

Despite all our recent technological communication advances and capabilities, the telephone has unequivocally proven itself a universal business staple. The telephone provides a unique opportunity to personally communicate while advancing branding efforts, and can be used unequivocally to help us *stand apart* and better compete in our global marketplace. Meaningful restrictions exist pertaining to travel costs and *per diems* for face-to-face meetings, which also involve time away from the office and family. We cannot overstate the importance of professional telephone training in order to be most effective in business and optimize our office time.

Many are challenged — and perhaps even a bit intimidated — when it comes to effectively using this inanimate object. As most things challenging in life, the telephone has its own skill set and rules governing accepted, even exceptional performance. And, as with most things challenging, the more we use the telephone and practice, the more adept we become. Being telephone savvy in business is an art and an area of productivity into which the savvy professional knows how to dial/tap (pun intended). The telephone is the only object which literally stands between, yet has the potential to quickly connect, us and our target. The all-embracing goals of this chapter:

1. To instill *confidence* in telephone usage.
2. To develop a professional yet authentic **fabulous** telephone style.
3. To standardize performance so clients will experience the same level of efficiency and internal consistency from you/your department/company.

Clients should come to expect the same degree of professionalism (and courtesy) each time they call you or hear from anyone in your firm. You are all part of the same brand. Standardizing telephone training to ensure consistent performance will be appreciated and valued by your staff and noticed by your clients and anyone communicating with your firm. This will enhance client *trust,* speaks to firm reputation and will positively perpetuate branding efforts.

Challenges

Inherent in the telephone are certain advantages and challenges. Neither party has a visual, therefore, neither is able to:

*   Look into the other persons' eyes ("eyes are a more exact witness to the soul")
*   Shake a warm hand
*   Assess how the other is attired
*   Make judgments and glean information from office surroundings and atmosphere
*   Present a complete picture and truly "be a man/woman well-met!"

Advantages

On the other hand, neither party need worry about:

*   Clammy hands
*   Bad breath
*   Being meticulously attired
*   Office surroundings/personal effects being scrutinized

Telephone vs. Electronic Communications

Electronic communications, while useful, still do not outrank the telephone in terms of potency. In the pecking order, after face-to-face meetings, the next best medium is the telephone. Reaching out to someone by picking up the telephone requires extra effort. Making this effort shows not only that you care, this effort makes them feel valued, special. (See the next chapter, *Fabulous @ Electronic Communications*, for tips on how to *stand apart* while managing technology.)

Voice

The human voice conveys valuable information. This medium is very different from, i.e., following someone's blog or tweets, sending a quick text, posting on their wall, or sending an email. Using your voice enables others to learn important information while hearing emotions such as enthusiasm, impatience, interest, boredom, excitement, annoyance, etc., and many other senses come into play. As savvy business professionals we use the medium of voice to our advantage. Picking up the telephone and using our voice enables a stronger personal connection. Simply stated, the telephone enables emotional involvement, and people buy with emotion.

STORY

I send out quarterly newsletters and have done so for the past twenty years to communicate with my clients. However, whenever I take the time to pick up the phone — the old-fashioned way — to connect with people, we have a chance to renew our personal relationship and business connection, and catch up with each other. Relying solely on electronic newsletters, blogs and social networking efforts is not the same as a one-on-one, live telephone call. Use the telephone to tap into, dial up and ring in business relationships (all puns intended!).

That said, the telephone is not easy to manage. Aside from Skype and various smartphone video-chat apps such as Tango, we still lack the luxury of physically viewing the other person, looking into their eyes, shaking a warm (or clammy) hand, and gleaning as much information as we do in a face-to-face meeting. We miss subtle clues about them, their office surroundings, body language, nuances, messages conveyed by attire, and so on. While the telephone is more personal than online communications, we still need to know how to optimize and manage the medium to best project ourselves and enable a most effective interpersonal connection.

1) General Telephone Techniques

Identify the immediate goal (as well as the ultimate goal) of *this* call before dialing. Rarely do things "just happen." We create opportunities. Being prepared will properly position us from the first "Hello!"

Initiating A Cold Call

Some are more comfortable and seem more natural and adept at making cold calls — however, are they really? While some find these cold calls challenging, many more are positively petrified at the thought of picking up the phone and calling a complete stranger, let alone have a live conversation. Make no mistake, those who seem at ease making cold calls have been coached and practice *a lot*. With the right tools anyone can get the edge and hone the art to confidently initiate and execute the dreaded "cold call."

STORY

I make it my practice to initially try to connect with the president or CEO directly, in order to personally introduce myself and our firm's services. I have learned painfully through the years (with large companies in particular) that unless I have already met this individual, trying to reach the president or CEO of a very large firm via a cold call more often than not requires other internal connections, even an internal champion.

However, there is a way to reach "Mr. Big/Ms. Grande."

Fine: Call the company and ask to speak with Mr. Big.

Fabulous: Place a call to the executive assistant/administrative assistant (who answers their telephone) and introduce yourself. The way you introduce and present yourself and your firm's service here is critical to getting to the next step.

Treat the admin as if they *are* the CEO and respectfully provide your full background information as it pertains to you, your firm, your services and what's in it for them. Advancing internally with the help of the CEO's admin is meaningful and gives you credibility to gain more access. More often than not, admins will refer me to a key department head. Calling (or even being transferred to) a department head at the recommendation of the CEO's personal executive assistant is strong.

When the CEO's admin connects you to the appropriate department:

Fine: Once connected, re-introduce yourself and state the nature of your call.

Fabulous:

- *Ask* if you may use the admin's name (the name of the CEO's office is implied).
- Use the admin's name when introducing yourself to the department head.

> *"Being fabulous is recognizing that admins run the world."*
> **—Matt Schiffman**

We may think we know who can help us, however, we may be wrong. We may believe Mr. Big/Ms. Grande is "the one." But what if we're incorrect? What if the individual who really makes these decisions is in a different capacity, in another department? Remember that decision-making power is not necessarily always implicit or inherent in hierarchy.

Fine: Be relentlessly persistent until you get through to your target.

Fabulous: Cultivate *relationships* with each individual encountered along the way, beginning with the first person who answers the telephone.

Administrative Assistants and Executive Assistants are often the most knowledgeable and best connected. Receptionists can also be helpful and extremely influential. Do not be in a rush to get off the telephone with the person who takes your message. They just may just be your access person or even your internal champion.

Speakerphones

Speakerphones can be useful, intimidating, even obnoxious. Practice to be confident and speakerphone savvy in order to *stand apart*.

Fine: Go ahead and just place others on speakerphone.

Fabulous: Ask, "May I place you on speakerphone?"

Rule: *Always* ask *before placing anyone on speakerphone, and then wait for them to answer.*

The gesture of asking is **fabulous**. In our present day instant-action culture, we tend to lose sight of how really nice it is when someone actually pauses and waits for us to answer a question. Personal courtesies, standard operating procedure a generation ago, are no less necessary today. While they may have been temporarily misplaced, make no mistake: acknowledging others and showing personal courtesies toward others is time-honored, noticed, appreciated and handily sets you apart, especially these days.

STORY

As regional director of Carlisle, I placed a call to one of my consultants regarding an urgent matter. I was in high gear and intense in an effort to resolve a delicate client matter. As we spoke, I sensed something had happened to our connection; my consultant's voice sounded more distant and her words trailed off. I asked if something happened to our connection and she said, "Yeah — I put you on speakerphone. I'm putting on my makeup... go ahead..." Do you think this action resulted in an instant connection or a complete disconnect?

Always ask before placing anyone on speakerphone. It is not necessary to explain why, especially when reasons involve matters pertaining personal hygiene.

Who's in the Room?

Fine: Host will announce names of everyone present at the start of the call.

Fabulous: Host welcomes everyone, thanks them for being present and introduces everyone at the start of the call. (Please refer to Chapter 6, *Fabulous @ the Meeting*, for more on business meeting introductions and protocol.)

Speakerphone (Meeting) Participants

How participants conduct themselves is noticed and presents another opportunity to *stand apart*.

Fine: Speak and respond normally.

Fabulous: Speak very clearly into the speakerphone. Voices tend to drift, and there is nothing more frustrating than being uncertain who is speaking or not being able to hear.

Fabulous: Re-identify yourself when you speak ("This is Judy again") allowing other participants the opportunity to once again associate your voice with your name; do not assume everyone has instant recall of the sound of your voice.

Videophones/Video Conferencing

Should you use a videophone program on your computer or cell phone (Skype, Tango, etc.), remember to observe general rules of etiquette, dress and appearance as discussed in depth in Chapter 1, *Fabulous @ Networking*, as well as in the later chapters on *The Meeting, The Presentation* and *The Interview*, as the visual impact is so important.

Video conferencing is a more personal and interactive form of communication than (i.e.) telephone calls or email. Non-verbal cues and facial expressions matter. (See Chapter 6, *Fabulous @ The Meeting*, for in-depth information about Video Conferencing.)

2) Telephone Sales Savvy

The savvy telephone sales professional will *use their surroundings* to their advantage to access (and eventually *own*) information, i.e., post key phrases, word tracks, etc.

STORY

When I worked at The Interface Group in Internal Sales, before I became proficient handling objections and closing sales, I used to actually write down anticipated objections and company-coached responses. As a result, I had little post-it notes all around me. Yes, eventually I owned this information, however, whenever a new objection or any issue surfaced, I could simply post another note to help me be more articulate, compelling and effective.

Preparation

Mental Preparation

1. Mentally prepare for the day's anticipated and unexpected activities.
2. Forever endeavor to project your professional best.
3. Know when to "*walk away!*"
    Rule: *Do NOT even place the call if you are not up to the task or distracted. Callers will sense this and you will not be effective.*

STORY

Also at The Interface Group, we asked for telephone training. Our manager presented us with a 3" x 5" mirror and said, "Here's your training: Use this mirror. Pretend your reflection is the other person and smile. You can hear a smile through the wires." I did. I do. It works!

Advance Client Research

Prepare for *this* call. Pre-qualify before you attempt the connection. (I cannot tell you how many times I was reminded of the importance of this by omission. Please learn from my missteps.)

Research your target company's internal activities, as well your target themselves. Anticipate and prepare responses for any objections which may arise. A quiet consult with the "mutually respected third party" for clarification or information is always advised.

Verbal (Presentation) Preparation

Inside telephone professionals have very limited time to get and keep their target's attention. Therefore, how we convey our message each time we pick up the telephone is essential.

STORY

Early in my career I read Camille Lavington's book, *The First Three Seconds*, and was so riveted by this concept that I called Ms. Lavington and requested a meeting. I flew to New York and had a very productive and most enjoyable chat with the author. Ms. Lavington's ideology made a very big impression on me, one which I share with you herein.

Actually, some say you have only one (second) to connect or give them a reason to disconnect! Given this limited time/attention span, we need to carefully prepare our introductory presentation and use hard-working words and word tracks.

- Make each call sound *fresh*, like what you are saying is being said for the very *first* time!
- Endeavor to make each caller truly feel special and valued, not like just the next person on your call list.
- *Be yourself!*

Remember, people do business with people they like and *trust*. I do business with XYZ company because I like you, I *trust* you, I choose to do business with you.

Voice

The impact of your voice, tonal quality and volume, together with clarity, grammar and diction, cannot be overstated. Speaking within the cubicle environment may tend to make us more self-conscious and speak at lower volume levels, however, volume is important as it gives our voice inflection and color. If we do not speak with normal volume, we risk sounding monotone and boring.

Articulate and enunciate clearly, authoritatively, with *confidence* and conviction.

Breathe! Oxygen flowing into your brain will help dilate blood vessels, enhancing performance.

A Few Style Notes

Fine: "I am calling for *a Matt Schiffman*."

Fabulous: 'I am calling for *Matt Schiffman*." (There is only one.)

Fine: "I hope all is well with *the both of you*."

Fabulous: "I hope all is well with *both of you*." ("Both" is inclusive and implies two. The expression "the both of you" may be a colloquialism, however, is grammatically incorrect.)

Physical and Logistical Preparation

Props: Use a mirror and pretend your reflection is the other person. SMILE! You can literally *hear* a smile through the wires. Smiling helps ensure a personable, energetic, confident delivery.

Position your seat upright so you are not comfortable. Your goal is not to come across as relaxed and comfortable, but to project professionalism. When you sit upright, you are focused forward, attentive and alert. Excellent posture is imperative. Best yet, STAND.

Yes, STAND (versus sit) for *every* call, to help project a stronger, more confident authoritative voice. Standing is: better for your physical health and well-being, opens your vocal cords, and helps you better project... not to mention that it burns more calories! Pacing may help to relieve tension and deflect anxiety, and will also re-channel any nervous energy.

Invest in a good headset so your target can hear you clearly.

Use a land-line (preferably) versus cell phone for better audio clarity and uninterrupted connection.

Have your notes from advance research and updated information specific to *this* call.

Jot down talking points in advance of the call to be better prepared to leave a succinct voice mail message if necessary. Customize your opening for *this* client.

Ensure surroundings are quiet and not distracting. No one wants to hear your radio in the background, phones ringing or other people talking on your end. This is unprofessional and distracting. Check that your cell phone ringer is off.

Have water available. Be conscious of drinking healthy, i.e., water or green tea versus coffee — *Note*: tea actually has more caffeine than coffee if you are looking for a burst! (However... don't drink directly in your mouthpiece/microphone.)

Have note paper and working pens at the ready. Or, if you chose to use an IT device be conscious of "clicking" sounds as you take notes.

Be Attentive and Aware

Listen to how they answer the telephone. Their first "hello" conveys or betrays powerful information which you can use to your advantage. Are they speaking in first gear or fifth, so to speak? Do they sound open and receptive, or abrupt, rushed, distracted, bored, arrogant, etc.?

Refrain from multitasking. Be "fully present" and give *them* your full attention.

Be engaging, genuine, authentic... even fun! Use some humor; it is okay to be a bit playful, depending on personalities. Presidents Ronald Reagan and John F. Kennedy were both renowned for their effective use of humor and playfulness which helps to deflect tension and can even be endearing.

Be inclusive... speak in terms of "we" and "us." Assume that "you" and "I" are a "we."

Adjust your tone, pace, inflections, etc. to match theirs; be chameleon-like and mirror *them* in order to help you better connect.

Placing The Call

The Number One Rule in Sales — *(on the telephone or otherwise): Identify the client need and fulfill that need.*

- Extend a warm greeting.
- Identify yourself, your company affiliation and the name of your target.
- STAND, SMILE, project positively and be enthusiastic.
- Use your referral's name to enhance your credibility and the recognition factor, i.e., "I am grateful to Judy Jones for suggesting we connect."
- Respectfully inquire about the timing of your call in a way which encourages a positive response.

Fine: "Am I getting you at a good time?" (This suggests a more likely NO response and gives them a chance to say no, i.e., "Well, not really... I'm just on my way out," or "I have a telephone appointment in about three minutes.")

Fabulous: "I am getting you at a good time, yes?" (Project *positively! Assume the Sale!*)

- Use their honorific and ask how they prefer to be addressed: "Dr. Jones, how do you prefer to be addressed?" Never assume the familiar form of address.
- You have researched and prepared your opening introduction for this client and customized your call.
- Refer to your notes; however, *own* your information.
- Be the diagnostician. Ask probing, open-ended questions so they must speak *first*. Endeavor to ascertain what is being said *between* the lines.
- Employ the same savvy dialogue and active listening skills you normally use in face-to-face communication. Give them your full attention.
- Know how important vocal tone, inflections, vocabulary and mannerisms are to a conversation. These elements will help prompt genuine dialogue.

- Take both business and personal notes, and use this information in future communication to help cultivate relationships.
- Send a personal follow-up, thank you email and personal note, even a greeting card when appropriate.
- Remember to ask for referrals in a respectful way — not one which implies "Okay, NEXT!" — for example, "Perhaps you could help point me in the direction of the appropriate individual there internally or at XYZ company who may have an interest in learning more about this opportunity, or who could benefit from our services."

How to Answer the Telephone (in Sales)

Use your greeting as an opportunity to welcome potential clients to your business and convert current clients into raving fans. Our goal in business is to let others speak well of us.

"(Good morning/afternoon), *thank you for calling XYZ company this is* (first and last name) *speaking. How may* (not 'can') *I assist you?"*

Use this greeting, even if you have caller ID or believe you know who is calling, as this is most professional. Project cheerfulness, be inviting, be sincere.

- As soon as they say their name, REPEAT it and use their name (often).
- Your voice is soothing, reassuring and constant. You are informed, professional, engaging.
- Always maintain *your* high professional standards and be courteous, especially when handling difficult callers. Never lower yourself or your standards. Work *with* this caller toward an acceptable answer to the issue.
- Recognize that every inbound call holds business potential.
- Become familiar with voices of regular callers and clients, however, still use the standard greeting to ensure consistency.

STORY

The Interface Group trained us as sales professionals to understand that incoming callers are a gift. When you think about it, what an incoming caller is really saying is, "I'm interested... please convince me!"

You had to do something really wrong to not get the close.

Scheduling and Confirming Telephone Appointments

Fine: "I want to schedule our telephone meeting for 4:00 pm."

Fabulous: "Let's take a look at when we can chat tomorrow. Does 4:00 pm work for both of us?"

Use words such as "chat" or "get together" versus "meet" or "schedule." Use inclusive and collaborative words whenever possible (us, we, let's) vs. individual words (I, me, you).

*Remember, we are courting and cultivating relationships in business! It is all about making a personal connection.

STORY

My brother Stephen was at one time Walter Mondale's chief fundraiser, and he was successful in raising more $$ than anyone else in the history of the Democratic Party up to that time. I asked Stephen how/why he was so successful, and he shared with me his technique:

"WM asked me to call you personally to let you know he would consider it a great personal favor if you would consider X."

I never forgot that: make it personal!

Top Tips for Confirming Scheduled Telephone Appointments

Always call or send an email the *day prior* to any pre-scheduled telephone appointment to reconfirm your telephone time together; the same practice pertains to face-to-face meetings. (I have had a few embarrassing instances where I did not, and fell off their radar. Please learn from my missteps!)

Send an email *agenda* in advance of your call so that you have an established starting point. (Be sure to include them on the agenda.)

How to Leave a Voice Mail Message

Fabulous:

- Extend a greeting, i.e., "Good morning!" and use their name.
- If applicable, state the name of the person who referred you or suggested that you contact them.
- State your name (first and last) and your position, company affiliation, date and time of call.
- State the nature of your call. For example: "I am calling to explore any interest you may have in XYZ."
- Be sure to let them know *what's in it for them,* i.e., "I have a marketing idea I wanted to run by you... I'd like to work on your campaign... Judy Jones suggested that we connect, and thought we might have some good business synergies..."
- Always repeat your telephone number (*twice*) and say it slowly and deliberately. If you rush, you will lose... e.g., their attention, their interest, them.

STORY

Through the years, I have been told by various very senior people that if they are unable to ascertain telephone numbers and callback information the first time, they will not bother replaying the message to hear the number again. They will simply hit "delete."

Something as basic as speaking clearly — even when it comes to saying your telephone number — shows you as professional and callback worthy!

- State when you may or may not be available.
- Convey any action items or special instructions.
- Provide your website in the event they want to familiarize themselves with you and your company/service in advance of the anticipated conversation.
- Leaving your email address is also good practice.

THIS NEXT PIECE IS KEY:

Fabulous: Follow-up each call with an email.

Sending a follow-up email provides you with another opportunity to leave yet another *impression* of you and the "Judy Jones" brand and shows you as thoughtful, thorough, professional.

The way you write and the way you construct this email, including your salutation and sign-off, conveys more information about you and provides another opportunity to demonstrate your professionalism and tenacity, and *stand apart*.

Your email message may say: "I just left you a voice mail message and write to follow-up."

- Ask them the best time to connect *real-time*.
- Be certain to include your standard signature line.

(See Email Etiquette in the following chapter, *Fabulous @ Electronic Communication*, for more email protocol.)

Sending Information

Fine: Assume everyone would like to receive your information.

Fabulous:

- Always *ask* if you may send them information.
- *Ask how they prefer to receive* this information. Use their name, i.e., "Mr. X, shall I send this via email or hard copy?"
- Send information ASAP. The longer you wait the less impact — networking, research, preparation, calling, leaving messages, emailing … all your efforts hold.

After The Call

Follow up your telephone conversation with a quick email note of thanks (only after you have determined that they are an e-culture person/company). Have a variety of greeting cards on-hand (i.e., birthday, anniversary, get well, etc.).

Never sign any card "Best regards, Jack." Always personalize the email and card. (See Chapter 6, *Fabulous @ the Meeting*, for more ideas on how sign off on emails and cards in a more personal way.)

Returning Calls / Follow-up Calls

Fine: Return calls on a timely basis.

Fabulous: Return calls as soon as possible — within 12–24 hours latest.

A quick response will:

- Make this individual feel valued.
- Demonstrate that you are eager to be of service to them.
- Reflect well on you, your efficiency and professionalism.
- *If the caller has referenced a mutually respected third party, you may want to consult with this individual in advance of the return telephone call.*
- If you have been unsuccessful at reaching someone during normal business hours they may be screening their calls. Call at atypical business hours, i.e., before 8 am or after 5 pm. If they are at their desk, they are likely to pick up.

Fabulous Tips for Sales Calls:

1. Exude a *positive* attitude! Mentally prepare before the call.
2. Research in advance; have your notes at hand.
3. Stand.
4. Have and use your "props" — including a mirror. Smile!
5. Check your voice for clarity, grammar, diction, tone. Speak clearly. (Acknowledge and apologize should there be an issue with your voice, without going into detail.)
6. Use their honorific and ask how they prefer to be addressed.
7. Reference any mutually respected third parties up front.
8. Make/take notes.
9. Adapt to *them.*
10. Be fully present. *Listen!*
11. Be engaging, genuine, sincere.
12. Make each call sound like it is being said for the *first* time.
13. To quote Kenny Rogers, "Know when to fold 'em!... know when to *walk away*!"
14. End the call if you initiated the call.
15. Follow-up ASAP.

3) Inside Telephone Staff Training for Admins (Receptionists, Operators, Administrative Assistants and Executive Assistants)

(*Note*: In previous editions of this material, this section is "required reading" for administrative staff in various departments of many major corporations and educational institutions.)

STORY

Twenty-five years ago, Jack Connors, then president of Hill Holiday, one of the top Advertising agencies in the country, told his young receptionist that she was the "face and voice of Hill Holiday." Karen Kaplan took this very seriously and considered her position to be the "CEO of Reception"... and in her next position with the company as the CEO of that job, etc. Ms. Kaplan had high ambitions and high expectations for herself. Her work ethic and dedication were noticed, admired and rewarded in each of the twelve positions she held at the company. Today, Karen Kaplan is the CEO of Hill Holiday.

Never approach a position believing this will be the job you will have forever, or that you are "just" the receptionist, administrative assistant, etc.

If you apply yourself in a similar way, this woman could be you.

ANOTHER STORY

In a conversation with Sandra Knott, President of the Greater Boston Chapter of the International Association of Administrative Professionals, she told me she was thrilled to have almost doubled their membership during her tenure. I asked to what she attributed this success and Ms. Knott explained that during our recent economic freefall, this was not only a tenuous time for admins but senior executives themselves as they were uncertain of their own futures.

Sandra Knott decided to leverage this condition and encouraged admins to hold themselves to a higher standard and show they were committed to their careers. She suggested that by showing that they weren't going anywhere, admins would be more valued, more respected and more sought-after as professionals in their field.

Ms. Knott advocated for professional credentials, certifications and urged admins to join professional organizations such as the IAAP. Ultimately, this advanced the position of administrative assistants while enhancing the admins' value to the company, as well as helping to grow the association.

How to Answer the Telephone

"(Good morning/afternoon). *Thank you for calling XYZ company. This is (first and last name) speaking. How MAY I assist you?*" Or, "*How may I direct your call?*"

Use this greeting, even if you have caller ID or believe you know who is calling, as this is professional.

- Become familiar with regular callers' voices (however, always use the standard introduction).
- Your voice is soothing, reassuring and constant. You are informed, professional, engaging.

- If you have a difficult or challenging caller, always maintain *your* high professional standards. Be courteous, show respect and never lower yourself or your standards. Work *with* the caller toward an acceptable solution. If needed, consult with a supervisor to resolve an ongoing issue.

How to Ask the Name of the Person Calling
Fine: "Who is this?" or "Who's calling?" (This sounds nosey.)
Fabulous: "May I tell Dr. Snyderman who is calling for her, please?"

How to Take a Message
Fine: "Can I take a message?"
Fabulous: "May I offer to pass a message along to Dr. Snyderman, or would you prefer to leave a message in her voice mail?"

Screening Calls
If you answer the telephone for another individual:
Fine: Try to guess if the person for whom you answer the telephone might like to take certain calls and avoid others based on your understanding of present circumstances.
Fabulous: Have a regularly scheduled time to get together with the person for whom you answer the telephone, and review the day's activities, including who gets through and who does not.

It is the responsibility of the person for whom you answer the telephone to inform you of their preference regarding accepting or screening calls. For example, if they prefer NO calls that morning or that day except from (i.e.) Gerry Doyle, those intentions should be made known to you. Ditto if they will take calls from anyone *except* Gerry Doyle. Communication is key; no one can read anyone's mind.

How to Screen a Call
Fine: Ask, "Who's calling?" They give their name.
"I'm sorry, Dr. Jones has just stepped out." (The perception *here* is this caller did not make the cut.)
Fabulous: DO NOT ASK WHO IS CALLING... YET. "I am sorry, Dr. Jones is UNavailable presently, may I ask who is calling and offer to take a message?"
TELL EVERYONE WHO CALLS THAT DR. JONES IS UNAVAILABLE.
"This is Gerry Doyle."
"Oh, Dr. Doyle, thank you for calling, hold for one moment please. Dr. Jones is expecting your call."
The perception NOW: Dr. Doyle is feeling very special indeed! He just got through!

How to Transfer a Call
Fine: "Hold on." "Hold on just a sec." "Just a second." "I can connect you to her now."

Incoming callers have the responsibility of identifying themselves, their position, and company/affiliation. If they do not, you should ask, "May I tell Dr. Jones who is calling, please?" Be sure to convey this information when you transfer the call.

- Avoid the dreaded dead silences
- Do not leave the caller hanging as they may wonder if they have been disconnected or whether you may have forgotten about them, etc.

Fabulous: "*May* I ask you to hold, (name of person), for one moment, please, while I transfer you to Dr. Jones."

Fabulous: Say, "Please allow me to connect you with Dr. Jones."

If you have been so instructed, ask: "Will Dr. Jones know the nature of your call?"

How to Place a Caller on Hold

Fine: "One sec." "Just a second." "Can I ask you to hold?"

Fabulous: "*May* I ask you to hold for one moment, (name of person), please, while I (i.e.) place you on hold and locate that information, etc."

First of all, it is never "just a second" — Remember, we say what we mean and mean what we say.

- If the nature of this call requires you to conduct research, ask if you may look into (topic X) and get back to them within the next (time frame) i.e., hour.
- Bring them to agreement.
- Honor time agreement and get back to them accordingly.
- Avoid idle chit-chat.

How to Refer to Callers

Remember: Never address clients by their first name unless/until invited to do so. Always use their honorific: Mr., Dr., Professor, Chancellor, Senator, Ms.* (pronounced: "Mzzz").

Note: "Miss" is reserved for young children under twelve. Use "Mrs." socially, or in business only after you have ascertained this is their preference.

Never refer to this person or the person they are calling as a pronoun, i.e., "him" or "her" — always refer to them by *name*. For example:

Fine: "What's her last name?" or "What's his first name?"

Fabulous: "May I ask Catherine's last name please?" or "May I ask Mr. Johnson's first name?"

Clarifications/Verifications

Listening, generally speaking, is a challenge for most of us.

- *Listen* to the caller and what they have to say.
- *Repeat* the information back to the client for clarity and understanding.

Verify:

- That you have heard and properly transcribed their message.

- The correct spelling of their name.

Fine: "Can you spell that?"

Fabulous: "*May* I ask you to spell your name for me please, Madame X?"

Telephone — Appropriate Greetings and Responses

The common greetings and responses below are really *not fine*. Let's focus on being **fabulous** here.

Fine: "Yo." "Hi." "Hey there."

Fabulous: "Hello." "Good (i.e.) morning, afternoon, evening."

Fine: "Yeah" or "Yup" or "Uh-huh."

Fabulous: "Yes" (name of person)

Fine: "Hey dude! How ya doin'?"

Fabulous: "How ARE you today? (name of person)"

Fine: "I'm good!" "It's all good."

Fabulous: "I am well, thank you for asking (name of person), and how are you today*?*"

Fine: "Not a problem" or "No problem." (These common expressions actually should be avoided, because they imply there *is* a problem and therefore suggests a negative.)

Fabulous: "With great pleasure!" "I'd be happy to." "Of course." "You are most welcome."

Remember The Power of "The Ask"

"*May* I help you?" (Let's eliminate "can" from our professional vocabulary! … And try replacing "but" with "however" whenever possible, too…)

"*May* I ask you to hold for one moment please, (*name of person)*?"

"*May* I tell Dr. Snyderman who is calling for her, please?"

"*May* I place you on hold, Mr./Ms. X, for one moment, please, while I (etc.)?"

"*May* I take a message or would you prefer to leave a voicemail?"

Vocabulary/Speech Issues

- Eliminate the *non-words*: "Um," "You know," "You, like, like, um, er, you know…"
- Be chameleon-like. Try to mimic/playback the vocabulary, pacing and speech patterns of the other party.
- Speak clearly, don't mumble or rush through your greeting.
- Smile! You can hear a smile on the telephone.
- Avoid gum chewing, eating or drinking when you answer the telephone.

Special Opportunities

- When given the occasion to engage in (brief) *small talk*, embrace and use this as an opportunity… to *stand apart* and connect!

For example:

Caller: "We just moved to Boston."

You: "Welcome to Boston!" Be warm, personable, genuine. Endeavor to make a real connection whenever possible.

- Anticipate issues and be prepared to pacify.
- When a client has a complaint or issue of any kind:

Fine: "I see." (Even worse would be to deflect in any way, for instance, to say something along the lines of "We're talking about something completely different here," or "That has nothing to do with me."

Fabulous: *Empathize!* "I am sorry you are experiencing this situation, (name of person) I understand how you feel. I, myself, have had the same experience." It is very important not only to sympathize but to empathize with callers; empathizing is validating.

Ending the Call
Rule: *The person who initiates the call is responsible for ending the call.*

Fine: Say, "Have a nice day." (Actually, this is NOT fine. Be careful signing-off on calls saying, "Have a nice day!" which is overused and may be seen as insincere, or as though you are simply going through the motions.)

Fabulous: Say anything else, i.e., "Have a wonderful afternoon" or "Enjoy the weekend!" or "I look forward to speaking with you again in a few weeks!"

How To Accept A Compliment
Graciously! Say, "Thank you!" Acknowledge their gratitude and say, "You are most welcome!"

Rule: *Never brush off a compliment, and never accept a compliment without also extending one.*

Fine: Say, "Sure, fine, whatever, no problem."

Fabulous: Say, "Thank you for your kind words, Mr. X. I have enjoyed speaking with you as well."

CHAPTER 4

Fabulous @ Electronic Communications

There was a time when it was common to be unreachable while we were in meetings, on the road or out-of- town. Today, technology enables access 24/7 — and actually being *unable* to access someone these days is rare. As a result, we all have very little "down" time. This reality should prompt us to use IT tools judiciously and in so doing show respect for others' time, their preferred *modus operandi*, and *stand apart*.

Business Versus Social

While one form of e-communication may be perfectly fine socially, this may evoke an altogether different response professionally. The **fabulous** professional knows this and will utilize e-communication accordingly.

Multiple gadgets and multi-tasking may give instant access, however, if not used prudently, could backfire. Grammar and spelling, meanings and even complete intentions can be tarnished or even vanish with one thoughtless choice or inadvertent keystroke. The medium with which we chose to communicate should be one selected with care, with our target in mind.

All means and mediums of communication present opportunities to make others feel valued and special versus just another (perfunctory) task. We may not understand how a tiny chip can enable a fraction of a split-second global connection, however, maintaining **fabulous** standards on everything from Skype and Twitter to Facebook and LinkedIn (etc.) is just as important as our *Professional Presence* in live networking.

Being Tech Savvy

Avoid the perception of being in fast and furious mode just trying to get the obligatory task done. When you rush, you risk making them feel like just another perfunctory (and unimportant) task — even showing yourself as sloppy and even disrespectful.

Remember all communication — form and substance — is, however subliminally, judged by others. You may believe that your communications are "just fine" — however, without realizing it, they may be failing to ramp up to achieve **fabulous** status to let you truly trump in business. While the focus of this book is on being **fabulous** in one-on-one, face-to-face interpersonal professional relations, many of the same basic rules of etiquette and protocol apply in the online environment. Maintain your professional standards when communicating via email or any social media platform, program or app.

Communicating electronically is not just about being "out there." Anyone can yell and be out there. **Fabulous** e-communication is still about *connecting* people to other people to form authentic relationships, which requires forethought and discipline.

Face-to-face communication and the telephone (in this order), while they may be more challenging than online contact, are still the most effective ways to connect with others… especially as we move into more senior levels. Nonetheless, in addition to possessing excellent interpersonal communication skills, professionals at all levels need to be tech savvy as colleagues expect to be contacted and courted in various modes. *Creative* competition is the rule today.

So, how do we get noticed using electronic modes of communication and be perceived as **fabulous** — without just creating more noise or going over the top? In this chapter, I will review these many opportunities.

Email Etiquette

Email, while certainly commonplace today, may be on the verge of extinction as the pace of technology continues to advance rapidly. That aside, email still presents another opportunity to show respect and *stand apart*.

Here are some basic guidelines governing email etiquette the world over.

Rule: *Treat an email like a letter; use a salutation and a sign-off. Emails should be well-constructed and properly formatted to project a professional image.*

Fabulous *Email Tips:*

Addressing Others

- Use their honorific or title (i.e. Mr., Dr., Ms., Chancellor, Professor, Senator) unless/until invited to do otherwise.
- Do not assume that because Dr. Snyderman signed her email "Nancy Snyderman" that you may call her "Nancy" in your reply. Rather, "Dear Dr. Snyderman... how do you prefer to be addressed?" or "May I call you Nancy?" is appropriate. Should Dr. Snyderman not acknowledge this in her reply, continue to use Dr. Snyderman's honorific.
- If your target has earned a Ph.D. (for example) and hence possesses a "Dr." status, be sure to use their "Dr." honorific in all written correspondence (as well as upon greeting in person, during conversation, when making introductions, etc.). Using this professional courtesy will be positively noticed and appreciated.
- *Note*: Women in <u>business</u> (who do not have another title such as "Dr." or "Professor" or "Senator") should always be addressed using the honorific "Ms." (pronounced "Mzzz.") even though socially, they may be a "Mrs." Only use "Miss" for young girls, up to about age twelve.)
- Personalize the email in some way, either in the body of the email or using the P.S. — (i.e.) "Enjoy the Islands!"

Referrals

- Ask before using your referral's name.
- When referring to another in email correspondence, always copy *them* in the email. Doing so enhances credibility and speaks to your professionalism and shows respect. Say, i.e., "I am grateful to Judy Jones, copied in this email, for suggesting we connect."

Subject Lines and Greetings

- Subject line should be consistent with content for quick reference and filing purposes; be careful about misleading subject lines.
- Do not mark "Urgent" unless it truly is.
- Begin emails by offering a cordial greeting such as "I hope this note finds you well!"... unless your intention is to be very direct. *Please note*: we can be direct and still be cordial.

Timeliness

- Respond to each question or topic raised.
- Reply to emails in a timely manner, which suggests within 24 hours of receipt. It is competitive out there — your prompt response is noticed.
- Should you anticipate a greater delay due to (i.e.) research or for whatever reason/s, ask, "By when would you like this information?"

Rule: *After three back-and-forth emails, if the subject matter still remains in volley, pick up the telephone or schedule a personal visit.*

Style Issues
- CAPITAL LETTERS IMPLY SHOUTING; use capital letters *selectively.* Better to highlight using *italics*, bold or <u>underlining</u>, if necessary.
- Be brief; less is more.
- When they write a short and concise email, *respond in kind.* Adapt your pace and language to *them.* If they use contractions, you do the same. When they refer to a meeting at 2pm your reply will replicate 2pm versus 2:00 P.M. Use *words* they use. If they greet you with "Hi" even though "Hello" is more professional, reply using "Hi" (unless "hello" is indeed, that which you wish to convey... and yes, there is a difference). Your goal should be more focused on your ability to connect rather than being correct.
- Consider using dashes and spacing in between topics for ease of reading. *Use structure, including headlining, bullet-points and paragraphs.*
- Emails sent from smartphones should acknowledge any misspelling, lack of punctuation, briefness, etc.
- Use asterisks or bullet points (versus numbers) when creating lists. This is a subtle distinction more common in High Context cultures because of the significance some numbers hold in other countries. However, this method highlights key points, and is just different enough to... *stand apart.*

Proofreading and Confidentiality Issues
- Be VERY careful regarding "Reply to All" unless you intend that your email be read by every person who received the original document.
- Always read and re-read your email before you hit "send" to ensure the note conveys your intentions (and is addressed to the correct person!) and that the content is concise, not wordy.
- Use your spell and grammar check, review for proper punctuation and capitalization... and be sure to proof proper names, addresses, emails, dates, numbers, URLs and phone numbers *closely*, since spellcheck can not correct those errors.

Situation. You hit "send" and then realize an error, a misquote, a misspelling, etc.:
- Correct the mistake
- Resend with the headline: "Kindly Disregard Previously Sent Email."
- Write "REVISED" along the top of the document.

Sending Personal Notes via Email
Sending a personal note in an email is tricky because email, by its very nature, is so impersonal. However, as always, there is a way to make email correspondence come across as personal, making the received feel acknowledged and special, while reflecting exceedingly well on the sender.

Fine: Mark "PERSONAL."

Fabulous: Subject line to read: "Personal Note from Judy Bowman."

Obtaining an Acknowledgment of Receipt for Emails

Fine: Use the "auto reply" feature.

Fabulous: Ask in your email, i.e., to "kindly acknowledge receipt of this email."

Email Greetings and Sign-offs

The greeting we use in an email may be traditional or creative. There is no right or wrong. The greeting we use is personal and should be predicated on the relationship we have or the one we endeavor to grow.

More **Fabulous** *Email Tips:*

- "Dear John" is considered the more traditional form of greeting.
- "Hello," "Greetings" or "Good morning, Ms. Jones!" are subtle yet important nuances which will help distinguish you while acknowledging them. These greetings also set email apart from a formal letter, making the email more akin to a conversation.
- *Make it your practice to insert your signature line after your sign-off to include: your name, title, firm, address and contact information and website.
- Resist the urge to sign-off on an email using "Best regards." This is the equivalent of saying, "Have a nice day," which is overused and may be seen as insincere or as though you are simply going through the motions. Signing a letter or email "Best regards" does not help you *stand apart* in stellar ways.
- Consider a more thoughtful sign-off, such as "My best regards," "My best wishes," "Warm regards," "Very sincerely," "Appreciatively yours," etc.
- "Respectfully yours" is a **fabulous** salutation which demonstrates respect for the other person while endeavoring to earn respect.

Email Signatures Lines

Your *authentic signature* is optional. However, always insert your professional signature which includes: title, firm, address and contact information including website.

Fine: Type your name and automatically insert your standard signature line. For example:

(Signature line here)

Judith Bowman

President and CEO

Judith Bowman Enterprises

DBA: Protocol Consultants International

Fabulous: Once you have "earned the right" (to advance)… use your *initials*. The shorthand of initials is more personal, suggests a level of intimacy that can help advance your relationship to an even more personal level. i.e.: My very best wishes, J, j or Jb or jb, jB or JB etc.

Photo? Logo?

Including a photograph in your signature line is appropriate in many fields. Your picture reminds others who you are, and when we may have met many individuals at a large function, this can be helpful.

If you have a brand or logo design, it is always good to reinforce that visual image by including this in your email signature line as well. You may care to consider using a truncated version (one *sans* graphics or a photo) for subsequent replies, so the email trail does not get too bulky.

Other Nuances

Their Email Address:

The way you write their email address presents another opportunity to make them feel special while reflecting well on you.

Fine: Type the recipient's email address as we normally would, in all lower case.

Fabulous: Type the first letter of their first and last name and perhaps even company name in upper case, for example: JudyJones@XYZCompany.com. This is very subtle yet highly effective.

Note: When sending email to those overseas, be aware that reversal of the surname is common in some countries. Because they are aware of this ambiguity, many already reverse their surname out of consideration for us and our ways. When in doubt, always *ask*. (See Chapter 10, Fabulous @ Business Travel & International Protocol, for more regarding reversal of the surname.)

Exclamation Marks

Fine: Use the "exclamation mark" or "urgent" mark to call attention to your email.

Fabulous: Save this for emergencies.

Make sure your emails always send a message of substance.

Interoffice Memoranda

Paper "memos" have become scarce, mostly because internal emails have replaced them in the communications landscape. For this reason, use emails as you would an interoffice memorandum.

STORY

Q. I recently intercepted an email intended for the CEO of our company. Believing it was intended for me, I automatically opened the email, only to discover an extremely intimate "love letter" from an administrative assistant in our firm, with whom he, our CEO, is clearly having a personal relationship (he is married). I was embarrassed and afraid that if I forwarded this email to our CEO, he would be aware that I knew of this relationship, which would be extremely awkward or more, for everyone involved. What would be the best way to handle this situation?

A. As real-time, real-life examples repeatedly demonstrate, this can and does happen. If you were to forward the email, your CEO would presume you read the note and hence were aware of the indiscretion. I suggest bringing this glitch to the attention of your IT manager, *sans* any detail, in order to help prevent this from occurring again in the future. In the meantime, in order not to cause embarrassment (or worse), I suggest discretion, particularly in this instance, and simply hit the "delete" button. The interception should never be mentioned.

Companies are aware of employee abuse and this is a glaring example of a potentially damaging explosive situation, which should serve as a reminder to all of us to honor and respect business and personal boundaries. This story drives home the importance of the notion: never write anything in an email that you would not mind having published in the *Wall Street Journal* or the *Salem News*... or on the world-wide web!

In Summary

1. Treat email like a letter.
2. Use a greeting, a sign-off and your signature line.
3. Use an appropriate subject line — readily identifiable and easily referenced.
4. Use easy-to-read font (size and color.)
5. Brevity is best.
6. Remember: CAPITAL LETTERS infer shouting.
7. Avoid abbreviations/slang.
8. Avoid requesting a "Reply" as this can be annoying.
9. Do not mark "Urgent" unless it is.

Email Taboos

People are more inclined to open infrequently received email from the same source. Be careful about over-sending e-correspondence, such as very frequent newsletters, specials, announcements which consistently boast of your accomplishments, etc. This may result in your communications becoming classified as junk mail and quickly deleted.

Chain mail, commercial emails and other links to random business contacts are taboo in business.

Jokes or politically charged content should also be avoided in the business landscape... (and be careful about even which friends you may choose to send these, as well). Avoid the traditionally delicate and potentially explosive topics of politics, money, sex, and religion, even if sent with humor.

Hacking email accounts is becoming more common, and others will try to use your account to send out phony emails under your name (asking for money, promoting strange products or websites, etc.); this has happened to me. Contact your email provider immediately to report the problem, and send an email to your entire contact list informing them of the breach.

Texting

Texting was once only used for casual communication with friends and family. Today, texting, an impermanent form of communication, has migrated into the business arena and remains used in epidemic *faux pas* proportions. Therefore, texting presents another opportunity to show we know our audience, show we know "the difference," and *stand apart*.

Texting is great for quick updates or letting someone know we are running late, however, the use of shorthand in texting can sometimes lead to miscommunication. Therefore, conducting formal and business transactions via texting can be risky, and how we text needs to be considered. I recommend if a client or colleague is texting sensitive or confidential information, we guide then to a more stable format. For example, should you receive a text regarding a new business venture, consider replying, "That's good news! May I suggest we continue these discussions live or at the very least have a preliminary telephone chat? I can be reached at 123-456-7890, or I will reach out to you."

*In this complicated age, it is unwise to automatically text another and assume this level of familiarity.

STORY

I met with a television producer recently who was actively interviewing candidates for a new internal position. The producer received a text while we were together. She read it, looked back at me and said, "Well, he just eliminated himself!" We discussed what just transpired and the producer felt the candidate assumed this level of familiarity (texting her) too soon. The television producer considers texting a more personal form of communication, hence the candidate was unprofessional and getting too familiar too quickly. As a direct consequence of this one, small, impulsive action, the candidate was not going to be given the opportunity to even be considered for the internal position they so direly sought.

Fine: Say, "I will text you that information."

Fabulous: Ask permission before sending a text; earn the right to advance: "How do you prefer to receive this information?" Be respectful of spoken and unspoken communication boundaries; do not text without being invited to do so.

Despite the fact that nearly everyone agrees that texting in front of other people is rude, we continue to text in class, at meetings, in church, during the family dinner table, in restaurants, on dates, in store check-out lanes, while walking, and even while bicycling and (horrors!) driving, which has led to horrific traffic accidents. We even text when another person is sitting right next to us trying to engage in conversation. This suggests that someone else is more important and texters are tuning out present company.

General Device Rule*: As soon as you reach your destination — and connect with your party — turn off and put away all smartphones and other IT devices.*

Cell Phones, Blackberries and other IT devices never belong on a (dining) table unless there is mutual consent. (The following story appears again in Chapter 9, *Fabulous @ Dining & Social Situations*, for it is worth repeating.)

STORY

Kathy Lee Gifford tells the story of how she actually cast off a friendship because of this. A friend whom she had not seen in a long time had been hounding her to get together and told her how much she missed her, wanted to see her and catch-up, etc. They finally arranged time together, sat down to dine, and the friend sat with her Blackberry out on the table, using it to read and send texts to other random people throughout the entire course of the dinner. Kathy Lee just sat there, looking around. These actions cost them both their friendship.

Why bother getting together if you are not going to interact with each other?

Texting:
- Is inherently a barrier; our focus, by design, becomes limited.
- Shifts our attention and suggests something or someone else is more important, causing our companion/s to feel less than whole.
- Detracts from quality time together (rare enough these days) and de-personalizes the connection.
- Does not lend itself to a true interpersonal experience.

Stop. Use technology to connect with, not disconnect from others.

Fine: Read and send texts in front of others.

Fabulous: *Read/send texts in the presence of others only with "mutual consent."* Receiving another person's complete attention is a gift, and one-on-one personalized attention is the foundation of every centered interaction.

Fabulous Texting Tips
- Keep texts short. Think of texts as the prelude to a conversation.
- Keep tone direct, i.e., "see you at 4 at Panera."
- Turn devices OFF or put them away upon meeting with another *unless* you are expecting an urgent notice. In this case, alert the other person in advance — without sharing the nature of the anticipated text.
- Do not text in class, during meetings, in a spa, gym, at the movies OR while a guest in another person's home — even if you are alone for a short while. Be fully present

and respectful of your "place" even during down time. Enjoy quiet moments; life is short.

- NEVER text while driving, bicycling, or walking in traffic. Your life, and the lives of others, are at stake.
- Reconsider using texting vernacular and abbreviations unless you are sure the recipient is well-versed in this and will not be offended.

STORY

I always thought that when my son wrote LOL this meant "Lots of Love" I later learned that this means "Laughing out loud." Ah well.

- Send texts (to smartphones) during respectful hours (as with the telephone). Basic guidelines: between 8 AM and 8 PM. If the recipient neglected to silence their phone, a beep will blast at unseemly hours.
- Never assume that someone else welcomes a text from you. Be reminded that IN BUSINESS, we need to "earn the right" to text. Never assume this familiar form of communication too soon in a business relationship; ask their pref*erred* method of communication or *ask* permission first.

Tweeting Etiquette

Whether you use Twitter for business or fun, you don't want to be a bystander. The essence of Twitter is interaction and *engagement* is key. As always, how you use this communication medium provides another opportunity to *stand apart*, optimize our time, energy and investment in this worthy medium of the social media world. Twitter has become more mainstream because information can go viral and enter the *T witterverse* quickly.

There is no right or wrong way to use Twitter and no two people use Twitter for the exactly same reasons. Twitter is largely rule-free although there are proper decorum standards which will help your Twitter identity become more renowned and even popular, should this be your objective, in just a short time.

Twitter has shown itself to be useful during elections and debates to instantaneously solicit, garner and gauge viewer opinion and reaction. Twitter is also widely accessed on:
- Television and radio talk shows.
- National contests and competitions (i.e., *Dancing with the Stars*, *The Voice*, *American Idol*, etc.)

Twitter has also proven itself to be an indispensable medium to help law enforcement worldwide. In an urgent and delicate situation, Twitter was used very successfully to identify, locate and apprehend the Boston Marathon Bombers.

Twitter Search

We can easily find others who share our interests. Use Twitter Search to look for some of the most obscure keywords related to your work, hobbies, or passions. Then click through to the profiles.

If you are just getting started, know that early days on Twitter will probably be fairly quiet. Other Twitterers are just getting to know us. Once our tweets appear regularly in the timelines and we add contacts to our network, we will be noticed.

Making a Good First Impression

To make a good impression on Twitter:

Fine: Dominate the network.

Fabulous: Be:

- Social
- Informal
- Gracious and say "thank you" often (use the @reply or @mention to publicly thank someone)
- Honest. Say who you are and state your intentions clearly on your profile bio (identify if you are a blogger, marketer, etc.)
- Genuine, non-deceptive
- POSITIVE. Use your words to make a *Contribution* and lift others UP, not to be negative and tear people down.
- Interesting, engaging
- Authentic

In addition:

- Keep a human voice.
- Have a sense of humor.
- Have fun; do not treat tweeting as a chore.
- *Listen!*
- Position *yourself* as a resource
- Provide value!

Fabulous Tweeting Tips:

- Promote others more than yourself (20:1 ratio advised).
- Let others promote you; let others tweet on your behalf.
- Talk about current events, other people.
- Vary your posts to keep interest.
- Do not tweet in the third person i.e. "Judy likes XYZ."

Remember: just a single click of the "Un-follow Button" can sever important relationships.

Number of Characters

Generally speaking, Twitterers expect to be able to read and absorb our tweet in one bite. Think about tweeting as offering content "snacks" versus three-course meals with coffee and dessert. The 140 character limit prevents us from rambling and sparks creativity.

Should you wish to tweet more than 140 characters, consider:

- Tweeting incomplete tweets and providing a link.
- Sending messages over several tweets — although this could come across as dominating the conversation.

This does not mean we should never break up a long tweet, nor does it suggest we should post uninterrupted tweets.

Conversation

Remember, we are having a conversation on Twitter. If we think about it, when chatting with a friend we take turns speaking. When one or the other dominates the conversation this can be off-putting.

Engage and show an interest in *them* before asking them to care about you; "be a friend to get a friend."

Ask Questions! Remember, people love to talk about themselves. (See Small Talk and Conversation Skills in Chapter 1, *Fabulous @ Networking*, for more information about drawing people out and making conversation.)

Fine: Share every minute of your life.

Fabulous: Tweet about notable moments in your day, or interesting thoughts or observations on current events.

Fine: Tweet and describe what you are doing, including that which you may be thinking about doing.

Fabulous:

- Only tweet and describe what you are doing — NOT what you may be thinking about doing — no one really cares.
- Tweet something that entertains your followers and sparks a conversation. (If they don't like it they can always read someone else's tweets.)

Frequency

Frequency needs to be considered: if over-tweeting is a mistake, then so is under-tweeting. Consistency is important.

Fabulous: A good rule of thumb is 20 tweets/day, max!

(If you would like to tweet more, use another program, i.e., *hootsuite* or *cotweet*, to schedule your tweets so they can be segmented.)

- Make the time to maintain your social media presence.
- Log in regularly, i.e., once/day or once/week.
- Post at least 5 tweets every time you log in.
- Reply/re-tweet your followers' tweets, which will also maintain your presence.

Tweeting for Business

Twitter (and FaceBook) are used more to interact, communicate and yes, *promote* yourself and your business/ideology, versus LinkedIn which is used more to *connect* with others.

Balance the number of self-promotional tweets versus (the number of) value-added tweets.

Use the 5:1 ratio as a guide: for every tweet about you, send out at least 5 tweets that inform, engage and add value for followers.

Spamming

Fine: Send countless self-promotional tweets.

Fabulous: Promote others, and position *yourself* as a resource; this will come back to you.

*Spam and automated hash-tag-filled tweets do not work. These will compromise your professional credibility.

Spelling Style

We are already aware that capital letters suggest shouting, and that in texting we often use cute abbreviations (such as "C U L8R" for "See you later"); however, know that with Twitter we should:

- Spell words out
- Avoid using numbers (to represent letters) whenever possible.

The language of tweeting needs to look like real words and avoid abbreviations.

Tone

It is easy to get caught up in the moment and carried away with emotions, and tweets are not censored. This does not mean that there are no limitations; other users *can* report or block you.

As with emails, do not write anything in a Tweet you would not want to see published in The New York Times, streaming around the newsfeed in Times Square or on the evening news… and always proof your Tweet before you post!

Emotional Tweeting

When new ideas are presented in business, our adrenaline speeds up. Any given topic can serve as a highly emotional trigger, and remember that nothing good ever comes from rage. Therefore, if you are angry or depressed or just "over-cooked" and not prepared to respond in a polite and respectful manner, as with the telephone, as Kenny Rogers says, "… know when to fold 'em… know when to *walk away!*"

Fine: Tweet whatever is on your mind, even if you are enraged. (THIS NOT FINE!)

Fabulous: Collect yourself. Choose your words carefully before you tweet. You cannot take something back once it is "out there" in the Twitterverse.

Be responsible and your tweets will be respected.

Re-tweets

Fine: Hound influential people and implore them to re-tweet or refer your blog to their millions of followers. (This is NOT FINE!)

Fabulous: Earn *trust* and influence by making the effort to help and be of service to others, first.

Re-tweets are best used to:

- Help and promote others.
- Make something go *viral!*

*It is generally not considered good form to ask others for random re-tweets — unless there is an important issue at hand.

Fine: It is fine to copy someone else's tweets and tweet it yourself.

Fabulous: Yes, it is acceptable to copy someone else's tweets and tweet it yourself however, be sure to give credit to the original Twitterer.

Following People

The way you follow people provides another opportunity to *stand apart.*

Fine: Follow only close friends and people you already know. (This may suggest that you are antisocial or cliquey.)

Fine: Follow random people.

Fine: Follow someone expecting them to follow you back.

*In the beginning you may want to reward anyone who follows you by following them in return.

Fabulous: Follow people because you are interested in what they have to say.

*Ironically, if someone does follow you, it is courteous but not necessary to follow them back.

Know that as your follower list grows you will need to be a bit more selective about who you follow in return. Your followers will have to understand that you are being "selective," not rude.

The ultimate test of Twitter etiquette is how you and other people react to any given topic. The Golden Rule still applies here! And, as with texting, reconsider tweeting or checking your Twitter feed on your smartphone when you are with someone else. Give *them* your full attention.

Social Media Platforms

LinkedIn and FaceBook, among other social media sites, present another opportunity to distinguish ourselves and advance on an altogether different platform. Hence, how we interact with others and promote ourselves and our services is primo. This section highlights ways to optimize our recognition in the social media network.

Overall, Facebook is more social, geared primarily to sharing with family and friends (although there is certainly a large and growing professional and corporate presence). Nonetheless, it is acceptable to make longer posts, use more extensive vocabulary and a more casual tone in your communications, especially with friends and family. LinkedIn, on the other hand, is geared specifically to the professional community. Therefore, use more professional verbiage and be more selective in sharing news with the LinkedIn community.

LinkedIn

LinkedIn is the largest, most professional, business-oriented online network in the world, accessed in over 200 countries with over 48 million members. The way we use our image, updates, posts and correspondence can affect our financial future. Be aware of this highly influential medium to help advance your network of connections as well as personalize and nurture relationships.

Use LinkedIn and other social media networks as an adjunct to — not a replacement for — personal, one-on-one networking to make new connections.

Use LinkedIn to:

- Expand our network of connections.
- Create value-added with social platforms.
- Enhance brand identity.
- Broaden our reach for a job search.

LinkedIn is quickly replacing many positions in the Executive Search Industry for a reason. There is a tactical and strategic way to stand out with recruiters as well as access connections to advance your own job search.

Sending Profiles

Fine: Send your profile to those you believe would be a good fit.

Fabulous:

- (Offer to) forward others' profiles to those you believe would be a good fit. ("Be a friend to get a friend.")
- Forward job listings to others, where appropriate. This also works to your benefit as it signals to your connections that you have access to opportunity, are a person "in the know" and are a "go-to person."
- Pave the way for introductions to others

Building and nurturing relationships is a multi-tiered process. Please consider the following:

Photos

The photo you use will either help your image shine or tarnish others' perception of you. Utilize the photo image option and show yourself to be a stand-up individual and *stand apart* professionally.

Fine: Use a photo of you at the beach, partying or looking provocative. (NOT FINE, especially the provocative part; this is also an instant turn-off for recruiters.)

Fabulous: Have a professional photo shot for your LinkedIn profile picture

*Note that LinkedIn has added 9 different apps, similar to those on other Social Media sites, to help your profile stand out. When used correctly and in the right places, they can help you with travel, blogging, workspaces and more. There is even a Google and slideshare presentation app to help you share your work strategy on your profile. Keep current with updates to your preferred social media network to take advantage of new developments.

Your Profile

Craft a clever, memorable headline/summary to help you be memorable and *stand apart*. Consider hiring a professional résumé writer to create a profile that clearly shows your best attributes and lets you shine. (See Chapter 8, *Fabulous @ The Interview*, for more on the importance of writing up your skills and accomplishments to highlight your value to potential employers, clients and customers.)

Accuracy

Employment history should be honored, accurate, and complete, going back at least (and usually not more than) ten years. Employment and education information older than ten years may be provided if it is particularly impressive or relevant to a new position.

Fine: It is okay to embellish your professional profile. (Actually, this is NOT FINE! Especially in law and banking, background research is very thorough, and misrepresenting yourself on your online profile, as on your résumé, can get you fired… if you get hired at all.)

Fabulous: Tell the truth. All dates and references to former and present employment should be true and accurate. Inconsistencies will be exposed and can severely tarnish your professional reputation.

Status Updates

Update Frequency

The number of updates we post should be considered. Updating several times per day can be annoying and connections may tune you out. Fewer updates may serve to pique the interest of others… or cause them to consider you as "out of the loop." Be sure to update often enough to show you are engaged, but not so often that you are seen as having no life offline.

Fine: Update as you will and get your name out there.

Fabulous: Maintain balance in your update frequency.

Note: Frequent updates on Twitter is acceptable.

Update Topics

Rule: Keep update topics professional.

Fine: Post updates regarding, i.e., your trip to Maui or your cousin's graduation.

Fabulous: LinkedIn is the *business* social media platform — post updates on your job, professional profile, a recent/current project or event, etc.

Posting Links

Fine: Add a random link and say "click here"

Fabulous: Get creative when referring to and recommending sites on which to click.

Post, for example, "Please click here to read even more: LINK." The latter (**fabulous**) draws members in and generates anticipation.

Recommendations

Requesting Recommendations

If you have not done so already, begin the practice of asking for recommendations. Who you ask and who you recommend should be carefully considered.

Fine: Ask everyone you work with and for to recommend you.

Fabulous:

- Select a few (raving fans!) who can articulate how you distinguish yourself. It is always **fabulous** to let others speak (well) on your behalf.
- Request recommendations after you have worked for/with them for at least six months.
- Offer to provide talking points.
- Be careful of pressuring anyone to write a reference.

Writing a Recommendation

Fine: Write a generic recommendation, i.e., "Judy is a good Protocol consultant."

Fabulous: Personalize a stellar recommendation or don't bother, i.e.:

"Judith Bowman is a dynamic and informed presenter and is terrific to work with. She has presented for our organization's Executive Women in Healthcare conference twice on *The Power of Protocol*, and both times she has been engaging and interesting. Our attendees rated her highly — even asking her to extend her talk during lunch so that they could ask more questions. I highly recommend Judith as a speaker at conferences that touch upon the critical protocol issues faced by business professionals."

—Kirsten Singleton, Executive Director, Massachusetts Hospital Association
Center for Education & Professional Development, Burlington, MA

"Dear Judy, Your presentation at the NEBTA meeting in Boston in October was tremendous! I was able to apply what I learned from you at a global conference in Rome the following week. Your advice was instrumental in helping me meet, greet and lead a panel of corporate travel executives from Russia, the UK, Asia and the Middle East. I have no doubt our presentation and success in presenting to a global audience was improved because of you."

— Kerin McKinnon, Director, Strategic & Global Sales,
Travel and Transport, Inc., Omaha, NE

Fabulous:

- Give more then you receive. *Endorse* others when you can.
- Offer to write *recommendations* for those you can recommend highly.

Number of Recommendations

The number of recommendations we have on our Profile is to be considered. If you give them out too freely, the perception is that they have no value. If you give out too few, then you are seen as being "out of the loop" (or ungracious to your clients/vendors). Again, balance is key.

Introduction Requests

Requests for introductions to other members is expected. How we do so presents another opportunity to be particularly heard or ignored.

Fine: Send a standard introduction request to another member.

Fabulous: Call the member first to personally pave the way for an introduction request. This is not only gracious but also encourages others to be more responsive.

Connection Requests

Requests to connect are what LinkedIn is all about. Use this everyday activity to *stand apart* and reinforce brand identity. As always, "How we say it" is important, and in LinkedIn the way we ask presents another opportunity to *stand apart*.

Fine: Use the standard generic "request to connect" blurb.

Fabulous: Use their name and personalize the request.

Accepting Requests to Connect:

How you accept requests to connect will also set you apart.

Fine: Accept every invitation you get and use this platform to expand your network of connections.

Fabulous: Be discerning.

Fine: Use the standard generic acceptance blurb.

Fabulous: Always personalize the message. Use their name and personalize the acceptance. Take advantage of this opportunity to also reinforce your brand identity, i.e. "Hello Lynn, Thank you for your invitation to join your network via LinkedIn. I look forward to our future association! Please consider us as your future XYZ needs evolve." Add a special newsworthy item if applicable.

Auto-generated Templates

Fine: Use LinkedIn auto-generated templates for congrats, recommendations or requesting a connection, etc.

Fabulous: Always personalize correspondence. For example, if you just met at a conference, mention the function or something discussed.

FaceBook

Facebook is considered by many the gold standard of social media. At its core, FaceBook is all about status updates. FaceBook's primary activity is to share and connect with current and long-ago friends and family. Many use FaceBook to connect with business colleagues as well, and most corporations have a company FaceBook page to promote and extend their brand online.

FaceBook for Business

However inadvertently, every employee engaging in social media is an instant online ambassador representing your company brand 24/7 — and without an understanding of parameters, the company's brand could be abused.

Avoid:

- Over-sharing
- Posting too frequently
- Negativity
- Vague posts
- Being loud versus being heard and understood.

Fine: Accept anonymous connection requests.

Fabulous: Accept connections from those you know or those with/for whom you have actually worked.

Fabulous: Use their email address when provided on the profile page after connecting.

Fabulous: Personally forward job opportunities to connections. This will also broaden your company's hiring pool for talent. This signals to your connections that you are a resource and are generous with them.

Status Updates:

Remember, never post anything on Facebook you would not want to see on a billboard or on the world wide web. This will be out there *forever* and can impact on your professional impression.

Fine: Post regular updates regarding your travels, people you meet and food you eat as the day unfolds.

Fabulous: Think before you post and ask yourself if you really need to share X with the world.

Fine: Post random, unedited, unproofed comments; hey, you're just being yourself.

Fabulous: Check your posts before you update your status. Proof them for grammar, punctuation, spelling, etc. — and double-check that you really want that content "out there."

This shows others that you take the time, are thorough and have good attention to detail — and implies that you conduct yourself in this same way in your life and business dealings. Once again, reconsider posting updates or checking your news feed on a smartphone or tablet when you are with others. Be present and engage!

Friend Requests

Fine: Use a template request.

Fabulous: Always personalize the connection and use their name.

Fine: Invite everyone to be your "friend" or to "like" your professional page.

Fabulous: Again, be discerning. Do you really want to see the feed from someone who has nothing to do with your business, or who goes on and on and posts every little detail about their lives? (And certainly, don't *be* that person on someone else's feed!)

Un-Friending

Fine: Announce that you are doing so.

Fabulous: There is no need to announce this; just hide them from your feed. Should others ask, simply explain that you need to reorganize. You can also limit the number of status updates you see from others (using the same menu) and delete without fear of offending anyone.

Selecting Your Medium of Communication

Whatever channel of communication you select, be intentional regarding format, tone, word choice. Proof for clarity and accuracy. Just as you strive to be **fabulous** in your work, respect the capability provided by texting, tweeting and posting updates to help reinforce your message, illustrate your professionalism, perpetuate your brand, and ultimately connect.

Using iPods

While iPod use is widespread and does afford one the opportunity to "zone out," one should be aware of the downsides of zoning out. Use of iPods (or other MP3 devices) without acknowledging this to others may make others feel slighted and be interpreted as rude. You are not-so-quietly implying lack of interest in present company and suggesting that this inanimate object is more important, which is insulting. Should you chose to use your iPod in the presence of others, it would be courteous to acknowledge the act and them, so they will not feel ignored, particularly when they address you.

Using an iPod while engaged in virtually any activity such as driving, working out, or even walking, i.e., down a busy street or an abandoned road, is also dangerous because we are not able to hear subtle or not-so-subtle sounds, such as oncoming motors, voices, screeching brakes, etc. We simply do not have the same good reflex reactions because we are otherwise mentally engaged.

STORY

Q. My younger sister has a very expensive iPod which she listens to all the time. I know this is her way of "zoning out" and having privacy. However, I find it annoying, as do others, who talk to her believing she can hear what is being said, when in fact she is listening to her iPod. What is going on with high technology these days that it continues to interfere with people and human relationships?

A. iPods are hot here in the U.S. and abroad, not only among adults but with teenagers and young adults, as well. iPods have capabilities in addition to playing music which include watching a movie, listening to radio broadcasts, playing a music video, downloading pictures, listening to recorded books, watching television shows, and more. People use iPods at random times which include working out or, zoning out, getting de-stressed or motivated, or simply for pure enjoyment, entertainment... Interestingly, iPods can also cause one-third hearing loss for those who abuse or don't pay attention to the decibel level.

High technology continues to advance at a very rapid pace. People themselves need to decide when, how and with whom to use this technology. When iPods or other high technology interferes with or compromises the quality of interpersonal relationships, it is time to draw the boundary line. Respect and consideration of others is still The Golden Rule.

iPad Etiquette

Many companies are investing in iPads (or similar tablet computers) and providing them to all employees. Training regarding the most effective use of iPads for presentations is imminent (or underway). Respectfully, please be reminded that the iPad is merely another new medium and another "prop" to assist with effective presentations and should be treated as such. As with all presentations, treat the iPad like any other "prop" and please note the following:

- No more than 3 bullets per view.
- Less is more.
- Own your material.
- Refer selectively to the iPad.
- Ensure their view not only includes the iPad/presentation, but YOU as well.
- Stand to the left of the iPad.
- When working with others, look at the iPad *together*. Be conscious of invading unspoken boundaries of personal space... and be sure you have your breath mints!
- Address timing issues as appropriate when referring to the big screen overhead.

Technology and Travel

(See Chapter 10, *Fabulous @ Business Travel & International Protocol*, for issues relating to traveling with smartphones, laptops, tablets and other ways to stay connected... and warnings about posting inappropriate updates to social media such as Facebook or Twitter while traveling.)

Conclusion

Whatever communications device or format you choose, remember these are tools to be leveraged to help us advance. How we communicate — the medium we choose, the words we use, the tone we convey — all represent us and our brand. Online etiquette and protocol are equally important as real-life etiquette and protocol. Stay current in online trends and remember to always maintain your own high standards. Just as we strive to be **_fabulous_** in our work, take the same care to ensure that our electronic communication efforts are respectful and distinguish us in all positive ways to help us better connect.

CHAPTER 5

Fabulous @ Professional Attire

Social vs. Business Attire

That pesky, age-old, perpetual question of "*What to wear?*" socially, evokes liberties and invites creativity, freedom and individuality. Professionally, "*What to wear?*" is contingent upon whom you plan to meet with that day. Today, many seem a bit confused by what is considered professional attire. Make no mistake, *professional business attire* is very specific. We may point directly to Hollywood, the celebrity culture and fashion-forward designers who are motivated to sell movies, new styles and trends, and might like to lead us to believe otherwise.

Attire communicates our intentions. Appearance sends a message. When we meet others for the first time, judgments and critical impressions are guided in large part by appearance. What we wear — including accessories and personal hygiene — are central to our message and reflect our intentions. In fact, the celebrated *Mehrabian Rule* suggests that as much as 55% of all first impressions are derived from a *visual* aspect (ref. Albert Mehrabian, *Silent Messages: A Wealth of Information About Nonverbal Communication*, 2009). Indeed, despite all our hard-earned book knowledge, technical wizardry, professional experience and amazing methodological expertise, studies show that how we look and what we wear are an integral part of our presentation to the world!

Certainly, intellectual acumen and technical knowledge are fundamental; however, they can easily be discounted and even dismissed if we do not "look the part." As a well-respected television producer once told me, "If given the choice of selecting a dull apple or the shiny apple, I'll choose the shiny apple." In the midst of today's tremendous global business competition, anything we can do to *stand apart* is critical to achieving business distinction — and dressing professionally is *never wrong*. To quote one of my esteemed business clients, "Dressing professionally in business today is the *Easy A*."

STORY

I was speaking with a friend who had just returned from the Kentucky Derby about how so many people these days do not dress up, even for special occasions. The Kentucky Derby is certainly an event where men and women know to dress up.

The Kentucky Derby is renowned not only for hats, of course, but that everyone is dressed "to the nines" (an expression referring back to the days when sailors would return from sea; their loved ones would dress up to greet them, the sailors would put up all nine sails of the ship, and arrive wearing full regalia).

My friend shared the observation that when people get dressed up, they look pretty. Every part of them is pretty. As a result, they walk taller and even smile more. They are polite, friendly and respectful. There is a distinct aura of civility and excitement at the Kentucky Derby.

The simple act of *dressing* shows respect for the tradition and those present — among them, the Queen of England and her husband are most notable — as well as the "greats" who have run and participated in this celebrated event.

Moreover, as a direct result of dressing in a thoughtful, respectful, more upscale manner, people behave in a more thoughtful, respectful and refined way. When they are dressed up at the Kentucky Derby, for instance, together they cheer, hope, pray, laugh and cry for those who have won, almost won, lost and even died.

The point is: when we dress up, we behave better. When we make the effort to dress our best, we definitely act our best. When you think about it, growing up as children, "dressing up" used to be a game. In so doing, children would put on airs and try to act "grown up." As we indeed grow, our real persona comes into play and we become individuals. So today, both socially and in business, when we take the time to dress appropriately, it perks us up and makes us feel and act better. My friend, who herself was an invited guest to the Kentucky Derby, is known for dressing on the funky side at times. And she was told, in no uncertain terms, in advance, upon receipt of her invitation, that if she accepted the invitation, she must *dress*. Her host "tucked it to her" and this was duly noted. Sometimes, we all need to be reminded and have it gently, clearly, tucked to us.

So, in this chapter, we urge you to take the time to dress. It's not about being over the top; it's about being complete. We come to feel comfortable with our new persona when we are dressed well. We project confidence, show respect, invite conversation and welcome new people into our lives. This chapter urges us to break through our comfort zone and the *Hakuna Matata[1]** mentality of "This is who I am" dressing if we want to *stand apart* at work™ to better compete.

When we dress and exhibit simple respectful gestures, such as saying "Please" and "Thank you," using someone's name, shaking their hand, etc., we instantly stand out in the workplace, especially these days. Remember, others notice: *"A nice gesture, a kind word, a fleeting glance, a warm smile."* Be that person. These words were spoken long ago by our dear family friend Shawny at a time when we were all young and single in Boston… some things never change! Dressing well encourages behaving well. Being gracious is a "way to be" and will help you *stand apart* and advance in the professional world.

Consider this chapter a walk-in closet. Together, we will tour through the many different options, and I will draw attention to everything you will need to be **fabulous***ly* attired from style and colors to accessories and more, so you can easily draw from and regularly update your **fabulous** wardrobe arsenal. I will define and delineate top flight **Business Attire** (and touch upon **fabulous business casual** and **formal** attire, as well). I will describe specific **fabulous** professional business attire for both men and women in their quest to advance to the next level in business today. (Note that some dressing guidelines pertaining to topics such as suit colors, briefcases, etc., relate to both men and women, and are repeated in each section. Therefore, if you read the entire chapter straight through, expect some repetition.) There are many sayings about the importance of dressing professionally:

- "Dress for the position you want (not the position you have)."
- "Dress to impress."
- ***The Number One Rule in Sales*** *(with respect to attire):* "Look the part!"

… and the quotes go on.

Professional Attire

Think *Quality* and *Investment Dressing*. When you buy a quality suit or even have one custom-made, you are making an investment in yourself because quality is unmistakable and quality endures.

---

1   * "No worries" in Swahili (similar in meaning to the English phrase "No problem"), popularized by the song of the same name in Disney's 1994 movie, *The Lion King*.

STORY

One celebrated tailor I know in Boston actually went out of business because the suits he made literally lasted a lifetime and his clients stopped needing yet another new suit.

Dressing well need not be costly. We want to emphasize that you can look **fabulous** and not spend a lot of $$. A well put-together look suggests having an eye to fabric and fashion and knowing what flatters you. Fabric and colors are key. You can wear a crisp dark blue suit with a crisp white shirt, shined shoes and look like a million $$. Crisp, clean, shiny and confident will win every time!

STORY

My mother told me long ago, "If you can only afford one, make sure it's the best, and that it is quality because quality lasts. Furthermore, you feel better in quality. Quality speaks volumes about who you are." To this day, I still wear clothes my mother wore when she was 40 (my mother is presently in her 80's). Quality indeed endures!

Carrying Off Special Looks

In this chapter, we review what is considered quality and classic, and discuss "Power Dressing." We cover accessories and even find some **fabulous**ly "outrageous" things that make a tasteful personal statement. While we should always make the effort to dress appropriately in standard business clothing (suit, tie, hosiery, etc.), when it comes to daring or fashion-forward choices, it is critical that one is able to carry it off. To quote a fashionably astute friend: "There is a difference between being able to put your clothes on and take them off... and *carrying it off*." Never wear anything you can't carry off. Adorning ourselves means knowing how we want to be viewed in the world with our audience in mind.

Be comfortable with who you are, but know your audience. Be mindful that while one part of your personality may be comfortably displayed with one group, not necessarily so among others in another setting. Everything you select to wear must shout of *authenticity*. A bracelet or pinkie ring? A lapel pin, a French cuff, or the "Wall Street" collar? If you can carry it off, fine. If this is who you are, wear it. Wearing cufflinks may be part of one person's persona while not so with another. The point is, if you do not feel completely comfortable in a French cuff shirt, braces, a bow tie, a vest, a statement necklace, chunky eyeglasses, or whatever, *don't wear it*. Ultimately, you need to be confident selecting and wearing any accessory or unusual combination of prints, stripes, colors, and know you can "carry it off."

Men

Suits

Invest in a quality suit. Even if you only have one (actually you need two), be sure they are quality. There are many outlets in this country and everyone has sales. Keep your eye out for "that one" that looks, feels and fits perfectly, or know that you can buy it for a steal when it goes on sale and have it altered to fit.

Recommended brands include Brooks Brothers, Jos. A. Banks, Hickey Freeman, Armani, and Ermenegildo Zegna … or consider a (bespoke) custom suit, especially if you know a reliable and reasonably priced tailor, or find yourself in Asia where having anything custom-made is extremely reasonable.

Colors — (for Men and Women)

The most professional suit colors:

- Black
- Blue (navy)
- Gray (charcoal)
- Pinstripe, in any color variation

*Off-white and khaki — a great clean look to be considered in warmer weather and tropical locales.

*Brown is still <u>out</u>.

Fabrics

Today, wools are lighter and will go the four seasons.

*Seersucker, seen more in Southern states, is acceptable for younger men and older gentlemen, typically worn in warmer climates.

Suit Jackets

Ensure suit jackets fit well. Check arm length, shoulders and chest particularly, and make sure you are able to button properly. While the three-button jacket was formerly more prevalent, today, manufacturers are making jackets with two buttons or even a one-button jacket, which is more of a European influence. However, the three-button single vent suit is still considered classic.

Double breasted suit jackets are generally considered *yacht-ish*.

Double vents: make no mistake — you need to have the lines to wear a double-vent jacket well. Double vents also suggest a more European influence. Wear what is most flattering with your body type in mind.

Lapels

Fine: Go with the latest fashion trend.

Fabulous: Think: classic, not trendy. Not too wide or too narrow.

Jacket Buttons

The top two buttons (on a three-button coat) or top one button (on a two-button jacket) should be buttoned, the bottom button should remain open to vent (for men and women). This is true both at the boardroom and dining room table.

Gentlemen: buttoning your jacket also helps protect your beautiful ties (while dining).

Unbuttoning Jackets

Fine: Randomly unbutton buttons.

Fabulous: Unbutton from the bottom and work your way up!

Tailors

Fine: Go to anyone nearby.

Fabulous: Have your own tailor even if it means traveling a distance and paying a bit more. A good tailor is worth it. A good tailor has your measurements, knows your body type, and will be candid regarding fit, sizing, colors, etc. A good tailor does it right. Never hesitate to visit your tailor for any alteration, especially if you have lost or gained weight. Your efforts to ensure a **fabulous** fit will make you feel great and not go unnoticed.

Suits and Travel

Fine: Carefully pack suits in a suitcase or garment bag.

Fabulous: When packing in a suitcase or even a garment bag, cover each suit and shirt with a plastic dry cleaning bag. This helps keep the item wrinkle-free.

Vests

Vests are a way to complement a suit look. Some men look simply stunning in a three-piece suit, and others look positively peculiar.

Fine: Wear a vest if it comes with your suit.

Fabulous: Wear a vest if this is authentically you — and make sure the vest fits.

Know that a well-fit vest has the power to create a long and slimming "column" effect — or, if not well-tailored, can completely cut someone off, especially someone who may be short and stout.

Wear vests with an attitude!

Shirts

Shirts are noticed — big time. Quality is essential, gentlemen. Careful consideration should be given to quality fabric as well as fit.

Fine: Purchase any name brand shirt with the most professional colors in mind.

Fabulous: Invest in quality shirts. Custom shirts, despite popular belief, can be considerably less expensive than store-bought shirts. Consider a custom shirt. You can select the fabric and are assured a perfect fit. As a result, this will help make you feel better and more confident.

Natural fibers — 100% cotton or a cotton and linen weave are recommended.

Fabulous: The "Royal pinpoint" is rich-looking and different.

Fabulous: The French cuff speaks of distinction. Further, the cufflinks you select from your **fabulous** arsenal of accessories can be used as a conversation launch. Share a story about the cufflinks which will involve others and help advance the relationship.

*Remember, only one-quarter inch length of shirt cuff should show beyond the sleeve of your suit jacket.

Shirt Colors

The following are considered the most professional color shirts for men (and women):

#1: White

#2: Blue (light)

*Dark blue shows a more European influence

#3: Stripe — the Power Stripe

#4: (Light) Pink for men and women is **fabulous**

*Windowpane shirts are a more casual yet a "confidence" look.

*Black shirts make an altogether different statement: actor or gambler? Smooth…

Collars

Men's shirt collars also make a statement. Make sure collars fit. This means you should be able to place two fingers — not your fist — inside the collar. Collars too tight or too loose are equal forms of self-sabotage.

STORY

For those of you who remember the television series "24" — do you recall President Logan, who in the series was initially portrayed as rather mealy, lacking character? In the beginning, President Logan wore shirts whose collars literally hung from his neck, making him appear weak and ineffective. As his character grew to be stronger, more aggressive and ultimately, actually sinister, his shirt collars grew tighter.

Something as seemingly insignificant as the fit of a shirt collar subtly yet powerfully reflects character, confidence and power. This nuance was extremely subtle yet highly effective in portraying the man as he transitioned in this popular television series… and so we take a lesson in life.

There are different collar shapes which complement or negatively accentuate men's necks. Therefore, ask your tailor or personal shopper, found in virtually all stores these days, to tell you what collar best flatters and complements your face, neck and jowls.

- A starched collar is professional.
- Button-down collars: suggests a more casual, even "preppy" look.
- A high neck British tab collar may better suit a gentleman with a longer neck, who could *carry* this.

- Flat collars, those leaning against the neck, may be more appropriate and flattering for someone with a large neck or jowls.
- The "Wall Street collar" — the white collar on a light blue, power stripe or light pink shirt, etc., is **fabulous**. Once again, can you carry this off? Are you comfortable? Is this authentically you?
- The white collar/white cuff is the pinnacle look. This makes a power statement, crisp and commanding.

*Incidentally: worn, frayed collars should be tossed. They are not chic even at the university level, professors.

Ties

Ties are the ultimate self-expression vehicle. Ties present a rare opportunity for men to express themselves and their personalities. And, if a powerful statement is your intent, you have a great opportunity through your choice of ties to do so.

Fabulous: Hermès and Ferragamo are rich and elegant; Brooks Brothers regimental is classic.

Once again consider — what do you want to convey about yourself? If you represent a professional conservative firm, you may want to rethink wearing your "personality" tie at work. A regimental tie with a light blue or white shirt is a great classic look, for example. A print or patterned tie with a striped shirt can make a very strong statement which would be more of a confidence look. Therefore, if you are feeling confident and authentic by mixing a regimental tie with a power stripe or patterned shirt, go for it.

When you find a good tie that makes you feel good, look great, helps achieve your desired statement and resonates well with your audience, stay with it!

Fine: Choose your tie to match your mood.

Fabulous: Select ties to match your mission.

Solid ties are a power expression which go in and out of style; they make a crisp power statement, as well.

Polka dots. Large polka dots: NO. You are not to be taken seriously. Small polka dots: Yes. Mitt Romney used to wear a (small) blue polka dot tie to death in an earlier campaign run.

Tie Knots

Tie knots present another way to *stand apart*. The Duke of Windsor popularized the famous Windsor knot, which, compared to other methods, produces a wide symmetrical triangular knot that commands attention. Add a single or double dimple for even more presence.

The "Full" or "Double Windsor," a very thick knot, and the "Half Windsor" today are referred to as *the* method of tying a necktie. The "Full Windsor" is usually worn with a medium spread or full spread collar. Knot size should be proportionate to the collar. For example, one would not necessarily wear a "Full Windsor" with a British tab collar.

*Many of the senior executives with whom I work wear large knots.

Perfecting the Tie Knot

The popular dimple in the tie knot is a must. Always have a dimple in your tie under the knot. This is a detail — a *nuance* and a flash. Consider the dimple of the tie like an exclamation mark after a sentence. "To what other *nuances* do you attend so meticulously?"

Learn how to properly tie a necktie to include the dimple (or even a double dimple).

The Single Dimple   The Double Dimple

Tie Colors and Their Significance

Tie colors are worthy of consideration. Understand colors and their significance.

For example:

    Blue: warmth, honesty

    Red: intense, passion, power — go!

    Yellow: personal power; generates enlightenment

    Green: friendship, trust

    Ice blue or *ice pink*: elegant

Further, we should know what colors flatter and complement us. For example, while the color red may suggest a power tie, think about how you, a redhead, look in a red tie? Is it flattering? There are also summer tie colors to consider. Know if you look washed out in coral and sage or if you need your summer tan to look great in these colors. Best not to wear summer colors (even though it may be summer) if they make you look washed out. Consult a personal shopper for assistance with color selection. Also, see Chapter 10, *Fabulous @ Business Travel and International Protocol* for information about the significance of different colors in other cultures.

Tie Length

Ties should touch the top of your belt within an inch. Back panel should never hang below the front.

Bow Ties

Some men prefer bow ties, which are perfectly acceptable. Bow ties make a personality statement and can look very chic. A bow tie needs to be worn with confidence and suggests the wearer has a sense of himself. Again, this is one of those looks that has to be authentic for you to be able to carry off.

Pants

Regardless of the latest fashion trend, pants need to flatter.

Fine: *A flat front or pleated pant.*

Fabulous: While pleated pants may flatter a long lean body type, they tend to distort a rather short, stout individual. The latter should consider wearing a flat front which is more becoming.

Fine: Cuffed or straight-legged.

Fabulous: Pants should always be cuffed, suggesting a more "finished" look, like the dimple in your tie. That said, for someone on the short/stout side, a cuffed leg tends to cut you off, so to speak. In this case, a straight leg would be appropriate and more flattering.

Pant Leg Lengths

Fine: The length of the pant leg is even to the floor.

Fabulous: Pant legs should be cut on a bias and slope at an angle so that the front pant leg rests along the top of the shoe and the back of the pant leg touches the top of the (shoe) sole.

Fine: Wear pants ankle-length.

Wearing pants ankle-length is not fine unless this is authentically you and this is the statement you wish to make; socks should be covered.

Shoes

You can wear a beautiful suit, shirt, tie, be meticulously groomed and well put together — however, when someone looks down at your feet and your shoes are scuffed, stretched out or shabby, you have negated all your efforts to make a professional statement.

Remember, shoes do so much more than just protect your feet if you know how to use them:

"Shoes are the soles of propriety!"
—an original quote from *moi*.

Good shoes make you feel good and take you good places.
—Old Chinese proverb

Fine: Wear whatever shoes you normally would, or consider debuting the latest fashion trend.

Fabulous: The "Presidential" shoe — black — is considered the most professional — with or without the cap toe; brown or cordovan take a back seat to black. You need to earn the right to wear the soft, supple, brown leather tassel loafers. Incidentally, the reason they are called *Presidential* is because presidents (of the United States and presidents of companies, as well as senior executives) wear them. In fact, Johnston & Murphy has a shoe called the *Reagan Presidential* because Ronald Reagan bought his Presidential shoes there.

STORY

Many years ago, President Clinton was speaking at the National Academy Foundation's Annual Conference in Anaheim where I was also a presenter. Sandy Weill, former CEO of Citigroup, was giving the scheduled keynote address, in which he emphasized many things to young adults about to enter the world of global business — including the importance of attire and specifically men's shoes. He said, "You need to wear the professional, conservative, black, laced-up, 'Presidential Shoe'," and pointed across the stage to the shoes Bill Clinton was wearing "...until you 'earn the right' to wear these..." referring to his own shoes which were soft, supple leather brown tassel loafers.

AND, speaking of Presidents and their shoes, the mere idea of President Nixon wearing anything other than the black, conservative, laced-up 'Presidential Shoes' seemed unimaginable. After the infamous Watergate debate wherein President Nixon confessed his role in Watergate, David Frost good naturedly gifted President Nixon a pair of black loafers (Gucci, of course!).

Cobblers

Fine: Frequent any nearby random cobbler.

Fabulous: Have your own cobbler and bring in shoes before they are noticeably in need of repair.

Shoes and Travel

Keep shoes well polished and buffed. Use a shoe tree or stuff toes with tissue paper to preserve shape. When traveling, use shoe bags for protection. The shower caps provided in hotels will do in a pinch.

"Being fabulous is having shiny shoes."
—Matt Schiffman

Fabulous: Have a professional shoeshine, or keep polish and a buffing cloth and brush on hand to do this yourself.

STORY

I am an expert shoe buffer... I started at age of six polishing shoes for my father and loved doing this.

Socks

Fine: Thick ankle length socks are fine.

Fabulous: Think long and thin (over the calf), executive-length gentlemen's hosiery. Bare legs and baring your own "mohair" is not advised; men's *fur* should not be visible when sitting (or standing). Black socks are "never wrong."

STORY

When I first met my husband and we were dating (he was in fact my fiancé by that time), he called me during a shopping expedition and announced, "Judith, I want you to know that I am now the proud owner of 'gentleman's hosiery' ... something I used to call 'Men's socks!'"

That said, wearing something very different such as argyles, "confidence" socks with outrageous color combinations such as blue, orange, purple and black can be fun — however, we need to earn the right to wear these socks in business. Once again, understand who you are, what image you wish to project — and what you can "carry off."

Accessories

Accessories are a tasteful accent as well as a great conversation launch. Items such as tie bars, tie ropes, tie clips and tie pins are all **fabulous** because they are not seen as much these days. Therefore, there is usually a great (personal) story, i.e., they belonged to your grandfather who... (xyz, etc., etc.). Cufflinks, watches, glasses, sunglasses and handkerchiefs are also great *nuances* which help you *stand apart*, serve utilitarian functions, are great accents and present opportunities to express **fabulous** you.

Watches

Men's watches are important in business because they are one of few accessories men are expected to wear and others notice in a big way. Once again, think: *quality.* I embrace the notion: "Wear the watch you can best afford." However, know your audience. Think twice before wearing your solid gold and diamond Rolex, for example, with a first-time client who may not have such a watch, for whatever reason. Also, these days, in this challenging economy, even if you have one, you may not want to flaunt it. Many have multiple watches to suit the occasion and your audience. For example, owning a GPS sports watch or heart monitor, a work watch, and maybe even a special occasion watch is not uncommon. Choose thoughtfully the watch you wear for each business occasion.

STORY

I remember sitting with a group of senior financial management executives who were all meticulously attired in gorgeous suits, shirts, ties, shoes and looked fabulous. I was a bit surprised to notice that several were sporting those plastic bubble top watches found at the local drugstore. There was an instant disconnect.

That said, some can carry off unusual watches, such as when a very senior person sports, i.e., a Mickey Mouse watch (especially if they work for Disney or a toy company)… or if they are a marathoner or tri-athlete (or work for a company that caters to that audience) and they wear a GPS/heart rate monitor watch, etc.

Bracelets

Some men wear bracelets. Remember, if you are not comfortable wearing a bracelet and cannot carry it off, if you are not authentic wearing a bracelet, do not wear it… although it is always touching when we wear a wrist band signifying our support of a special cause or one made by our children — also a (personal) conversation opportunity.

Rings and Pinkie-Rings

Other than a wedding band, some men wear rings including diamond rings or symbolic rings representing an organization, fraternity or family crest. Once again, you need to be authentic wearing these rings and prepared to tell the story. These items can serve as an immediate conversation launch and may help you learn something of a more personal nature.

Lapel Pins

A lapel pin is a little thing yet represents a big opportunity to convey powerful personal information while acting as a great conversation launch.

Fine: Wear the pin on either lapel.

Fabulous: Wear the pin on your left lapel, close to your heart. The American flag, a family or an honorary crest, company logo, fraternity/sorority or organization pennant, yellow or pink ribbon, etc., on the lapel is a celebrated accessory as well as an impressive conversation launch.

Belts

Fine: Black or brown is fine.

Fabulous: Quality — black belts will complement your black shoes and a gold buckle is considered a notch above (pardon the pun) silver and no more expensive. These days, we see more stainless steel and nickel.

Either way, be sure to match the color belt with your shoes and coordinate the belt buckle with your watch and cufflinks.

Pant Supports

Aside from belts, pant supports come in two forms: braces and suspenders. Braces are worn professionally as an accent or statement while suspenders are typically worn by, i.e., farmers to literally suspend their pants.

Fine: *Clip-on suspenders* are intended to be functional and help support your pants.

Fabulous: *Braces* actually button onto the inside of your pants and are worn more as an accent piece. Braces were especially made popular when Michael Douglas sported these in the movie *Wall Street*. However, if you are a person who likes this look as a sense of self-expression — if it's *you* and it's *authentic* — go for it. Do not wear braces if you are trying to be someone you simply are not (yet). This is one of those looks you really have to be ready to carry off.

Handkerchiefs

There are two types of handkerchiefs — the utilitarian handkerchief which you use when you sneeze, and a silk or cotton handkerchief used as an accent piece in your jacket pocket.

Utilitarian Handkerchiefs

Fine: Use a Kleenex.

Fabulous: A pressed monogrammed cotton or linen utilitarian handkerchief kept in your inside jacket pocket is at the ready. Think Rhett Butler and... Dr. Phil!

(*International protocol note*: Some societies, notably Japan, consider it extremely unhygienic to use a fabric handkerchief. For utilitarian purposes, only use paper tissues to blow your nose. Do your cultural research!)

Accent Handkerchiefs

Fine: A big colorful silk plume!

Fabulous: Cotton or linen weave — straight, three or four points (five is a little much), showing very little above the pocket edge. Less is more! Think: subtle, understated.

Handkerchief colors should complement, not necessarily match, your tie. Wear a big plume only if you want to attract like a peacock or if this suits the nature of your business and is the message you intend to portray.

Undershirts

Not wearing an undershirt or tee shirt is fine, however, tee shirts are frequently worn for warmth in cold weather, or in very warm weather to absorb perspiration. And on this note, remember, there is a difference between an antiperspirant (prevents/minimizes sweating) and deodorant (prevents/minimizes odor); know your body. (See the next section below regarding *dress shields* to provide extra protection for your clothes.)

Fine: Wear a regular (crew neck) white tee shirt under your dress shirt which helps keep you warm and/or dry.

Fabulous: Wear a v-neck tee shirt, which is no more expensive than a regular tee shirt, except that you cannot see this when wearing an open collar. Seeing a man's undershirt, especially if frayed or dingy, is (not good and) the equivalent of seeing a woman's bra straps: it's tacky.

Dress Shields

Dress shields help protect and preserve good suits from perspiration. Have dress shields sewn into suit jackets.

Nails

Nails reflect health and personal hygiene. It is important to get regular manicures and pedicures for a well manicured state of being and professional look, for men as well as women.

Fine: Get a manicure

Fabulous: Use clear polish for a truly "polished" look!

Beards and Facial Hair

Many men sport beards or the "Brad Pitt" look (e.g., a day or even several of not being clean shaven). There are many different types of beards and some can help project a great "look" while others don't look so great. Some men (feel they) need facial hair to enhance their appearance although for others facial hair is downright distracting. Also, while some professions are receptive and may even lend themselves to a bearded look, for others facial hair might be considered positively taboo.

Fine: Sport a beard, mustache or facial hair if you want to or just feel like it.

Fabulous: Should you decide to sport a beard or mustache make sure this is well-kempt, clipped and clean.

Hats

Hats present another opportunity to *stand apart* and make a statement. Know that whatever you choose from your *fabulous* arsenal to place on your head can positively accentuate or actually detract from your overall look. For example, if you are short, stout and balding, know that a watchman's cap will accentuate that which you may be trying to offset.

Fine: Wear a baseball cap.

Fabulous: The fedora is always distinguished-looking. Select a hat that flatters. Hats can be fun, stylish and rakish. You need to love your hat and feel good about wearing it.

Wear hats for warmth, to stay dry or, as an accent. For whatever reason you are wearing one, wear your hat with confidence and panache.

Whenever entering a building or home, or when dining, remove your hat, a sign of respect. Interestingly, the origin of this custom dates back to the Middle Ages when knights would meet each other in their armor. In order to be identified they had to remove their helmets. Today, taking off one's hat is a sign of respect, particularly when encountering a lady.

Baseball caps are one of my pet peeves. The baseball cap is a hat and therefore, even when dining at an outdoor café, the cap should come off. *Exception*: anyone with extreme sensitivity to sunlight (or another medical condition) should feel free to keep hats on to cover their head, face, eyes, of course; *acknowledge* this to dining companions.

Gloves

Gloves are both utilitarian and make a statement. Utilitarian — they help keep your hands warm. The statement they make suggests your attention to detail, says you are well put-together and have good taste. As with the dimple in your tie, wearing gloves may be analogous to the exclamation mark at the end of a sentence.

Fine: Wool, acrylic.

Fabulous: Quality — leather. Make sure gloves fit well, e.g. tightly. Black is classic. Brown and cordovan take a backseat to black.

Remember to remove your right glove when shaking hands — yes, even if it is zero degrees! We want to remove any barriers to our connection. The Queen of England is the ONLY person in the world protocolically permitted to shake hands with gloves ON.

Interestingly, *The American Heritage Dictionary of Idioms* defines to "handle without gloves" or "take off the gloves" to mean harsh treatment, nitty-gritty, down and dirty. They suggest that "handle without gloves" was an antonym arising from "handle with kid gloves" (meaning to treat gently) However, other sources suggest that "take off the gloves" comes from boxing, where the padded gloves soften the blow, so removing the gloves suggests rough treatment. Etymology is a wonderful thing!

Overcoats

Fine: Wear whatever you have always worn; it's fine.

Fabulous: If you have a particularly **fabulous** or a particularly un-**fabulous** coat, leave it in the car, which you should do anyway as you endeavor to un-encumber prior to your meeting or meal.

Emphasis on longer versus short overcoats — nothing frayed, worn, or in need of dry cleaning… you never know when your overcoat will get noticed and the overcoat itself as well as its condition is another reflection on you.

*No ski parkas or car-coats over suits. Think: calf-length.

That said, a cashmere or shearling car-coat, falling below the hem of your suit jacket, may be considered. The Chesterfield coat — classic, timeless, **fabulous**.

Colors: Black, dark blue, charcoal gray, camel are classic.

Cars

Similarly, if you have a particularly **fabulous** or a particularly un-**fabulous** car, park this out of public view, for obvious reasons.

Briefcases

Briefcases are an essential accessory in business. Consider owning different size briefcases to match your mission. As always, all things about you should speak of quality. (See Chapter 6, *Fabulous @ The Meeting* for more regarding selecting your briefcase to suit the event.)

Fine: Canvas — practical and lightweight. (Not fine: A slightly-worn canvas bag still looks worn.)

Fabulous: Quality — leather. Black, brown or cordovan. Monogrammed. A worn leather briefcase has character.

*Metal or silver briefcase — think: James Bond, who carried guns and $$. Carrying a stainless steel briefcase is also a major style statement.

Portfolios

A portfolio is often used in lieu of a briefcase, again, to suit your mission.

Fine: Use the company-provided portfolio… which may be vinyl.

Fabulous: Think quality — leather; black, brown, cordovan. Monogrammed. If a particular fabric or color suits your business, go for it absolutely.

I still use the leather portfolio I received as a college graduation gift. It still looks great and is in great condition and shows some character as well… if that portfolio could talk!

Eyeglasses
The Glass

The glass in your eyeglasses is a detail frequently overlooked, however, it has the potential to cast a dim reflection on you (pardon the pun). Wearing linty or scratched glasses is also a reflection of you, your personal hygiene, and can be seen as a metaphor for your eye to detail, so to speak. If you cannot see clearly through the lens… what else do you not see clearly? The glass of sunglasses and prescription glasses should be pristine.

Fine: Clean with whatever's handy. Use a household glass cleaner, rub with your shirt sleeve or a paper towel.

Fabulous: Clean daily with a lens cleaning gel/spray and a professional lens cleaning cloth. (Household glass cleaners actually destroy lenses and rubbing with cotton fibers or paper towels can damage the glass.)

Sunglasses

Sunglasses are functional and present another opportunity to make a personal statement.

Fine: Wear sunglasses as needed.

Fabulous: Like gloves, remove sunglasses when shaking hands to eliminate the barrier between you and the other person.

Prescription Glasses

Fine: Wear as needed, of course.

Fabulous: If you have the luxury of wearing prescription eye glasses selectively, take them off upon encountering another to eliminate the glasses (as a "barrier"); use as needed, certainly. This split-second nuance is a most respectful gesture which speaks volumes about you. Removing your glasses shows you know "the difference" while demonstrating respect and shows you are "fully present" in the moment.

Frames

Sunglasses and prescription glass frames should highlight and complement, not hide or detract from your face or eyes. Save fun, loud or "personality" frames for social occasions — unless you choose to make this personality statement in business, of course, and feel confident to carry it off.

Eyeglass Cases

As with briefcases and portfolios, these are noticed, and your selection should reflect your professional position.

Fine: Any pleather/vinyl/plastic case with your optometrist's name on it.

Fabulous: Leather, metal, crocodile, monogrammed, or something that reflects your personality and/or suits the business occasion.

Tattoos

Tattoos are a personal expression that have become more popular today among men (and women) of all ages. Some want their tattoos to be seen while others do not. Tattoos may be a fad, a phase or a stage. One may get a tattoo on impulse and later regret that decision. My suggestion, if you are considering a tattoo: get one that does not show when professionally attired. Discretion is the better part of valor.

Business Casual

Even in a "Business Casual" culture, we urge you to "dress a notch above."

The definition of business casual varies from company to company. For some, this may suggest khakis and a polo shirt and for others may simply mean "no tie." There are no hard and fast rules here and so, whenever in doubt, never hesitate to inquire.

Fine: Blue jeans and a tee shirt.

Fabulous: Even if the culture suggests blue jeans and a tee shirt, dress a notch above. Think: clean, crisp, pressed and well-fit. Your shirt is bright white and *pressed* not dingy, wrinkled or frayed and jeans are clean, pressed and fit well.

Fabulous: Consider khaki slacks and a white polo shirt; have a blue blazer on hand, just in case — this is a clean, professional, great business casual look.

Shoes and accessories are key. Instead of sneakers, wear boat shoes (Topsiders) without socks, a leather weave shoe or tassel loafer with argyle socks. And, if you do opt for sneakers, be sure they do not appear ancient or emit a 100-year-old fragrance!

Blue Jeans

There was a time when I could not imagine addressing the issue of blue jeans in the workplace. It was so far outside the realm of appropriate business attire that no one would ever have considered it. But the dot-com era has changed many aspects of our lives and jeans in the workplace is one of them. I point directly to Bill Gates who started it all. However, Bill Gates "earned the right" to wear blue jeans and cowboy boots; there is no excuse for the wrinkled tee shirt.

There are some guidelines regarding jeans:

1. Never assume you may wear them. If this is your first trip to the company for a job interview, consulting gig or business meeting, do not assume jeans will be fine.

2. If you work in a setting where jeans are appropriate, chose jeans that fit well. Make sure they do not sag and are not faded or torn. Pair them with a pressed white tee shirt (**fabulous**), or a polo shirt (black or light pink is special); a classic navy blue blazer is "never wrong."

Formal Wear

Technically speaking, when an event says "formal" it suggests that men wear tuxedos and women wear floor-length gowns. However, today the word "formal" is up for a modern-day interpretation and can mean many different things to many people. The formality of the event and whether the event will take place during the day (before 6:00 pm in the evening) or after 6:00 pm will determine the dress code. Whenever in doubt, always ask your host. Here are some guidelines for men:

Formal Event:

Fine: A tuxedo, tailcoat or cutaway jacket of any color, regardless of season.

Fabulous: BLACK tails or a gray cutaway jacket is traditional and **fabulous**.

Semi-formal:

Fine: A tuxedo, tailcoat or cutaway in any color is fine and contemporary, regardless of season.

Fabulous: Black or charcoal colored tuxedo is traditional and **fabulous** (for winter); white dinner jacket (for summer).

Pants (in formal wear)

Fine: Any color as long as they match the jacket.

Fabulous: Gray pinstripe, matching the jacket

Black pants are the traditional choice for formal and semi-formal wear. Contemporary looks suggest pants match the color of the jacket for both formal and semi-formal events.

Shirts (in formal wear)

Formal (and Semi-formal):

Fine: Flat, lay down collars work for traditional daytime events.

Fabulous: White piqué wing-collar (evening).

Fabulous: WHITE — regardless of formal or semi-formal.

Semi-formal (only): White pleated front or piqué shirt.

Accessories (in formal wear)

Fine: Vest or ascot.

Fabulous: Vest, ascot or cummerbund and/or bow tie to complement jacket and pants.

Evening Accessories:
Formal Traditional: White piqué vest or waistcoat, white bow tie, and white gloves.
Semi-formal:
  Fine: Vest or cummerbund with bow tie matching the jacket and pants.
  Fabulous: BLACK vest or cummerbund with bow tie.
Shoes
Fine: Leather or any type shoe and any toe, as long as they blend.
Fabulous: Black patent with a smooth toe.
Daytime Accessories:
Formal Traditional: Gray gloves, top hat and spats. (Spats are a short cloth gaiter covering the instep and ankle.)
Semi-formal: Traditional gray gloves.

"Dress for success," "Look the part," and the quotes go on. Remember, adorning ourselves means knowing how we want to be viewed by the world with your *audience* in mind. Dressing dictates how you feel, how you project, how you are perceived and ultimately received by others. Remember, dressing *well* is the "*Easy A*" in business especially these days, and will help you catapult to the next level. Lead by example.

In summary, the way you dress speaks volumes about who you are, your confidence, attention to detail, style. The way you chose to present yourself to the world is a reflection of how you feel about yourself, present company, and your future, and is a reflection on the company you represent. Dress to feel good about yourself and show respect for the nature of the event and others around you.

Women

STORY

I was honored to speak at a women's business conference which drew over 6500 women. The governor and his lovely wife were in attendance a well as other luminaries. As I looked around during the course of the day at the women attending this professional event, I saw women dressed in construction boots and blue jeans carrying backpacks. I also saw women wearing fishnet hosiery, stiletto heels, plunging backs and necklines. All this and more at a professional women's business conference?

ANOTHER STORY

I was asked to work one-on-one with a promising young woman at a Fortune 500 firm. She had beautiful long hair and wore it down. She wore short, tight skirts and tight-fitting tops. Her superior believed this young woman had exceptional potential and arranged to have us spend some time together to help develop her professional presence skills.

Two years later, she supervised a staff of 60 professionals and hired me to work for her, to train her staff in professional presence, etiquette and protocol. To this day, she tells me how embarrassed she was to think of how she used to dress, believing that this was how to "get ahead."

As more of our workforce is being hired back, two-thirds are men. This suggests that women, despite admirable efforts to reach the proverbial glass ceiling, are actually regressing. And, while women may need help in matters pertaining to life/work balance, negotiation skills, finance, getting to "the ask" and more… aside from all that, I believe many women are shooting themselves in the foot the moment they walk out the door in the morning to go to work, because they are not dressing professionally.

There is much confusion in the workplace today regarding what is considered "professional attire" for women, particularly among younger women in business. Please know emphatically that what is worn by actors on television and in the movies, and what we see in stores being pushed by cutting-edge designers, is not necessarily appropriate professional attire. Make no mistake: short tight skirts, plunging backs and necklines, fishnet hosiery and stilettos, while they may be fashionable, are *not* considered appropriate business attire. If women want to be taken seriously and advance, we need to dress *professionally*. We can all be reminded that we are professionals first, and should dress and act, walk, talk and sit accordingly.

STORY

We may recall the woman at JP Morgan who ended up on the nightly news not long ago. YouTube and all the newspapers covered this story because her company felt that she dressed too provocatively. She wasn't getting promotions and wondered why.

Conversely, giving *no* thought to our appearance is equally ineffective in the workplace. While some women are unable to advance because they follow every fashion trend, and are basically too sexy for the office, others are left back because they do not consider their visual impression at all. In a global marketplace, American women are losing their edge. Walk through any airport, look around any random street in New York or on any cruise ship. You can easily distinguish American women from European women, for example. There is a distinct difference in overall appearance including clothing, style, personal demeanor… plus, the shoes are a dead giveaway: European women do not wear sneakers to work. They rarely even wear them when visiting a theme park!

There is much we can learn from some of our cross-cultural neighbors in terms of the importance of that visual first impression and making the effort to look our best in each situation. Remember the *Mehrabian Rule*: 55% of all first impressions are derived from a *visual* aspect. Women have an opportunity to use their femininity to their advantage the same way men have always used their assets to achieve success forever!

FIRST PERSON

"I'm often in a room of gentlemen and I say, 'Who do you think they are going to remember, the 10th guy in the gray suit or the one woman?' Being a woman (in business) is an advantage, not a disadvantage. In a room full of gentlemen, it's easy to stand apart. Embrace what makes us different, ladies."

—**Karen Kaplan**, CEO, Hill Holliday

Suits

As always, make an investment in quality suits. Even if you have just one (actually you need two), be sure they are quality. There are many outlets and everyone has sales. Be on a first-name basis with sales consultants in your favorite stores and ask them to keep you in their little black book for sales and something that "has your name on it" when in arrives in the store. Always be on the look-out for "that suit" — you know the one that is perfect and beyond flatters. They are more difficult to come by than we might think. You may be able to buy it for a steal and have it altered to fit. Also, consider a custom suit, especially if you know a good tailor or find yourself in Asia where having anything custom-made is quite reasonable.

STORY

I used to be a District Sales Manager for Carlisle, an upscale women's clothing house based out of New York. They designed, manufactured and sold upscale women's clothes out of homes by invitation, and later through their own fabulous private showroom. Carlisle sold designer looks, i.e., similar to Gucci, Chanel, Escada, etc., but not at designer prices (not that they were inexpensive). However, the point is, they were investment pieces and customers literally passed on their Carlisles from generation to generation. I have a friend in New York who inherited her mother's Carlisle suits and had every one of them altered so she could continue to wear these classics. (The Worth Collection has since taken over the Connaught Group/Carlisle.)

Think *quality, classic,* investment dressing. Natural fibers or knits (they breathe!) — although there are some great synthetics out there these days as well. Ann Taylor, Pendleton, Hickey-Freeman, Ellen Tracy and Brooks Brothers are perhaps best known for their classics. St. John knits are classic and great for travel; they don't wrinkle. Wait until they go on sale and you can even find many at consignment shops these days — or online! Invest one piece at a time and add to your wardrobe which you will have forever.

Suit Colors

Knowing your "season" and what colors flatter you is important. However, please note the following are considered the most professional color suits to wear in business for women (and men):

- Black
- Blue (navy)
- Gray (charcoal)
- Pinstripe, in any color variation

Ladies, you need to "earn the right" to wear the confidence blues, the power reds, even pink. "Earning the right" refers to work status and client relationship status. In other words, when meeting with a first-time client from a conservative financial services firm, you probably would want to wear your quality, traditional, understated, professional black suit. Save the confidence colors for after you earn their business. When in doubt, classic colors and styles are "never wrong."

A classic suit (e.g., skirt/dress and jacket) is still considered the most professional business attire the world over; pantsuits take a backseat universally, particularly in other countries.

The Pantsuit

Hillary Clinton is known for wearing pantsuits while she ran for the highest political office in the land. Remember, though, that Hillary Clinton used to wear skirts as First Lady of Arkansas and as First Lady at the White House in the early 1990's. Secretary of State Hillary Clinton has clearly "earned the right" to wear pantsuits… and ponytails!

It is important to acknowledge that some women look and therefore feel better wearing pants while other women look and therefore feel better wearing a skirt or dress. Know what most flatters you, how you feel most comfortable and dress accordingly. We embrace the notion: "The beauty in knowing the rules is knowing when it is okay to break them." Therefore, if you feel you look and therefore feel and perform better in pants, break the rules and wear a pantsuit versus skirt and jacket and vice versa.

Suit Jackets

Fabulous: Longer jackets are considered more business classic and are also generally more flattering. That said, longer jackets are not as flattering on someone who is rather short and stout. Consult with an image consultant or personal shopper for advice on which cut best suits your figure.

Jacket Buttons

The top two buttons on a three-button suit or the top button on a two-button suit should be buttoned, the third or bottom button should remain open to vent (for men and women). This, at the boardroom and dining room tables.

Unbuttoning Jackets

Fine: Randomly unbutton buttons.

Fabulous: Unbutton from the bottom and work your way up.

Hemlines

Fine: Follow the latest fashion length.

Fabulous: Consider the length that most flatters you. There is great merit to the notion: the more senior the executive, the longer her hemline.

*A short tight skirt does not make a professional statement.

Blouses and Tops

Ladies, our blouse, shirt, sweater or camisole will make or completely break our entire professional statement.

Colors and Styles:

The same colors apply for men and women:

#1: White

#2: Blue (light)

#3: Stripe — the Power Stripe

#4: Light Pink is **fabulous**

- Flowers, lilacs and animal prints do *not* make a classic professional statement.
- Lace and ruffles, while from time to time a major fashion trend and socially completely **fabulous**, do *not* make a professional statement.
- Low-cut blouses (front or back), exposed bra straps, and especially cleavage (!), do *not* make a professional statement.
- Consider quality, as always, and natural fabrics. Although today, there are some beautiful polyester and cotton spandex blends. Check proper fit and make sure blouses are pressed. The body of the blouse should not be too bulky or tight fitting.
- Turtlenecks — should fit well around your neck, not be bulky or hang off your neck, and should only be worn in cold weather.
- Only one-quarter inch fabric at the suit cuff should be revealed, as this extends from your jacket's arm.
- French cuffs — **fabulous**. Again, the opportunity to wear cufflinks presents the opportunity to share personal information (who gifted them, where you found them) and place the other person at ease while allowing you to get to know each other a bit more.

Clothes and Travel

Cover each suit, blouse, etc., with a plastic bag to help eliminate the wrinkle factor. Dry-cleaning bags work perfectly for this purpose.

Collars

Shirt collars always seem to evoke questions. Should they be worn inside the jacket, outside, stand up or lay flat across the neckline of the jacket? There is no right or wrong, better or worse. If you are able to keep your shirt collar up, wear it up. If it is easier and more flattering to have collars lay flat against your jacket neckline and you won't have to adjust it or think about it, go for it.

Hence, a crew neckline is a great alternative as this allows you to basically forget about the collar and focus on business. The classic crew neckline is "never wrong," never a thought, never a challenge. (For some, the v-neck is more flattering, creating more of a vertical line.)

Shoes

You can be beautifully attired, have hair, nails and accessories all meticulously in place — however, if one were to look down at our shoes and they were scuffed, poorly maintained or old-looking, we will have instantly negated all of our efforts to complete a well put-together professional look. Remember, "*Shoes are the sole of propriety!*"

If nothing else, splurge on shoes. Think: classic and comfortable and affordable. Stuart Weitzman never disappoints. Some of the most costly shoes are actually very uncomfortable. One of my puppies is apparently very discerning!

Fine: Wear your comfortable shoes.

Fabulous: Invest in shoes for classic styling and comfort. The classic pump is "never wrong." Suede is considered by some a notch above leather and no more expensive. A fabric shoe is considered a notch above patent leather (summer months) and no more expensive. Patent and grosgrain is a **fabulous** look.

Leave slingback, open toe and stilettos for social events — they will not enhance your professional statement or credibility at work. You want to be fashionable yet want the statement you make to be all about professional you — not your high fashion shoes or "look at me" accessories.

White shoes

Fine: Chalk white: think nurses, baby shoes and brides.

Fabulous: Off-white, champagne, beige or spectators (white and black/dark brown/dark navy blue). *Note: Shoes should be darker than your hemline.

Cobblers

Fine: Go to anyone nearby.

Fabulous: Have your own cobbler and visit before the need for repair is actually noticeable. Have toe/heel tacks affixed as soon as you purchase shoes to help preserve them.

After wearing shoes, use a shoe tree or fill with tissue paper to help preserve shape. Also, when you travel, use a shoe bag or covering to prevent scratches, scuff marks, etc. In a pinch, use a hotel shower cap.

Hosiery

Always wear hosiery, regardless of temperature. Wearing hosiery is being "finished" and a presents a polished look.

Beige, tan and neutral shades of hosiery are always appropriate leg colors for women. One of the biggest *faux pas* I see among women in business is with respect to black hosiery. Please be reminded that *sheer* black hose is the most elegant, the most formal and therefore, reserved for evening. Black *opaque* hose, which comes in different weights — light, medium and heavy (good for warmth) — is appropriate day hosiery in cooler months. Very light gold or slightly silver hues are usually matched with a dressy dress or dress suit. White hosiery is "out" in business, except for nurses.

*Always make sure shoes are darker than your hemline and legwear, i.e., never wear black hosiery with white or tan shoes.

STORY

I worked fairly regularly with the Tourism Department in St. Maarten with a woman who was the Director of the Department of Tourism. Even though it may have been 98° outside, this woman — and every professional woman whom I encountered there — wore hosiery. If they can do it, we can do it.

I am frequently asked about navy shoes and hosiery colors: wear blue opaque hosiery (in cooler months) or beige, tan and neutral shades, any months, with blue shoes, if possible. If not, black shoes with navy hosiery is "never wrong."

Dress Shields (for men and women)

Use dress shields to protect your good suits from perspiration. Many women wear a jacket *sans* blouse and so dress shields need to be changed every wearing. Therefore, we advise women consider disposable dress shields rather than sewing dress shields into their jackets.

Accessories

Accessories are truly *everything!* It's all in the detail. Use accessories to silently complete the statement about who you are and convey your message.

There is a big difference between accessorizing socially versus in business.

Jewelry

Fine: Bangles, dangles and glitters are fine socially, as is cheap and faux if you are in a fun, glitzy business.

Fabulous: Wear real gold, silver, stones in business, especially overseas. And, less is more; if you need to think more than *three* seconds and wonder "Is this — too much?" It probably is. Take it off. When in doubt, do without.

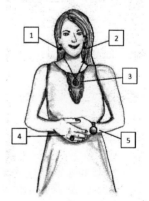

Think: The Rule of Five: Ears (earrings: 1, 2), Neckline (necklace: 3), Left or Right Hand (ring: 4), and Wrist (watch or bracelet: 5).

Gold and pearls are still considered the most classic; silver takes a back seat, however, is still appropriate — and of course, preferable if silver is more flattering to you and complements your coloring, complexion, other accessories.

Handkerchiefs

Fine: Use a Kleenex

Fabulous: Carry a cotton or linen monogrammed handkerchief. White, pastels, Wedgwood blue, etc.

International Protocol Note: Some societies, notably Japan, consider it extremely unhygienic to use a fabric handkerchief. For utilitarian purposes, only use tissues to blow your nose. Do your cultural research!

Of course, women, like men, sometimes wear an accent handkerchief in their suit pocket. As previously noted, this may be straight, have three or four points (five is a little much) and show very little above the pocket edge. Subtle and understated is best; less is more. Colors should complement your blouse and accessories such as scarves or purses.

Pins

Pins make a statement and provide a great conversation launch. Madeline Albright feels so strongly about this topic that she wrote a book entitled *Read My Pins*, a play on the famous George H. W. Bush quote, "Read My Lips." The theme of Ms. Albright's book (and significant in her life) is that she would always wear a pin to suit the occasion. For example, when she was accused of being serpent-like by Saddam Hussein, at her next meeting with him Ms. Albright wore her serpent pin which sent the signal she was aware of her reputation and characteristically and good-naturedly wore this. Madeleine Albright owns thousands of pins and wears them to suit each audience. Ms. Albright's pins always evoke reaction *et plus de* conversation!

Watches

Watches make a statement about you. To quote one of my mentors: "Wear the watch you can most afford." Wear a quality watch. Be careful about wearing a high-priced platinum or solid gold and diamond watch at work. Save these for special occasions… or know your audience, and your ability to "carry it off," and break the rules. Dress to be authentic but with your audience in mind. Many will own several watches reserved for various occasions such as a sports watch, a fun watch, a fashion-statement watch, a watch for work and perhaps a special occasion watch. Or if you have an heirloom piece, which might also be a conversation launch, you might consider this for an important meeting or presentation.

STORY

My editor met a gentleman on a cruise who owned a jewelry store. They were discussing the high-end watches for sale onboard the ship, and Denise initially resisted paying such high prices for a watch. The jewelry store owner asked her to consider how often she looks at her other jewelry such as a necklace, earrings, etc. Then he asked her to consider how often she looks at her watch. His point was when we consider the CPV (cost per view) index — a term I endearingly borrowed and clearly adapted from my friends in "bond land!" — the price is in truth minimal. Denise did purchase a beautiful investment watch, noting this is the most expensive item she owns, however, the watch provides value in expressing her (own) statement of quality and brings her *plus de plaisir* whenever she looks at it... many times a day!

Briefcases

Briefcases are an essential accessory in business. Consider owning different size briefcases to match your mission. As always, all things about you should speak of quality.

Fine: Canvas — practical and light weight. (Even a slightly worn canvas bag looks worn.)

Fabulous: Quality — leather. Black, brown or cordovan. Monogrammed. (That said, Louis Vuitton is vinyl, and I must tell you that I invested in mine twenty-five years ago and still use it today. For those of us who are animal lovers, we can easily find high-quality, non-leather products.)

Name brand briefcases such as Louis Vuitton, Adrienne Vittadini, Kenneth Cole and Coach are professionally appropriate, should this be the statement you wish to make.

Colors — all have significance. A rich, subtle tan or hunter green vs. a bright, fun red or even bubble gum pink all convey completely different messages about you/your firm/business.

*A metal or silver briefcase is a major style statement. As always, the size briefcase you use should suit your business mission.

(See Chapter 6, *Fabulous @ The Meeting* for more guidance in selecting the appropriate briefcase for the occasion.)

Portfolios

A portfolio is often used in *lieu* of a briefcase again, to suit your mission. I still use the leather portfolio I received as a college graduation gift. It still looks great and shows some character as well... if that portfolio could talk!

Fine: A company vinyl logo portfolio is fine.

Fabulous: Professional — think quality — leather; black, brown, cordovan. Monogrammed.

If distinctive fabric or colors or a brand name vinyl, i.e., Louis Vuitton, suit your business image, go for it absolutely.

How to Hold a Portfolio

Many women hold a portfolio the way they are most comfortable, often in front of them, like a baby or a box.

Fine: Hold a portfolio however you are most comfortable.

Fabulous: Hold a portfolio in the left hand, at your side (like a large book), leaving your right hand free to shake hands.

Scarves

A scarf pulls your look together and helps complete your professional statement. Even if you don't know how to tie them, wear a scarf and drape this over your shoulders.

Fabulous: Scarves are a great accessory and a conversation launch.

Fabulous: Burberry, Ferragamo, Hermès are among my favorites. (We may find many designer scarves at consignment shops … and on eBay (!) these days.)

Outerwear

Leave your overcoat in the car if possible, and un-encumber when calling on a client or attending a networking event. However, should you choose to wear in or carry your coat, make sure you do not have a particularly **fabulous** or a particularly un-**fabulous** overcoat. Even if you believe you will be hanging this in the reception area upon arrival, your host may (graciously) offer to help you on with your coat as you leave, and if your coat is either of the above, *en garde!*

Coat Length & Colors

Despite what *fashionistas* believe, coat length should be longer than your dress or skirt and certainly longer than your suit jacket.

Fine: Wear a parka or whatever coat you normally wear.

Fabulous: Save your ski parka for the slopes; a business setting calls for business outerwear. Invest in a professional cloth coat versus jacket.

Black, dark blue, charcoal gray, camel are classic coat colors. Be careful with white/off-white (easily soiled), bright red or other eye-catching outerwear (be sure you can carry it off).

Fur Coats

Unless you work in Chicago, leave fur coats at home. Think: Pat Nixon and her conservative, classic Republican cloth coat.

Unbuttoning Coats and Jackets

Fine: Randomly unbutton your coat or jacket.

Fabulous: Start from the bottom and work your way up.

Cars

Similarly, if you have a particularly **fabulous** or a particularly un-**fabulous** car, park this out of public view, for obvious reasons. Speaking of cars…

Getting Into or Out of a Car/Limo

When you think about it, the valet who stands in front of our car door, holding our door while we get in and out, may sometimes have cause to blush! There is a way for women to get into and out of a car more demurely, whether you are wearing a dress or pants:

Getting Out:

Fine: Take one leg out of the car, place this on the pavement and lumber out of the car — grab onto something if need to pull yourself out.

Fabulous: Knees together, swing your calves around to face away from the car — in one fell swoop — then lean your weight forward and get out. If someone is standing by to assist, do not hesitate to offer them your hand.

Getting In:

Fabulous: Sit down in the car first, and then with both knees together, swing your legs around and place them in the car — in one fell swoop.

Gloves

Gloves are both utilitarian and make a statement. Utilitarian — they help keep your hands warm. The statement they make suggests a finished look and a professional statement. You are completely well put-together in good taste. Gloves should be taut on the hand, and are analogous to the exclamation mark at the end of a sentence.

Fine: Wool, acrylic, nylon, down-filled mittens or gloves are functional.

Fabulous: Leather or kid gloves. Black gloves are classic; brown and cordovan take a backseat to black. If, however, you want to make a statement wearing your red, purple or green (leather) gloves and this is authentically you, go for it.

Note: "Kid gloves" are made from the skin of a young goat or lamb and are softer and finer than (harder) leather and so became a symbol of elegance and gentility in the early 1800's. The term "handle with kid gloves" thus means to be very gentle, genteel or tactful.

Remember to remove your right glove when shaking hands — yes, even if it is zero degrees! Gloves are a barrier and you want nothing to stand between you and the other person when you shake hands. The Queen of England is the *only* person in the world protocolically permitted to shake hands with her gloves *on*. (See the *gloves* section under <u>Men</u> above for interesting etymological history of "taking off the gloves.")

Hats

Hats are worn socially as a fashion statement or outside for practical reasons such as warmth or as protection from the sun or rain. The Royal Wedding of William and Catherine evoked a renewed fashion awareness regarding wearing hats. Please know that generally speaking, hats are worn more for social occasions and are not necessarily appropriate in business. Yolanda of Boston is an exception and is known for her **fabulous** hats socially and professionally. Yolanda has "earned the right" to wear hats.

With respect to hats, as one journalist put it, "You're either all in or all out," because once we put on a hat we get "hat hair," meaning our hair is completely flattened and recovery is a challenge at best.

Eyeglasses

The Glass

The glass in your eyeglasses is a detail frequently overlooked, however, it has the potential to cast a dim reflection on you (pardon the pun). Linty or scratched lenses are also a reflection of your personal hygiene, and can be seen as a metaphor for your eye to detail, so to speak. If you cannot see clearly through the lens… what else do you not see clearly? The glass of sunglasses and prescription glasses should be pristine.

Fine: Clean with whatever's handy, use a household glass cleaner, rub with hem of your shirt or a napkin.

Fabulous: Clean regularly with a lens cleaning gel/spray and a professional lens cleaning cloth. (Household glass cleaners actually destroy lenses and rubbing with cotton fibers can damage the glass.)

Sunglasses

Sunglasses are functional and present another opportunity to make a personal statement.

Fine: Wear sunglasses as needed.

Fabulous: As with gloves, it is gracious to remove (or at the very least make the gesture of raising) your sunglasses upon encountering another and when shaking hands to eliminate this "barrier" between you and the other person.

Prescription Glasses

Frames should complement (not hide or detract from) your face or eyes. Save fun or loud personality frames for social occasions, unless you choose to make this personality statement in business.

Fine: Wear prescription glasses to see, of course.

Fabulous: If you have the luxury of wearing prescription eyeglasses selectively, take them off when first meeting another to eliminate the glasses as a "barrier." Use as needed, of course.

Eyeglass Cases

The sunglass and eyeglass case you carry is noticed and is another accessory worthy of consideration. Designer Cases such as tapestry, animal prints, Vera Bradley fabrics, etc., all express our personality. Many have multiple cases to match our mood or project a personality statement. Generally speaking: Leather is classic… Metal is chic… Plastic is cheap.

Fine: "Pleather" (vinyl/plastic) case with your optometrist's name on them.

Fabulous: Select a case which reflects your personality and suits the business occasion; all are very subjective.

Tattoos

Tattoos have become more popular today with men and women. This may be a fad, a phase or a stage. One may get one on impulse and later regret the decision. My suggestion is that if you are considering a tattoo, get one that does not show when professionally attired. And, if you already have one in a conspicuous place and you are interviewing for a position with a conservative company, cover this up. There is professional makeup on the market today especially designed to cover tattoos.

STORY

A woman in one of my classes approached me with her dilemma regarding what to do about the tattoo she had strategically placed on the top of her foot, which was clearly visible when wearing pumps. She explained that she had gotten the tattoo when she was much younger and had no idea she would ever end up working for this conservative professional firm where she was presently employed. I suggested makeup to help camouflage the tattoo.

Tattoos can also have dire consequences, especially in other countries. For example, in certain countries, if you have a suggestive tattoo, you can be tossed in prison.

The Holiday Office Party

Make no mistake: the Holiday Office Party is no party. You are still at work and this is a business affair.

Fine: Wear your favorite holiday outfit and party!

Fabulous: The classic black, red or green holiday suit is "never wrong." Accessorize with rhinestone earrings and a bracelet (found in flea markets and even garage sales these days), a formal (small) evening bag, higher heels and even fabric shoes, a festive holiday pin and a beautiful scarf; black sheer hosiery here is appropriate.

Outrageous hair, plunging necklines, *trop plus de parfum,* etc., will undermine your professional credibility; save outrageous anything for purely social occasions.

Business Casual

The definition of business casual varies from company to company. For some this may suggest a sweater-set, blue jeans, shorts, khakis (skirt or pants) a polo shirt, a vest or sweater or even a navy blazer with gold or white buttons. There are no hard and fast rules here, however, whenever in doubt, know that dressing conservatively is "never wrong." Never hesitate to ask, so that you do not show up inappropriately attired.

Fine: Blue jeans and a tee shirt

Fabulous: Khaki or white slacks, or a skirt, and a white tee shirt or polo shirt with a blue blazer, funky chunky jewelry (i.e., turquoise, coral, jade) or classic pearls/diamonds and ballet flats is a clean yet professional great business casual look. Big name brand purses are very appropriate here.

Everything is pressed.

Blue Jeans

There was a time when I could not imagine addressing the issue of blue jeans in the workplace. It was so far apart from appropriate business attire that no one would ever have considered it. But the dot-com era has changed many aspects of our lives and jeans in the workplace is one of them. Here are some guidelines regarding jeans:

1. Make sure you look great in jeans.

2. Never assume you may wear jeans at *this* company. If this is your first trip to the firm for a job interview, consulting gig or business meeting, do not assume jeans will be fine.

3. If you do work in a setting where jeans are appropriate, choose jeans that fit well. Make sure they do not sag and are not faded or torn. Pair them with pressed tee shirt (white is **fabulous**) or a polo shirt. Black or light pink is special, a little sweater, vest, sweater set or classic navy blue blazer.

Formal Wear

Technically speaking, when an event says "formal" it suggests that men wear tuxedos and women wear floor-length gowns. However, today the word "formal" is up for a modern-day interpretation and can mean many different things to many people. Whenever in doubt, always ask your host. Here are some guidelines for women:

Choose a style, fabric and color to suit you and match the event. The classic little black dress is "never wrong" and always appropriate for any occasion; pearls are also "never wrong."

STORY

My friend Jackie, once again, had been invited to the White House for dinner with her husband. My first question upon her return from her first White House dinner was, of course, "What did you wear?" Jackie found a black (spaghetti strap) dress on a $10 rack on Charles Street... simply added pearls and, knowing Jackie, looked like a million $$$ ... which speaks to the fact that we don't have to spend a fortune to look fabulous. Also, the classic "little black dress" is "never wrong," anywhere.

Daytime formal events: Sparkles and glittery gowns are reserved for formal evening events and should not be worn during, i.e., an afternoon summer wedding.

STORY

Many (many!) years ago, I had a fabulous, electric blue sparkly dress I found at Bloomingdales and had worn this only once to an evening, black-tie evening in the cooler months. I received many compliments on this, and so, when my husband at the time told me we were invited to his company president's daughter's wedding, I thought this dress would be ideal.

However, this was a summer wedding, held at one of the beautiful estates in Massachusetts. This was an afternoon event on a very warm day. Every other woman there was dressed in light pastels, pale linens, summer silks, etc. I wanted to hide in the restroom for the duration because I felt so hideously attired.

What was perfectly appropriate for an evening black-tie evening fell way short of being appropriate for another altogether different venue, season, time of day, etc. I hope you learn from my mistakes and fashion faux pas. I have made them all!

Personal Hygiene

Hair

A professional cut is essential. Check your roots (!) and use a good hair conditioner. Also, if you know that your hair type requires washing every day and you wake up one morning saying, "I think I can get away with this one more day…" chances are, you cannot. Wearing "day old" hair makes you feel "day old;" more importantly you are not as effective. Wash hair daily if your hair type requires this.

Makeup

Less is more. Lipstick (light) and lip-gloss always. Consult a makeup artist to learn how to apply cosmetics. I have had many "experts" advise and even teach me how to properly apply makeup through the years and I have been sold many products. Why is it the last person always seems to contradict the previous person's advice? The result: we end up spending a small fortune and look no different. (Well, I speak for myself.)

STORY

A friend who happens to be a beautiful, very successful actress and model quietly asked me one day if anyone had ever taught me how to apply my makeup(!). She gently suggested I put a call into Kriss Cosmetics in New Hampshire.

Do you remember when Hillary ran for President? There was a newspaper headline that read "Hillary Gets Facelift." It wasn't a face-lift at all. It was a fabulous makeup artist, Kriss Soterian, who helps so many famous and not-so-famous people look and feel their best.

I did go to New Hampshire and had a consult with Kriss and highly recommend you do the same. Having the right makeup for your skin type is key and applying makeup is definitely an art.

Nails

Nails reflect health and personal hygiene. It is important that we get regular manicures and pedicures for a well-manicured state of being and look.

Fine: Fun colors — bright colors, green, fuchsia, brown, etc.

Fabulous: Glazed French nails with or without a light overlay, light corals and light pinks, even beige are understated, classic, especially in the warm summer months.

Perfume/Cologne

Perfume (or men — cologne) presents another opportunity to express ourselves. Actually, not wearing perfume or cologne can send an altogether different message.

Fine: Buy the fragrance branded by the latest Hollywood celebrity. Change fragrances often and use whatever free samples you have or receive as gifts.

Fabulous: (for men and women) Have a "signature scent" for which you are known… and remembered! Experiment with different fragrances until you find the fragrance that is "you!" This is typically measured by the number of random compliments we do or do not receive. Women, layer body lotion, powder and perfume or cologne for a longer-lasting scent; however, use in moderation. Remember, as with jewelry and accessories… when it comes to fragrances, "less is more."

*Do not wait for a "special occasion" to enjoy perfume. Use regularly as this is your signature fragrance. You need not spend a fortune in perfume or cologne. If you find one you like that mixes well with your body chemistry and happens to be inexpensive, go for it! Otherwise, splurge and enjoy… you are worth it!

*Be aware that many people have allergies to fragrances and may react to being in close quarters with someone wearing too much (or even any!) perfume or cologne.

Skin Care

It seems if you're not young in business these days, you're out. Everyone — even some twenty-plus year olds and teens — yearn for The Fountain of Youth. If you are among some of the older generations in the workforce today, it is especially important to look healthy and (many feel) youthful to be competitive. Skin care is so important, and integral to looking our best and having a polished appearance. Our face, e.g., our skin is what people see every day. It is important to take care of our skin.

Dr. Oz tells us that, interestingly and amazingly, most women do not even wash their face at night, let alone exfoliate. I had the good fortune of meeting a representative from Beauti Control who came to my home (yes, they come to you!) and taught me how to properly cleanse and exfoliate my face. She emphasized the importance of exfoliating and explained that: "Exfoliation is necessary for stimulating the production of new skin cells and helping to repair past damage and encourage the skin to act and look younger." So, if we do nothing else for our skin, which everyone sees every day, let's do one thing, once (or even twice) a week: exfoliate!

Facial Hair

Facial hair on women is downright distracting, not to mention unappealing. I was reading Buddy Cianci's book, *Pasta and Politics*, and smiled when he mentioned his willingness to do anything for a vote — including "kiss women with mustaches." Ladies, please look in mirror with your eye glasses on if need be and really look. Or, ask someone you trust to tell you the truth about your facial hair. Electrolysis, laser hair removal, depilatories, waxing, threading and tweezing are other options, and there is a new process called hydroplaning that may be considered.

Botox

Consider Botox or any facial enhancement that looks natural and makes you feel better about yourself to ultimately enhance self-confidence, better project and ultimately, be more effective.

Conclusion

In summary, please be acutely aware that the way you dress speaks volumes about who you are. The way you choose to present yourself to the world is a reflection of how you feel about yourself, your life, your future. Dress to feel good about yourself and show respect for others around you. Adorning ourselves means knowing how we want to be viewed by the world with our *audience* in mind. Dressing well will help dictate how we feel, how we project, how we are perceived and ultimately received by others. Remember, dressing well is the "*Easy A*" in business, especially these days, and will help you catapult to the next level. Lead by example in order to *stand apart* and advance.

CHAPTER 6

Fabulous @ the
Business Meeting

The Business Meeting

The ever-present, time-consuming, always looming, "very important" — sometimes boring (!) — business meeting remains an integral part of the professional landscape. So much time is spent in and around meetings that we need to wholly acknowledge their unlimited potential to advance business relationships. How we get the highly coveted meeting and the way we prepare for it should be both tactical and strategic. Think of business meetings as fertile judgment grounds where others instinctively and almost relentlessly evaluate us, our conduct and behavior, because business opportunity is on the table, so to speak. Therefore, if we are well-informed and well-prepared — or short-sighted and short-tempered — this is observed and evaluated. If we are equipped to negotiate, ready to counter and prepared to respond to any possible objection, glitch or question, this is noticed and judged. (Interestingly, other countries place much more emphasis on *pre-planning* for the objective of having only *one* meeting in order to emerge victoriously. There is much we can learn from our cross-cultural neighbors.)

The Number One Rule in Sales: "Identify the client need and fulfill that need."

STORY

Many years ago, I was working in the Corporate Travel and Incentive Award arena, selling Boston as an inbound destination, a concept which was way ahead of its time. My mentor was a very seasoned gentleman named Ozzie who took me under his wing and offered to bring me with him to a very important meeting with a Fortune 5 (!) company. The president and four other senior executives were present. Ozzie and I were both dressed "to the nines." He had prepared for this meeting for some time and I was honored that he invited me to go with him to see first-hand how it was done, and observe "the Pro" himself in action!

We arrived early and waited outside their offices. Ozzie was busy putting together last-minute notes and I could tell he was a bit anxious (in a good way), anticipating the presentation. Before we went in, Ozzie emphatically said, "Judy, say nothing. <u>Watch</u> and <u>listen</u> to me. This will be a good learning experience for you."

Ozzie and I entered the building, announced ourselves and were escorted to the meeting room. Greetings and introductions were exchanged, and there was very little small talk; we were seated almost immediately, Ozzie was introduced by the company president and began his presentation. I watched, I listened, I took notes and I observed. Ozzie looked and sounded so awesomely professional and no one uttered a word. Ozzie had clearly captivated everyone's attention and then concluded.

The president stood and said, "Ozzie, that was a great presentation."

Ozzie: "Thank you, Sir."

"The incentive program you presented was excellent. However," the president continued, "it is not what we wanted. You never asked us what we needed to incentivize this group. Sorry."

Company officers left the room and Ozzie and I walked out with our tails between our legs. Ozzie said to me, "Judy, let this be a big lesson to you as it is most certainly a reminder for me. Never forget the **Number One Rule in Sales:** *Identify the client need and fulfill that need."*

I never forgot.

High technology capabilities and social media connectivity aside, the one-on-one, face-to-face business meeting presents an opportunity to demonstrate as well as earn respect and *trust*. This is essential because the fact is *people do business with people they like and trust.* At some point, you will want to or should meet your business partners.

STORY

While watching the popular entrepreneur show Shark Tank, there were two entrepreneurs with an amazing product who received multiple offers from almost all the sharks. Two sharks were willing to give more money and take a lower percentage of the profits while another (team of) sharks was offering less $$$ and wanted a higher percentage of the profits.

Without hesitation, the entrepreneurs embraced the offer from the shark with whom they preferred to work, regardless of the financial offer because, when asked, they said, they "liked this shark, they felt 'culturally connected' to this shark and they wanted to swim and soar — with this shark." This demonstrates that often, regardless of financial terms and conditions, we choose to do business with those we like and trust.

Social media is amazing, however, it does not enable a personal connection, does not afford us the luxury of shaking a warm hand, looking into another person's eyes, observing body language and picking up on non-verbal cues which convey or can betray feelings, energy, emotion and more information. Face-to-face contact activates sensory perceptions and provides us with personal information communicated through nuances such as attire, demeanor and hygiene. Photos, bookshelves, office décor, professional plaques and awards convey additional valuable information, providing further personal insight that can help advance relationships.

This chapter will detail specific ways to *stand apart* and be **fabulous** when you participate in or conduct any business meeting with anyone, anywhere in the world.

Prelude to a Meeting... Getting the Meeting

Question. How do you get the (impossible) meeting with the much-sought-after potential new client?

Fine: Pick up the phone. Ask for Mr./Ms. X and schedule a meeting.

There is nothing wrong with this method except it has an exceptionally high failure rate. A high-ranking executive will typically not take a call from a total stranger.

Fine: Go to their office and wait... (Stalk them?)

Fine: Get creative. Appear outside their office, hold balloons or wear a sign that says, "Please meet with Judy Jones."

After initial rejection, some have resorted to what I call "meeting stalking." A particularly ambitious individual may wait at their office, show up at their fitness center or even attend charity events they support, hoping to connect with their target.

While stalkers may come across as ambitious and *creatives* do get noticed, they are not viewed in a favorable light. Stalkers are just plain annoying and high-ranking individuals are rarely fooled when a "nobody" keeps popping up on the Stairmaster or Yoga mat beside them, or at a charity ball, auction or dinner. Remember, people do business with those they like and *trust*. These activities do not garner respect, trust or even likeability — let alone the sense, "I want to do business with you." Rather than helping advance the relationship and secure a meeting, stalkers merely succeed at acquiring a reputation as desperate.

So, what can we do?

Fabulous: Work through the *mutually respected third party* to secure an introduction.

In fact, the only way to get the much sought-after meeting with the highly prized person the world over is through someone you (both) know. And, how do you expand your repertoire of contacts? Through *Networking!* Think about people you know who may know your desired target, or consider someone you know who may know someone they know, etc. The *Six Degrees of Separation* rule says that you will identify an individual who is able to pave the way for your introduction, in six steps or less. (See Chapter 1, *Fabulous @ Networking*, for more information about *Six Degrees of Separation*.)

Although central to your mission, your connector merely enables passage. Your journey — and the real work — begins now.

Work the Connection

Once you have identified the "mutually respected third party," work your connection.

Fabulous:

- Ask your connector if you may use their name; never assume you may.
- Ask honestly if they are willing to speak *well* on your behalf. Never assume that because you happen to know them or have met their acquaintance or been put in touch with them through someone else, that the connector will speak well of you.

STORY

I had been interviewing for a new Administrative Assistant and finally met my ideal candidate whom I wanted to hire. I asked for three references and she gave me six. Only <u>one</u> out of the six references spoke well of my choice candidate. Of course, I was not at liberty to divulge why I did not offer her the position. However, the point is, the candidate merely asked these individuals if she could use them as references. She never asked them if they were willing to speak well on her behalf.

Situation. The connector has sanctioned use of their name.

Fabulous:

- Ideally, you want the connector to personally pave the way for your introduction; ask them if they would be so kind as to do so. Also ask the connector if you may keep them apprised of your progress.

- Copy your connector in initial correspondence and reference their name in the body of your email/letter, i.e., "I remain grateful to Judy Jones (copied in this note) for suggesting we connect…"

Situation. The connector has given you a contact name; however, they ask *not* to be identified.

When you make contact, say one of two things:

- "Several individuals have suggested that we connect, that we might have some significant potential business synergies I would like to explore."
- "The individual who suggested I contact you asked not to be identified (for whatever reason)" — play this down. Quickly resume the nature of your call: "I believe we have some significant potential business synergies I would like to explore and wanted to call to personally introduce myself and my firm's services as they pertain to XYZ…"
- Be positive and upbeat. *Assume the sale!* When you are positive and compelling this is contagious and you will be successful in your mission. You will get the highly coveted meeting.

Initial Overtures via Telephone

1. Thoroughly research this firm and your target.
2. Customize your "tagline" (to appeal to, i.e., Donald Trump) and practice confidently articulating this in advance of any call.
3. Practice your self-introduction and tagline out loud until you own it.
4. Stand when you speak.
5. Use a mirror and pretend your reflection is the other person.
6. Smile and project energy. A smile is literally "heard" through the wires and positive energy is contagious.
7. Know how to properly pronounce names.
8. *Listen* attentively.
9. Ask probing questions.
10. Use their name often in conversation.
11. Record personal notes and use this information in subsequent communication.

Initial Overtures and Sending Information via Email

After we have spoken with our target, they may ask for (or we may offer to) send company information. Sending company information presents another opportunity to *stand apart*.

- *Ask* if you may send them your (company) information.
- *Ask* how they *prefer* to receive this information (i.e., via email or hard copy). Honor their preference.
- Verify email address and clarify their *preferred* mailing address.

Fine: Send information within a few days.

Fabulous: Send information the same day for optimum impact.

STORY

Most of my clients prefer receiving information via email. However, recently, I was speaking with a client and wrongfully assumed (!) that they preferred to receive our information via email as this has become so commonplace. I was ruefully reminded to assume nothing when my request for their email address elicited the unexpected reply: "No, please send this hard copy."

FAUX PAS! Please learn from my missteps!

Never assume anything. Always ASK.

If you are sending something more than merely company information, such as a proposal:

Fabulous: Ask, "By **WHEN** would you like to receive this?" and honor the time specified.

Email Correspondence
Fabulous:

- Treat an email like a letter.
- Use a formal greeting and sign-off.
- Create an appropriate subject line — one which will be readily identifiable and easily referenced.
- Use an easy-to-read font/size, and black or blue text (i.e., not green, fuchsia, yellow, etc.).
- Brevity is best.
- CAPITAL LETTERS imply that you are shouting. If you must highlight text, use underline, *italics,* or **bold** text... or some combination of these (e.g., **bold and underlined**, ***bold and italicized***, or *underlined and italicized*). However, the most professional presentation uses regular text only.
- Avoid abbreviations, slang, and emoticons.
- Do not mark "Urgent," unless it is.
- Avoid requesting a "Reply" as this can be annoying.

Greetings/Salutations, Sign-Offs
Begin your email formally with "Dear Mr./Ms. X*" — you wouldn't start a typed hard-copy business letter by saying "Hi John," therefore do not do so in a formal business email, either, unless portraying yourself as more informal is your intention.

*Note: Reversal of the surname is common in some countries. Most are aware of this ambiguity; therefore, many have already reversed their surname for us, out of consideration and respect for our ways here in the West. When in doubt, always ask, "Is X your first or last

name?" (See Chapter 10, *Fabulous @ Business Travel & International Protocol*, for more on reversal of the surname.)

The way we close a letter or email conveys more telling information and presents yet another opportunity to *stand apart*.

Fine: Sign your email, "Best regards,"

Fabulous: Sign off with anything other than "Best regards," which is like saying "Have a nice day." This expression is overused and may be seen as insincere, or as though you are simply going through the motions. Sign off with "My best regards" or "My warm regards," "Warm wishes," "Warmly," or even "Respectfully yours," which conveys respect while quietly endeavoring to earn the same.

(See Chapter 3, *Fabulous @ Telephone Skills* and Chapter 4, *Fabulous @ Electronic Communication* for more detail about protocol regarding business communication by telephone and email.)

Sending Documents Hard Copy

Fine: Use regular mail service. (U.S. Postal Service or the postal service of the country where you are located.)

Fabulous: Send via overnight delivery service (e.g., Fed Ex, UPS, DHL, USPS Express Mail/Priority Mail, etc.).

Fabulous: For optimum impact, have hand-delivered by messenger or courier, especially when conducting business overseas.

Document Delivery Procedure

Plan your work and work your plan. Follow the *Call-Send-Call* rule to pitch, present, forward information, confirm receipt and follow-up.

- *Call* (to say you will be sending material)
- *Send* (the agreed-upon material)
- *Call* (to make sure it arrived)

This method shows you to be thorough, *politely persistent*, and professional.

Note that there is a fine line between being "politely persistent" and being annoying or an outright pest; overtures should be tactical, strategic and brief.

The Introductory Call

Interacting with the Receptionist

The way we first present ourselves to whoever answers the telephone is noticed. Therefore, our telephone demeanor should be cogent and respectful. My personal experience is that anyone may answer the telephone: operators, receptionists, administrative assistants, junior or senior executives, sometimes even company CEOs pick up a ringing line. You never know who may have just stepped in to answer the telephone and/or what influence anyone may hold internally.

Fine: "Yeah, can I talk to Jerry Jones?" (Actually, this is NOT fine!)

Fabulous:

- Say "Yes" versus "Yeah."
- Eliminate "can" from your professional vocabulary; you are not asking permission. State your intention: "I would like to…"
- Say you would like to "*speak with*" versus "*talk to*"
- Use their honorific: "Mr./Ms./Dr."
- Greet and identify yourself first (first and last name), state your business affiliation, and then ask to speak with your target. Do not rush to get through this. Speak clearly and authoritatively.
- Treat whoever answers the telephone with supreme respect and courtesy.
- Be professional. You are NOT speaking with your best friend. Do not assume familiarity.
- Ask how they prefer to be addressed.

Example: "Good Morning! (use receptionist's name only if they have shared this when they answered the phone) … This is Judy Jones, Marketing Director with XYZ Company calling for Mr. Jerry Jones. Is Mr. Jones available, please?"

Taking the initiative to identify yourself and your business affiliation before being asked perfunctorily by the receptionist saves them the step (of asking), shows you as **fabulous***ly* professional, and helps you *stand apart*.

Fine: Expect to be placed on hold and simply wait to be put through to your target.

Fabulous: Listen for even the smallest bit of information shared, however inadvertently, by anyone on the other end. Information is useful and powerful.

For example, from previous attempted calls you may understand that Ms. X has been in China on business, Hawaii on vacation, out on maternity leave, etc. Mention Hawaii, the China trip, or offer congratulations on their newborn. Perhaps you may have an opportunity to share a personal experience (you also had) in China, Hawaii, etc. *Connect, Connect*!

Endeavor to develop a rapport with the gatekeeper (executive secretary/administrative assistant) and encourage them to want to help you. Do not assume familiarity or be too chatty.

Once on the Telephone with Your Target

Remember, thus far your valued connector has (merely) enabled the connection. It is now *you* who must portray yourself as "meeting-worthy" and actually *get* the much-coveted meeting.

The way you conduct yourself on this initial call is critical. It matters not who you know or how you got through to Ms. X now, because unless you project well on the telephone, you will not advance. Be thoroughly prepared to confidently articulate who you are, the nature of your call and let them know "what's in it for them."

Fine: "Hey Ricky, Dude, Buddy, how ya doin'?" "You got a minute?" (Again, this is **NOT FINE!**)

- "Hey" or "hi" is not professional.
- "Dude" "Buddy" is not professional.
- "You got a minute?" is rude, grammatically incorrect, is not a sentence, and the close-ended question also quietly implies a more likely negative response.
- Avoid colloquialisms, slang and close the "-ing's" (never say "How ya doin'," "What's happenin'," etc.).

Fabulous (as in the initial telephone call):
- Stand when you speak.
- Use a mirror and pretend your reflection is the other person.
- Smile! … and project energy. A smile is literally "heard" through the wires, and positive energy is contagious.
- Extending a warm greeting is most welcome, especially in a rigid business environment.
- Identify yourself, your position, and your company affiliation. ("Good morning! Dr. X. This is Judy Jones, CEO of Protocol Consultants.")
- Assume the positive! ("I am getting you at a good time, yes?")
- Use honorifics until/unless invited to do otherwise. *Ask* how they prefer to be addressed. ("Dr. X, how do you prefer to be addressed?")
- Do not presume you may call Elizabeth "Liz," "Beth" or "Betsy," or Richard "Rick", "Dick" or "Ricky."
- Know how to pronounce names properly.
- *Listen* attentively.
- Ask probing questions.
- Use their name often in conversation.
- Be sincere.
- Record personal notes to use subsequent communication.

Remember: "Buyers are liars." If they say, "I've got about one minute," what they are *really* saying is, "Please convince me." If you have done your homework, you may find yourself speaking for more than one minute.

This individual may not be your ultimate contact; however, they may have the potential to be another connector or even your (internal) champion!

How to Speak

Fine: Just be yourself and talk the way you naturally do.

Fabulous: Match their verbal pace and use the words they use from the outset. If they are speaking in "fifth gear" and you are in first, kick it up a few notches to reflect their pace and vocabulary in order to be together and "connect." (Otherwise your personalities will clash from "hello.")

For example, if they refer to their "new product launch," use the word "launch" when you inquire (rather than "new product introduction" or "release" or "unveiling"). Reflect their use of language and terminology. *Connect, Connect!*

Further Advance Work

Fine: Dust off your tried and true presentation materials and you are good to go.

Fabulous:

- Thoroughly research the company. Endeavor to learn their needs and anticipated needs. Learn their mission statement.
- You have practiced your self-introduction and own it.
- You are ready to confidently articulate how <u>you</u> differentiate yourself from your nearest competitor.
- Ask <u>them</u> how they differentiate themselves from their nearest competitors? (*Note that a high percentage of CEOs surveyed are not able to do this.*)
- Have an idea of the answer before you ask. Springboard your expertise to complement what they share.
- Listen! Be *fully present. You are prepared, articulate and compelling!*

Proceed:

- Mention something specific you have read or heard about them/their firm such as an internal promotion, a new product release, a recent industry initiative, etc.
- *Ask* if you may present your firm's overview and be sure to let them know "what's in it for them."
- Be inclusive, bringing their answers into your next point of delivery.
- Bring them to agreement every step along your journey to *connect.*
- Based on what you have shared, ask THEM how they believe YOU can help them; have *them* articulate this.

Although your immediate goal is to get "the meeting," remember (long-term) you are cultivating the relationship. When we think about it, we are really *courting* new business, yes? Therefore, use courting words.

Fine: "I want to a meeting, let me look at my schedule. How about you? What's your calendar look like?"

Fabulous: "I do look forward to us *getting together* soon. Let's look at our calendars and see when can we *connect*?" (Speak inclusively: "us," "let's," "our" and "we" versus "I," "me," "my" and "you," and "your/s.")

Summary

Thus far, you have:

- Networked well and identified "the connector."
- Asked the connector if they are willing to speak *well* on your behalf.
- Identified talking points with the connector, if appropriate.
- Connected with your target's office and gotten through to your target!
- (Asked permission and) earned a first-name basis.
- Piqued their interest. They want to learn more and know how you can help them.

ASK for the Meeting

When we stay focused on cultivating the *relationship* we will get "the meeting." In the business world, people expect to ask and be asked for meetings, favors, connections. However, be sure you a*sk*! We need to use the word.

Getting to "The Ask"

The human spirit is over-endowed with the element of compassion. A natural human reflex is to help others. Remember, to *ask...* for help, for the connection, the business, the favor, etc. ... as did Pope Francis on day one of his new post: "Before I give you my blessing, I need to ask you a favor... I ask you to... pray for me..."

Remember to *ask* for the business! After all the time, effort and energy invested in networking, meetings and more, we need to be reminded to ask for their business.

Women especially tend not to ask because they, by nature, are nurturers. Generally speaking, women must work harder in this area.

STORY

In her book, *Knowing Your Value: Women, Money, and Getting What You're Worth*, Mika Brzezinski shares this story: When she was asked to co-host "Morning Joe," a morning talk show with Joe Scarborough on MSNBC, she was thrilled and took the post. Ms. Brzezinski never asked for more $$ and never negotiated. She was flattered that they thought of her, offered this position to her, wanted the job and embraced the opportunity to host the show, and eagerly accepted the position along with its terms.

It never occurred to her to ask for a higher salary. Ms. Brzezinski later learned that her co-host was earning considerably more $$ than she was, and became quite upset. Apparently, Mr. Scarborough offered to personally give her the difference, however, Ms. Brzezinski declined and wrote a book to help others be aware and guard against falling into the same situation.

ANOTHER STORY

My husband attended a seminar where the speaker stood in front of the room and asked anyone to give him a $20 bill. Someone gave him a $20 bill. He then asked if someone would give him their wallet. Someone gave him their wallet. He asked for a gold wedding band. Someone gave him their gold wedding band. Then he asked for a Rolex watch. Someone gave him their Rolex.

The speaker said, "I have a lot of valuable things here. People I don't know gave me these willingly. People whose names I don't even know gave me these items. Why? Because I ASKED."

Sometimes, we talk so much and get so caught up that we lose sight of our *raison d'être*... we forget to ASK. There is great power in asking. Use the power and ask. My ex-husband told me to think of any client who doesn't pay me on time as him... (Apparently I had no trouble asking my ex-husband for $$ he owed me.)

Meeting Preparation

Every client is different, and every meeting is different.

The Number One Rule in Sales: "Identify the client need and fulfill that need."
Remember my Ozzie story!

Customize handouts and tailor your presentation for *this* client, *this* meeting. *Anticipate* questions and objections and be prepared to respond, clarify, negotiate, counter and close. This preparation method is a winning *modus operandi* of High Context Cultures. As global business people, there is much we can learn from our successful cross-cultural neighbors.

Company Materials

Support materials in and of themselves silently convey information and present an opportunity to *stand apart*. Quality material speaks volumes about your quality, professional firm. Cheap, flimsy materials *avec* typos, run-on and incomplete sentences convey the same impression.

Fine: Proofread closely

Fabulous: Have a second pair of eyes review your material. Professional editing and proofreading help is always available and well worth the expense for the improvement in your critical first impression.

Handout Material

The handout material you distribute holds another silent opportunity to convey valuable information. Again, be sure to layout effectively and proofread to ensure a professional look.

Fine: Have handouts available for the number of those in attendance and distribute them neatly stapled or clipped together during the meeting.

Fabulous: Prepare customized handouts and place at each seat in advance of the meeting. Have a few extra on hand, just in case.

Fabulous: Prepare and present handouts in a personalized cover. Consider superimposing their logo or monogram. They will always have this thoughtful remembrance of you. As always, *the presentation…* is everything!

An Agenda

Fine: Providing an agenda is optional.

Fabulous: Have an agenda prepared, even if this only has one or two bullet points. Be sure to include *them* (the person/firm with whom you're meeting) on your agenda!

STORY

I had a series of meetings with several Senior Vice Presidents of a major brokerage firm, and distributed my agenda at each meeting. The last SVP with whom I met reviewed my agenda, looked at me and said somewhat sardonically, "Were you planning on placing <u>me</u> on your agenda?"

After this humbling experience, I always place THEM on the agenda.

Dressing for *This* Meeting

Meeting attire is important and presents another opportunity to *stand apart*.

*Remember, the Number One Rule in Sales (with respect to attire): "Look the part!"

Socially, we dress according to how we feel that day. In business, we dress according to whom we plan to meet that day.

Fine: Dress to match your audience.

Fabulous: Learn the company dress culture and dress a notch above. You want to "fit in" yet present yourself so that others look *up* to you as the consummate professional in your field.

When in doubt, know that *"Professional attire is never wrong."*

(See Chapter 5, *Fabulous @ Professional Attire* for more details on dressing for business meetings.)

Briefcases

The briefcase you carry presents yet another opportunity to *stand apart*.

Carrying your largest, filled-to-the-brim briefcase to a 15- to 30-minute meeting with one person suggests that they are one of *many* you are meeting with that morning/day/week, etc. Remember that your goal is to make them feel special, as if they are your "one and only" most valued client.

Fine: Use your everyday briefcase — it works just fine.

Fabulous: Invest in different size briefcases — small, medium and large — and select the appropriate size to match your mission. As always, briefcases are *quality*.

STORY

My brother Ron is involved in the Energy and Real Estate fields and works all over the world. Many years ago when he had his own firm, he had just opened a new office location across from the Waldorf-Astoria in New York, which he invited me to see. When he opened the door to his private office, the first thing I noticed were his briefcases. Lined up and sitting side by side along the wall were three gorgeous briefcases, all different sizes.

I said to my brother, who has a reputation as a man of many excesses and everything he has is total quality, "Why do you have three briefcases?" He gave me the reason stated here, which I abide by and endorse. Thank you, Ron!

Directions

Fine: Get directions to your destination and familiarize yourself with the best route. Judge time/distance and plan accordingly.

Fabulous: If possible, make an actual advance run to your meeting destination. Be sure to check updated traffic and weather reports that may affect travel time on the day of the meeting.

On Time

This meeting, upon which you are about to embark, has been the result of much time and effort; make it count. Follow the *15-Minute Rule*: Being "on time" means arriving 15 minutes early — however, no more than 15 minutes early. You want them to feel as though they are your "one and only" — but not quite literally your *only* client. You have other people to meet, places to go, things to do!

Arriving early:

- Distinguishes you as a professional.
- Affords you the opportunity to familiarize yourself with your surroundings, the company "culture," energy, etc.

Running Late

Running late presents another opportunity to *stand apart*.

Fine: Call out of courtesy and alert your host. Explain in detail what has happened.

Fabulous: Certainly call out of courtesy and alert your host, however, "the less said the better" rule applies here.

Apologize and say you are experiencing an unavoidable delay. There is no need to embellish. You might explain what happened at a later time, if appropriate.

When Does The Meeting Actually Begin?

When you arrive on their company property or are in the vicinity, be as close to 100% at the ready as possible. These days, security and cameras are everywhere and you never know who is watching or listening when, where or how.

STORY

I was quite early for a meeting at a hospital and parked three blocks away from the building. As I sat in my car, working and preparing for the meeting, a security guard stopped and asked me to move on. Although I was not on their property or in their parking lot, I was apparently on their radar. Heightened awareness pertaining to security issues today is real.

The individual who sees you killing time in the parking lot may be the one with whom you are scheduled to meet. You should anticipate being seen, overheard and yes, judged — and act accordingly. Do not idle away your time on their turf; if you arrive too early, consider waiting at a nearby coffee shop.

Freshening

Fine: Freshen upon arrival.

Fabulous: Stop and freshen as you near your destination, particularly if you have had a long journey. You may also want to take this time to refer to notes one last time.

Cell Phones and IT Gadgets

*The General Device Rule regarding cell phones, pagers, IT gadgets: as soon as you reach your destination: cell phones and pagers — OFF. Leaving your cell phone out for viewing with the vibrate option on does NOT make you appear more important; it is merely rude and NOT fabulous.

Fine: Leave devices on with vibrate option activated.

Fabulous: Wait until all parties have arrived safely, you have made contact and then turn devices off (bend the rules here for obvious reasons).

*Exception: If you are expecting an important call, alert your host *in advance* (no explanation necessary), set your phone to vibrate and, if/when the call comes through, excuse yourself and take the call outside the meeting room, outside the building — any place other than in the presence of your host, which would suggest someone or something else is more important to you than them, the reason you are there.

Accoutrements

Fine: Carry everything and endeavor to appear organized, professional, *balanced*.

Fabulous: Un-encumber!

- Overcoats. Unless it is 36 degrees below zero (!) leave overcoats in your car. If you must wear a coat in to the building, attempt to leave overcoats out of public view, especially if you have a particularly **fabulous** or a particularly un-**fabulous** overcoat.
- Ladies' Purses. Ladies, do not bring your large name brand pocketbook into the meeting. Leave it in the car, if possible, or at your office, and carry lip gloss, a small comb, and some cash or a credit card and some form of ID in a jacket pocket, or tucked away in your briefcase… OR carry a small shoulder purse.

    If you must carry a larger purse, please know that purses should never be seen on the meeting room table or flung on the back of a chair. Large bags belong on the floor, along with briefcases. (However, see Chapter 5, *Fabulous @ Professional Attire*, for issues relating to placing one's purse on the floor. If the area where you hang or store your coat at the meeting is secure, you may consider placing your purse there.)

- Cars. As with overcoats, if you have a particularly **fabulous** or un-**fabulous** car, park out of public view and scrutiny. Regardless, always ensure your car is clean — inside and out — just in case.

STORY

I had arranged to get together with a prospective new client and have lunch. We had decided in advance where to meet and I would drive. When we met, for several reasons, I asked him if he would mind driving (us) to the restaurant, and I believe he may have been embarrassed by the condition of his car. This happens; however, be aware and try to prevent any potentially embarrassing or awkward moments. Incidentally, this was embarrassing and awkward for me, as well... although, as a former single mother with a baby and three dogs, I can totally relate to the difficulties of keeping one's car in pristine condition!

Greeting the Receptionist

Fine: Announce yourself, stating your name, time of your appointment and the name of your host.

Fabulous:

- Greet the receptionist warmly and enthusiastically.
- Use their name (refer to their name badge).
- Introduce yourself, stating your name, company affiliation, and the name of the person with whom you are scheduled to meet and time.
- *Ask* if you may offer them your card.

Handing the receptionist your card:

- Assists them perform their job more efficiently.
- Helps them properly announce you.

*Have your driver's license readily accessible in case ID is required for security or identification purposes.

The Restroom Check

Fine: You just stopped; no need to revisit the restroom.

Fabulous: A quick visit to the restroom prior to being introduced is advised.

- Perform a final visual of everything including stray hairs, buttons, zippers, ties, dandruff, lipstick, mascara…
- Pop a breath mint.
- Wash and dry hands thoroughly (this helps to eliminate body oils which encourage *clammy hands* — the "kiss of death!!")

Waiting for your Host

Situation. Your host has been detained 15 to 20 minutes. The receptionist invites you to "have a seat and make yourself comfortable" in the lobby area and wait.*

Fine: Accept and be seated. It is fine to pick up a newspaper, make a call or refer to last-minute notes while you wait.

Note: In High Context cultures, being asked to wait is customary. While you wait, resist the urge to open your briefcase, review papers or use your cell phone. You are being evaluated and doing anything other than standing, waiting respectfully, suggests that something or someone else is more important than the purpose of the visit.

Fabulous: Thank the (well-trained) receptionist, graciously decline their invitation and remain STANDING… yes, even if your host is detained 15 to 20 minutes.

In reality, wait time is rarely 20 minutes. Nonetheless, when your host does appear, you do not want to be caught off-guard or appear flustered as you attempt to juggle several tasks simultaneously, i.e., closing the newspaper, terminating the call, reaching for your briefcase (and ladies, your purse)… all while trying to stand with dignity and maintain your professional presence.

Question. What have you lost in exhibiting the latter?

Answer. Timing, eye-contact, momentum, "it," the X factor… you have come unraveled. So much for *First Impressions!* … and they say "you never get a second chance!"

Therefore, while the rest of your competition has customarily accepted the receptionist's offer and are all seated comfortably, we **fabulous** professionals remain standing and:

- Hold our briefcase in our left hand, leaving our right hand free to shake hands.
- Look pleasant and approachable.
- Look up, out and interested in anything such as the view, their artwork, etc.
- Resist the urge to pace or even speak (too much) with the receptionist who is presumably busy and trying to execute their responsibilities.

When our host arrives, we are truly a "man/woman well-met!"

(This particular nuance is universally well-received and achieves notable results!)

Do not be concerned about offending the receptionist, who may even repeat their offer to be seated. Respectfully, your focus is your host, not the receptionist. Worrying about declining the receptionist's offer of hospitality is not your top priority; rather, your first impression and the way you appear when you first meet your host is paramount. That said, in order to maintain pleasant relations, and to make the receptionist feel "acknowledged," offer a pleasant comment such as, "Oh, I've been sitting/driving, I need to stretch my legs," or "We'll be sitting in the meeting, I would rather stand now," or something that indicates you are not ignoring their offer, hovering, or suggesting in any way that you are growing impatient as you wait for your host. This way you maintain a cordial atmosphere while remaining at the ready.

The Host Arrives

The Initial Greeting

The host's arrival hastens "the viewing" and the all-important *First Impression*.

Fine: Collect your belongings, then stand as the host approaches. Exchange pleasantries and proceed to the meeting room. Shake hands only if the host initiates this, particularly if you are a woman.

Fabulous: Remember, you are already standing!

- Definitely shake hands. There are no gender rules in business — regardless of gender, whoever initiates the handshake, as well as the eye-contact and conversation, initiates, acquires and maintains *control*.
- Make eye contact.
- Say their perfectly pronounced <u>name</u>.
- Exchange <u>pleasantries</u>.

Situation. If your host does not return their hand for the handshake:

Fine: Say/do nothing.

Fabulous: Say, "I would really like to shake your hand, Ms. X." This, said with sincerity, will make them feel flattered, not insulted.

Forms of Address

Forms of address should be considered and present another opportunity to *stand apart*.

Fine: "Hey Jack, how ya doin'?" (This is NOT FINE.)

Fabulous: *Ask*, "How do you prefer to be addressed?"

- Use honorifics ("Mr./Ms./Dr.").

When Meeting for the First Time:

Do not assume familiarity. Even if Dr. X may have (previously) given you permission to call him "Jack," suspend the privilege when meeting for the first time, particularly when in the presence of their subordinates, as a gesture of respect. *This is particularly important in High Context Cultures.*

Proceeding to the Meeting Room

The journey to the meeting room presents another opportunity to *stand apart*. Who leads, who follows, and even order of procession are all considerations.

Fine: Host defers to guest, especially a woman, to precede them.

Fabulous: The host always leads, regardless of gender because… they know the way and, remember, there are no gender rules in business.

Hosts should *acknowledge* their role and say, "Please allow me to lead the way."

Conversation Skills and Small Talk

Silence may be "golden"… or deafening!

The journey *en route* to the meeting room presents another opportunity to display your expert interpersonal communication skills by engaging in the art of *small talk* to help place others at ease, to build *trust* and advance relationships.

Fine: Let conversation ensue naturally, or not.

Fabulous: Small talk is absolutely essential here and is an art. Small talk is in fact "very important" talk because it serves as an ice-breaker. Small talk may be initiated by either party, however, it is truly incumbent upon the meeting host to initiate small talk, with the goal of eliminating any awkwardness and encouraging discourse. Practice helps us all become more proficient at this kind of easy conversation.

*Rule: *We always want to be the Initiator and initiate the conversation.* Being the initiator accomplishes three important tasks:

1. Takes the burden off you to talk first (answering or responding to their questions).
2. Allows you to hear <u>them</u> speak first (in answer to your thoughtful inquiry).
3. Keeps you in the *control* position (by establishing the conversation topic and flow).

Voice is a powerful medium which generates volumes of powerful information we can use to our advantage. Listen to their tone, pace, grammar, diction, inflections, etc. and then adapt your voice to match theirs in order to *Connect, Connect*.

Small talk is analogous to the prelude before a performance or the preface of a book. As for topics, anything in view or outdoors is fair game, such as awards, plaques, sports, weather, traffic, etc. Avoid more substantive and even personal topics, especially those pertaining to health or personal finances.

The Art of Conversation

Conversation is also an art. Many struggle to make conversation with people they do not know as well as those they just met. Making conversation seem natural and unforced is not always so easy and effortless. This is work and presents another stupendous opportunity to take the lead, place others at ease, build *trust*, and *stand apart*.

Fine: Answer questions and interact.

Fabulous:

- Initiate conversation by asking open-ended questions — all about <u>them</u>.

- Ask a *generic* question such as, "How are *things*?" or "What is new in your world?" These are open-ended questions which allow them to set the topic and tone of conversation; follow their lead.
- Encourage them to talk about *themselves.*
- Share some of your own similar experiences... let them know you are relating to them, that you are "with them" as you endeavor to *Connect, Connect.*
- Be an *active* listener. Listen with not only your ears but also your eyes, facial muscles and body language. Be "*fully present.*"
- Think twice before you speak. Share some personal information; however, not too much personal information. (Be careful about getting too personal too quickly.)
- Think before you interrupt!

(See Chapter 9, *Fabulous @ Dining & Social Situations*, for more tips on making conversation with low-key individuals and appropriate conversation topics.)

Pre-Meeting Activities

Many are unsure of what to actually *do* in the meeting room while waiting for the meeting to start. The time we spend in the meeting room before the meeting begins presents *plus des* opportunities to *stand apart.*

Fine: Be seated, wait for people to arrive and the meeting to begin.

Fabulous: Use this time judiciously and embrace this *opportunity* to meet every individual in the room:

- Circulate. Take this time to get to know colleagues, break some ice and enhance everyone's comfort level.
- Shake hands and exchange cards; use your prepared tagline for this group.
- Ask people how they prefer to be addressed.
- Banter a bit... engage in small talk (see above).
- Share (some) personal information.
- Learn (some) personal information.
- Make/take personal notes *sub rosa* (to help you remember the other participants during and after the meeting).

Once seated, strategically align (collected) cards around your portfolio so that cards correspond with seating. In so doing you are able to address others by name, which is strong.

*Note: In High Context cultures such as Japan you honor the most important person by placing their card on the top of your portfolio. Doing so in Low Context cultures also demonstrates your respect and professionalism and sets you apart.

Sitting and Seating

There is a protocol relative to seating arrangements at a meeting. When, where and how you sit in the meeting is strategic. Proper seating should be considered and will demonstrate that you are aware of protocol, shows you as a person "in the know" and will help you *stand apart*.

WHERE to Sit in the Boardroom or Meeting Room:

Situation. Your host invites you to "Sit down anywhere you'd like and make yourself comfortable."

Fine: Take a seat (*bien sûr*) — "Anywhere you'd like and make yourself comfortable!"
The host is seated at the head of the table.

Question. Where is the "head of the table?"

Fine: Anywhere the host says it is.

Fabulous: This notion may have some merit; however, in terms of protocol, the "head of the table" is the one *facing the doors*. Here, the host has full view, knows who is coming, going, approaching, etc., and is in complete *control* of their room. Sitting anywhere other than facing the doors will compromise the host's *control* and when they turn to (look at) the door, may miss seeing someone at the table glancing at their watch, rolling their eyes, etc., and thereby miss an important element of what really may be occurring during their meeting.

STORY

The first time Wild Bill Hickock sat with his back facing the doors, he was shot in the back!

Fabulous:

- We honor the most important person by seating them to the host's RIGHT.
- The second most important person is seated to the host's LEFT.
- If co-presenters are present, co-presenters are seated directly *across* from the host so that together they have the ability to communicate with each other (i.e., through body language, eye contact and silent signals) to respond incisively to any situation.

Something as seemingly insignificant as knowing our "place," e.g., knowing where to be seated, will distinguish us and allow us to stand (or sit!) apart.

STORY

A friend was keynoting with Carolyn Kepcher at Bryant University and invited me to attend to "see her in action" and meet Ms. Kepcher in person, as I was a big fan from CK's days on *The Apprentice*. Carolyn Kepcher told us this pre-Apprentice story, which she also shares in her book.

At the time, Carolyn Kepcher was the only woman in the Trump Organization. The anteroom was filled with men and one woman — herself. They all heard "the voice" permeate through the walls and say, "You may now enter the boardroom." Even though there are no gender rules in business, thankfully, most of the gentlemen with whom we work are traditional gentlemen. These gentlemen graciously deferred to Ms. Kepcher to precede them and enter the boardroom first; she graciously accepted.

(*Note*: We all tend to have our own "space." When we attend a conference and return the next day, the chances of us selecting the same seat on the second day are real. When we drive to the grocery store, drug store or church, etc., we tend to park in the same "space" or at least the same area. We are creatures of habit.)

Carolyn Kepcher visually panned the room and identified Donald Trump's seat. She chose the chair to Donald Trump's RIGHT. (Remember, the most important person is seated to the host's RIGHT). This became "her seat" and Ms. Kepcher became Donald Trump's "right arm" — his most valued person. This simple act of selecting the right seat also got Ms. Kepcher on *The Apprentice*, her own book, etc., all because she chose this seat.

Therefore, the next time we hear the words "please have a seat anywhere you feel comfortable" ... think twice, and consider the invaluable opportunity that sitting and seating presents.

WHERE to Sit in an Office Setting:

Chair Selection: In an office setting, we are generally offered a choice of chairs. Yes, even the chair we choose is significant and reflects intention.

Situation. We are offered the least comfortable or most comfortable chair._

Fabulous: Choose the *least* comfortable chair as:

- This virtually forces us to look more alert.
- Hard chairs encourage good posture.
- Getting into and out of it is easier.

Sit two-thirds of the way back which automatically propels your upper body forward, forming an invisible "V" between you and the back of the chair. Your focus is automatically forward and your attention is on *them*. (Leaning back in the chair creates the impression that you are laid back, and perhaps a bit *too* comfortable.)

Situation. We are offered the chair across the desk from or the chair angular to the host.

Fabulous: Choose angular, or even next to your host. This eliminates the desk as a barrier and allows us to more personally connect, unless having a barrier is your intention.

Shaking Hands

*Rule: *Never shake hands across a desk.*

Fabulous: Come out from behind the desk to shake hands, eliminating the desk (barrier) and allowing you to personally connect. Your extra effort in doing so will be noticed and valued.

If logistics are such that this would be virtually impossible, shake hands (over the desk) however, *acknowledge* the desk (barrier) and say, "Please excuse this desk."

High-end front-office hotel personnel checking guests into their properties are generally trained to come out from behind the desk to personally welcome guests, hand them their room key/ card and even personally escort them to the elevator.

WHEN *to* Sit:

When to sit presents another opportunity to show we know "the difference" while demonstrating the ultimate respect toward our host, and all those present.

Fine: Be seated after you have met everyone in the room and collected cards.

Fabulous: Wait for your host to be seated and then be seated yourself.

The Number One Rule regarding seating: Always permit your HOST to be seated first.

Think of a courtroom and the judge: the judge enters... "All rise," the judge is seated, then everyone else is seated.

When we are hosting others, gracious hosts may defer to the person of honor to be seated first. We may observe seasoned television talk show hosts who invite their guests to sit before they do.

HOW *to* Sit:

The *way* you sit is noticed.

Fine: Simply sit the way you normally would and be comfortable.

Fabulous: Think of sitting as a three-step process:

1. Approach the chair and pivot on the balls of your feet, maintaining eye-contact with colleagues.
2. Touch the back of your legs against the front of the chair (so you don't miss — yes, I have missed!)
3. Place your buttocks on the edge of the chair, slide two-thirds of the way back so that your upper body is focused forward... no plopping!
    Be conscious of:
    *   Exhibiting good posture (invisible "V" between you and the back of the chair).
    *   Planting both feet firmly on the floor (ladies, legs together, please).
    *   Sitting focused forward (with attention on *them*).

* *Note*: In Japan, women are taught to keep chin parallel to the floor when sitting down as well as when standing up. They learn to do this by practicing sitting and standing while balancing a book on their heads. (Earlier American and European etiquette guides prescribe similar exercises to improve posture and present a refined image.)

Standing

To stand, reverse the process:

1. Slide forward
2. Lift/stand up
3. Walk away, chin parallel to floor.

Crossing Legs

The way you cross your legs should be considered for many reasons and also presents another opportunity for both men and women (women in particular) to *stand apart*. We all know "crossing" is bad for our backs and circulation, however, if we are going to cross our legs, consider the following:

Fine: *Perception of this sitting position:* Body Language 101 — Lower body is "closed." This man's defenses are UP.

During Oprah's famous world-viewed interview with Lance Armstrong, Mr. Armstrong sat in this closed, cross, guarded, defensive position for the duration. (Photo credit: George Burns - AP)

Sitting in this position is also considered highly offensive in other countries because one is exposing the sole of the shoe. Be aware that throughout Europe, Asia, Latin and Arab countries the lowest form of "being" is the sole of the foot. We are global, and to expose the sole, however inadvertently, may be misinterpreted as an insult.

STORY

Remember when the Iraqi journalist threw both of his shoes at President George Bush in Baghdad during a press conference and could be heard yelling in Arabic: "This is a farewell... you dog!"

The soles of the feet are considered the lowest form of "being" throughout Asia, Northern Europe Latin and Arab countries. Hurling shoes at anyone, or even sitting so that the bottom of a shoe faces another person, is considered a great insult.

This reporter was dragged away to jail and released three days later. However, had the reporter done this previously, he would have been jailed for up to two years; they had just changed the law in Baghdad.

The European Cross

Rather than sit with the foot across the knee, exposing the sole of the shoe, consider the **European Cross**.

Fabulous: This style of crossing leg over leg is appropriate, with both soles facing the floor.

Ladies Sitting

Ladies, the same approach, touch the back of your legs with the front of the chair. Plant your buttocks on the edge of the chair and slide two-thirds of the way back so there is an invisible "V" between your back and the back of the chair. You are now focused forward.

Fine: Keep knees together and feet planted firmly on the floor.

Fabulous: Keep knees together and feet planted firmly on the floor, and hands resting on your lower thigh, just above the knee.

Note: Knees should be kept together whether you are wearing a skirt, dress or pants.

Ladies Crossing Legs

If you are going to cross your legs:

Fine: Cross your legs, making certain that the soles of your shoes face the floor.

Fabulous: (Knees together!) Calves should *slope* — either to the right or left. If you do not want to cross your legs, still slope your calves together, or, if you are going to cross at the ankles, cross, yet still: slope!

Sloping is an especially lovely *nuance* for ladies.

*Planting both feet firmly on the ground for both genders (knees together, ladies) is "never wrong."

*Note: When attending a large meeting or conference where the table may have a protective skirt concealing legs from view, it is still important to follow these guidelines. If we cross the leg over the knee, or (ladies) allow our knees to separate, this will compromise our posture, and will be apparent to others even though technically we can only be viewed from the waist up.

Hands

Where you place your hands in a meeting should be considered. Do they belong on the table or in your lap? Does it matter?

Yes, even where you place your hands matters and transmits powerful information which involves professionalism and *trust.*

Fine: Hands may be placed on the desk or on your lap, whichever is more comfortable for you.

Fabulous: Hands and forearms (versus elbows) belong on the table. This shows you to be "above board," not "underhanded" or concealing anything, e.g., a weapon/sword! Positioning hands in this way also shows you to be more professional.

Note: Historically, keeping your hands in view on the table conveyed that one was not concealing a weapon or about to draw a sword ("underhanded"). Knights of yesteryear would charm fellow diners and (with the serrated edge of the knife facing outward) wait for the right moment to decapitate their dining partner! This is why when dining today, the serrated edge of the knife always rests on the plate facing INWARD toward YOU — not outward (toward them), where it might be perceived as a threat. (See Chapter 9, Fabulous @ Dining & Social Situations, for more details on dining protocol relating to silverware placement.)

Today, the rules remain intact, however, the reasons have changed. Hands and forearms (not elbows) belong ON the table to show you are "fully present" and not hiding anything, reading, texting, recording the conversation, etc.

The following are professional hand positions on the table:

1. Both forearms (not elbows) rest on the table. Forearms and hands may be used expansively to gesture, transitioning from hands clasped together (as in prayer) to a full expansion (the width of your body or even a bit more).
2. Hand over wrist
3. Folded hands (be careful of fidgeting thumbs!)

When There Is No Desk:
Fine: Randomly rest hands wherever comfortable.
Fabulous: Rest hand over hand on the lower thigh, just above the knee.

Space

The amount of *space* we occupy sitting at the table during a meeting is another seemingly small consideration, yet one which presents another significant opportunity to *stand apart*. When we consume greater *space* at the table, others perceive us as more significant, authoritative, powerful, in *control*. When we take up less space, the perception of us is "small," "slight," "insignificant."

Fabulous: Consume *plus de* space. Spread out personal belongings and *accoutrements* on the table and be conscious of consuming much "space." Strategically place your (i.e.) calculator far to the left, your business card holder high above your portfolio, reposition your water glass far to your right, etc.

Note: While men often take up additional space by spreading their legs apart in an aggressive position, women command their space by maintaining an erect posture while keeping knees together, whether wearing skirt or pants.

Accepting Gestures of Hospitality

A gracious host will offer guests refreshments such as coffee, tea, etc. Whether we accept or decline is another point of consideration and another way to distinguish ourselves.

Fine: Heartily accept offers of hospitality, especially when your hosts are imbibing and have encouraged you to join them.

Fabulous: Graciously decline offers of hospitality — unless your host has (clearly) gone to considerable lengths to have, i.e., your favorite soy latté, chocolate apple cinnamon scone, or if they bring out a porcelain or silver tea service.

*Note: When meeting with international clients, research ahead of time to be sure that a refusal of hospitality is not viewed as an insult. Historically, to decline offers of food or drink suggested suspicion that the host was trying to poison you. Accepting such an offer is a gesture of goodwill and implies trust, which is something we endeavor to cultivate.

Have your coffee (or snack) *before* the meeting. Remember most adults (94.7%) are somewhat nervous/anxious. You do not want to be remembered for:

- Spilling your coffee or for your trembling hands while holding your cup or drinking the coffee. Plus, consider the dangers of:
- Crumbs landing on your lapel.
- Food getting stuck in your teeth.
- Coffee breath (!) is real.

Stay focused on your *raison d'être* and graciously decline offers of hospitality.

STORY

A recent article in the Wall Street Journal highlighted this topic as it pertains to candidates interviewing for a job. The ONLY reason cited for refusing offers of hospitality in this article was "Coffee Breath!"

However, should you decide to indulge, whatever you do, *Don't Take the Last Donut!* *(Sorry, I couldn't resist!)*

Beginning the Meeting

Seating Order

Seating at the table should be consistent with rank/status (as noted above under <u>Sitting and Seating</u>).

- Hosts are seated first (at the head of the table).
- Guest/s of honor at the host's *right* (most important) and *left* (second most important).

Opening the Meeting

There are many elements of a well-run meeting. Knowing how to conduct yourself as the consummate professional will distinguish you as **fabulous**.

Fine: Someone should suggest everyone be seated and get started.

Fabulous: The host is responsible for:

- Opening the meeting.
- Providing introductions.
- Extending welcoming remarks.
- Concluding the meeting, thanking everyone for coming.

During The Meeting

Host's Welcoming Remarks and Introductions

How we welcome and introduce those in attendance presents another opportunity to *stand apart*.

*Ask if you may take notes during introductions.

Fine: Announce those present saying their name, title, company affiliation.

Fabulous:

- *Welcome* everyone and *Thank* them for coming.
- *Introduce* (vs. announce) those present using either the professional or the formal business introduction (see Chapter 1, *Fabulous @ Networking*, regarding business introductions).
- *Look* at each person as you say their name; *acknowledge* them.

For example: "Good Morning ladies and gentleman! Thank you all for coming such great distances to be with us here today. We value your presence. I would like to personally welcome you to ABC and thank you all for taking the time to be with us here today to discuss XYZ. At this time, I would like to introduce *TO YOU* Senator Jack Jones, (his State), Dr. Judy Jones, (affiliation), DEF, Mr. Don Johnson (capacity) from GHI company, etc."

Introducing vs. Announcing Those Present

Fine: Host will randomly announce those present.

Fabulous: Host will *introduce* (versus announce) those attending the meeting (saying their name, title/position, company affiliation). A **fabulous** host knows how to properly execute a formal business introduction. This includes introducing individuals in order of their rank/status. **Fabulous** hosts use inclusive words such as "we" and "us" versus "I" and "me."

Fine: Host will remain seated while making introductions.

Fabulous: **Fabulous** hosts will stand to welcome their guests — walking behind their own chair (enter/exit from the chair's right) and assume the *Presidential Pose* (left arm behind back). Then lean IN and make strong eye contact with all those present.

*A **fabulous** host has practiced name pronunciation in advance and executes with ease and fluency.

Self-introductions During The Meeting

Introducing *yourself* at the meeting presents yet another opportunity to *stand apart* and be noticed positively. (This may be done in lieu of formal introductions, or as a second self-introduction prior to speaking or making a presentation.)

Fine: Remain seated, go around the table and introduce yourself adding a tagline, i.e., "Hi, I'm Judy with ABC." (Remember, "Hi" is only fine socially, not in business.)

*Remaining seated does not help you stand apart; you merely blend in.

Fabulous:

- STAND (enter/exit your chair's right). Standing sets the professional tone.
- Assume the *Presidential Pose* (left arm behind back).
- Lean IN to the group.
- Make eye contact with each person as you speak.
- Do not rush to get through this.
- *Guest*: Begin by making eye-contact with your host and thanking them for inviting you. Express the honor you feel to be among such an esteemed gathering and the delight you hold (for whatever — the reason you are there).
- Say "Hello" (not "Hi") and confidently, clearly articulate your name, title/function, company affiliation and your tagline — customized for this gathering. (Taglines may and probably should change from audience to audience, meeting to meeting.)
- Say your first and last name.
- Share something personal you hold in common with your host and/or colleagues. *Connect, Connect.*

Situation. You are not the first to introduce yourself — and no one who precedes you stands.

Question. Is it still appropriate to stand?

Answer.

Fabulous: If you are the first or among the first to initiate the self-introductions then by all means stand. However, if you are positioned toward the end in order, rather than the full stand, consider the "half-stand."

The *half-stand* eliminates any possible misperceptions such as being viewed as grandiose or over the top. Making this gesture, however, demonstrates that you know "the difference," shows respect for yourself and all those present and you instantly, yet quietly, *stand apart. Remember, the beauty in knowing the rules is knowing when it is okay to break them!*

Situation. If you are last to introduce yourself and <u>no one else before you has stood,</u> it is probably best to err on the side of being conservative; when in doubt: do NOT. Rather than stand in this instance, remain seated. Yes, you want to stand out and be noticed, however, you want to fit in and be remembered in all positive, not potentially awkward ways.

Guest/Presentation Handouts

Fine: Make sure you have the appropriate number of handouts for all those in attendance.
Fabulous:
- Have a few extra just in case.
- Personalize each handout.
- Present handouts in a special covering. Remember *"The Presentation is everything!"*
- Consider superimposing their logo or their personal monogram. They will always have this special covering with thoughts of you. (See the earlier section on <u>Handout Material</u> for more information regarding handouts.)

Fine: Refer to your back-up materials regularly during the course of your meeting. (Referring to your handouts during your presentation takes their attention off of *you.*)
Fabulous: *Own* your information. Refer to support material selectively.

Paperclips

Something as simple as the paperclip you use will help you *stand apart.*
Fine: Standard silver or multi-colored paperclips are just fine, especially if you are in a fun, children's or graphics industry.
Fabulous: Use gold which suggests a hint of elegance, if this is your intention. Gold paperclips are no more expensive, just a notch above and unexpected.

Paper

Yes, even the paper you use matters!
Fine: Use regular Xerox copy paper to reproduce handouts.
Fabulous: Use quality paper — as close to 100% cotton/linen as possible.

Pens

The pen you use during the meeting also makes a statement about you and presents another opportunity to *stand apart.*
Fine: Use whatever pen you happen to have with you.
Fabulous: Invest in a *quality* pen. This need not be solid gold or silver, however, a high-quality, brand-name pen is noticed and a positive reflection on you, just as pulling out a gnawed-on plastic ballpoint is not.

Taking Notes and Other Nuances

No one expects anyone to remember everything discussed during the course of the meeting; therefore, we will be taking notes.
Fine: *Bien sûr!* Go ahead and take notes!

Assume nothing (!) as we continue to earn the right to advance, grow *trust* and forge important business relationships. Therefore —

Fabulous: *Ask*, "Would you mind if I took a few notes?" (*Asking* shows respect, and is a positive reflection on you.)

To Underscore a Point

> *"There are times when the speaker needs to underscore*
> *a point with the audience. A proven way to get cooperation*
> *(and a smile) is to say, 'I would be flattered and honored*
> *if you would write the following down.' Never fails!"*
> **—Matt Schiffman**

Closing the Deal

Your presentation is a success, and leads to an agreement, proposal, plan to work together. What's next?

Fine: "Let's sign that contract and get started!"

Fabulous: "I have so enjoyed this opportunity to meet and get to know you and your colleagues. Based on my understanding of your needs, I am confident in my ability to make a significant contribution to your organization's short and long-terms goals and objectives as it pertains to (i.e.) training, financial, etc., and would be honored to have this opportunity to work with you and your esteemed colleagues."

The Conclusion of the Meeting

Concluding the meeting presents the host with yet another significant opportunity to *stand apart*.

Wrap-up & Farewells

Fine: Adhere to appropriate meeting protocol. The appointed organizer summarizes decisions, lists next steps and assigns tasks. Once agenda has been covered, stand, extend farewells, adjourn and depart.

Fabulous: Hosts have the responsibility of initiating and concluding the meeting. A **fabulous** host will also:

- Walk attendees to the door (just as if they were guests in our own home).
- Shake hands with each attendee.
- Thank them for attending and for their contribution.
- Attendees will thank their host and even compliment them on a productive meeting.

Running Over-Time

Some meetings may run over-time. What to do?

Fine: Acknowledge the over-time and apologize. Announce date/time/location of next meeting.

Fabulous: A *fabulous* host is aware of time and will honor time parameters. Honoring time shows respect for others and their commitments, while reflecting very well indeed on you.

> *"Being **fabulous** is running a tight meeting."*
> **—Matt Schiffman**

Video Conferencing

Video conferencing is simply another type of meeting where the protocol is similar to face-to-face meetings.

*Rule: Conduct yourself on a video conference call as you would during a live face-to-face meeting.

Business etiquette guidelines have evolved largely from the *audio* conferencing world. This section highlights many nuances to be considered pre-, during and post-VC to help you know how to *stand apart*. Please note the following accepted courtesies:

Fine: Be on time.

Fabulous: Arrive early to perform technical tasks and room check, i.e., lighting, staging (and your own image).

Less than perfect conditions on one end of the call can greatly affect the entire meeting experience; preparation, as always, is key.

Pre-Video Conference Call

When we take the time to prepare for the video conference call, we show ourselves as prepared, respectful of others' time, and this will reflect well on us.

Fine: Provide an agenda and other relevant materials.

Fabulous: Send an agenda and other pertinent materials in advance — at least one day prior to the meeting. Have extras on hand just in case.

- Handouts should be sent to the remote sites in advance, by email or hard copy. Provide website links so remote sites can bookmark and access them during the meeting.

*Save lengthy text for handouts.

Presentation Materials

Prepare document-ready presentation materials for the document camera.

Paper (for Video Conferencing)

The paper you choose for presentation during the video conference provides another opportunity to *stand apart*:

Fine: Black ink on white paper.

Fabulous: Black print on pastel paper, i.e., pale yellow or pale blue, for best image on video. (No: red, orange, pink)

Fine: Glossy or shiny materials.

Fabulous: Matte materials.

Stage a Background

Performers do it… Presidents of the United States do it… We should make it our practice to stage a professional background prior to the video conference call. Our surroundings are subject to scrutiny and say as much about us as the points we are making and provide another opportunity to *stand apart*. Consider your environment with a professional eye. Be acutely aware of items on your credenza such as photos, trophies, books, etc.

Room Conditions and Environmental Noise

Eliminate distractions. Noises and side conversations can sidetrack a video conference. Therefore, when you are the host of a VC:

- Close windows, doors, drapes, blinds; daylight can conflict with interior room lighting. Adjust lighting to optimize video.
- Turn off fans, mute cell phones and beepers.
- Lower volume of office telephone and computer alert sounds for incoming email and IMs. The microphone can intensify these normal sounds.

Camera Tips

- Use the picture-in-picture — "near side" view function to see how you will appear to others on the far end.
- Check camera angle and incoming view window. Focus camera on a neutral area with a professional background; move your latté out of view!
- Use camera presets to focus on different people/speakers. Adjust and fill the screen with people versus tables, chairs, floor, etc.
- Ensure your line of sight is relatively level. Make sure that you and everyone are visible in the frame.
- Adjust the camera as you introduce participants so they can be seen and others can establish voice/facial recognition.

Onscreen Attire

In a video conference you are face-to-face (as in a live meeting), and what you wear speaks volumes about you; professional attire is "never wrong" (See Chapter 5, *Fabulous @ Professional Attire* for more details). However, for video, the **fabulous** professional is cognizant of colors and patterns.

Fine: Wear bright colors or busy patterns, such as paisleys, stripes, plaids and houndstooth. (*Note*: these are NOT fine, as they detract and also create a strobing effect on video).

Fabulous: Wear neutral or muted colors.

Audio/Volume

Check volume inset so you are audible to them and they to you. (Others in the conference room before you may have adjusted volume or even set on "mute.")

Fine: Simply turn on volume and hope it is the proper frequency level.

Fabulous: Deliberately set volume at mid level or slightly higher to enable a clear connection.

Test

Fine: Ask people on the other side if they can hear you.

Fabulous: Talk. "Testing, testing, 123!"

*If remote participants are having challenges hearing:

Fine: Ask (loudly) "Hello, hello, is anyone there?"

Fabulous: Simply say the word "comment" or "question" so the host site can give you a chance to respond.

Microphones and Muting

There are several **fabulous** points to consider with respect to the microphone:

- Place microphone on the table in front of people in the meeting.
- Limit sidebar chatter which gets picked up just as readily as core meeting points.
- Mute the mic before moving it or moving materials during a meeting.
- Mute the mic until the video conference begins.
- Mute your mic when you are not speaking.

If we leave microphones on when we are not speaking, we may get some unexpected entertainment or embarrassment!

*Muting is especially appreciated if you have called into an audio conference from your cell phone where the signal is prone to background noises.

Headphones?

Fine: Use a good headset. Small is better, less unobtrusive and not distracting. (Sorry, no two ways about it: headphones are distracting!)

Fabulous: Use an echo-canceling microphone or a good integrated mic/speaker system so participants don't need headsets to hear each other.

Technical Adjustments

Fine: Make technical adjustments during the VC call. (Not fine; this can be distracting and disruptive.)

Fabulous: Ensure your presentation is ready to show-test before you start the call. Set up equipment before the scheduled time so you can test the system and resolve any issues before the meeting. As with the presentation (Chapter 7), the perception of failed equipment? Yes, a failed video conference call.

Host Responsibilities:

As in a live meeting, the host here has many responsibilities and taking the lead to demonstrate your knowledge will help you *stand apart* and help keep your VC running exceedingly well.

The host/host site is responsible for initiating (and concluding) the video conferencing call; remote sites follow.

Fine: Announce other participants.

Fabulous: Introduce those present and include title, company affiliation (if applicable) and perhaps something relevant to the meeting. Use introduction time as an opportunity to warm up the audience and duly acknowledge those in attendance. (See <u>Host's Welcoming Remarks and Introductions</u> above for more information.)

Fine: Say, "Over to you, Judy," or "Take it away!" (*Note*: This is never fine to say.)

Fabulous: "And now we will hear from Judy Jones. Welcome, Judy, thank you for joining us today."

Fine: Assume the familiar form of address with other participants

Fabulous: Use honorifics until they suggest otherwise or ask, "How do you prefer to be addressed?"

Fabulous: Let each person extend a greeting in their own voice. This will help others make the voice/facial association

Fine: Tell a joke to break the ice.

Fabulous: Some jokes can be offensive and are less funny on a video conference call. Tell a real story that has humor as well as perhaps an element of self-deprecation.

During the Video Conference

Sitting

Fine: Be seated anywhere as soon as you come in the meeting.

Fabulous: Designate (or follow designated) seating arrangements.

If there is no prearranged seating, select an uncomfortable chair which will help you look more alert and professional. Be aware of posture and sitting focused forward toward the camera; look interested, even if you're not. (See <u>Sitting and Seating</u> above for more information.)

Hands

As with the meeting, where you place your hands needs to be considered:

Fine: Place hands on your lap or touching your chin; gesturing animatedly is fine.

Fabulous: Rest hands on the desk (hand over wrist, which shows you are aboveboard — literally not "underhanded"), not fidgeting, multitasking, or over-gesturing.

- Use neutral gestures when you speak — open palm, two finger wave, thumb over fist.
- Never touch or stroke your face, or hold your head up with your hands.

Demeanor and Facial Expression

Be attentive, respectful.

Be aware that the expression on your face is powerful and people respond, however subconsciously, accordingly.

Fine: Project your natural expression.

Fabulous: Consciously endeavor to have a pleasant, attentive expression on your face.

Eye Contact

Where to look when others are speaking should be considered, and permits us another opportunity to show respect, show we know the difference and *stand apart*. Remember that our visual impression is different on video than it is in a live meeting, particularly if cameras show each person in close-up.

Fine: Look at the person who is speaking. (This is actually not fine on video as it makes you look "squirrel-like.")

Fabulous: Look into the SCREEN. Otherwise, you look like you are looking off into the distance, which is what people do when they are lying. You look untrustworthy.

STORY

John Kennedy used eye-contact very successfully in his famous debate with Richard Nixon. He used the medium of television and looked directly at the camera, making his audience feel he was looking at THEM. As a result he connected with THEM. Richard Nixon was looking sideways and appeared shifty. President Kennedy "won" the debate to anyone who viewed this televised debate.

Looking elsewhere, including talking off-frame, IM-ing someone, typing on your keyboard or other multitasking are the VC equivalent of suggesting that someone/something else is more important. It is also distracting, disrespectful, rude; focus on people and topics at hand.

Speaking

Fine: Speak when it is your turn to proceed.

Fabulous: Wait 2-3 seconds, due to the technical delay in audio. Be aware of your voice and know how you sound to others. Do not interrupt when others are speaking.

Rule: Two people cannot speak simultaneously

Fine: When speaking, say whatever comes to your mind.

Fabulous: Contribute! Think about what you want to say and how you are going to say it and deliver with confidence. Speak as you normally would without shouting.

Repeat key questions or comments to be sure that the remote site heard them. Often, people at remote sites will wait to see if someone in the host location has a comment or answer to the question before they will respond.

Fine: Address the remote participants individually.

Fabulous: Use collective phrasing: "Does anyone else have anything to add?" with a pause long enough to accommodate them.

However, when asking a question to a specific remote participant, identify them by name *first* and then ask the question so they have a chance to turn off their mute and respond.

Tips:

- Avoid eating, gum chewing.
- Coffee, other drinks: keep out of camera view.

Conclusion

Host is responsible for bringing video conference to a close. Allow approximately five minutes for a meeting wrap up and farewells.

Review action items and confirm next meeting date. Request a "next steps" summary (if one is not forthcoming) at meeting conclusion

Post-Meeting

The "Meeting after the Meeting"

Before we rush out the door after a meeting, know that you are about to embark upon the legendary "meeting after the meeting" which unequivocally presents yet another stupendous opportunity to *stand apart*, while holding the potential and power to have everything — and more (!) — come together.

Situation. You have been in an all-morning meeting which finally concludes and your host asks you to take a walk with them (anywhere, i.e., to the elevator or outside). You have a flurry of activity which awaits you including several scheduled already over-due calls, time-sensitive unanswered mail/email... not to mention you are famished... Question: What to do?

Fine: Apologize and politely explain that you have other commitments (there is no need to embellish). Arrange to reconnect at a later time.

Fabulous: Forget about your emails, calls and appetite for now. Eagerly accept and know that this invitation holds an invaluable opportunity!

The "meeting after the meeting" is the time when questions not asked during the meeting, for whatever reason, are asked, a time when thoughts not aired and views not expressed have the opportunity to see the light of day. During the "meeting after the meeting" glitches are overcome and deals get done. This is when you get the grant, the contract, perhaps even the lunch date or golf game!

When you think about it, the minute you step outside the (vacuum of) the boardroom or the doors of the building — as soon as you step outside and into the fresh air — *everything* changes. We are out of view and away from the scrutiny of others, and we speak freely. When this new element is introduced, our mood, our mind-set, our frame of reference is somehow inexplicably altered. Therefore, the next time your host asks you to "take a walk," despite anything else you may have planned, we respectfully suggest you suspend these activities temporarily, graciously accept and go for it!

STORY

The well-documented ("60 Minutes") story of the World Economic Forum Annual Meeting in Davos, Switzerland, reveals that prominent individuals such as Bill Gates, Donald Trump, Queen Noor, etc., all congregate annually in this tiny little town for one week. The documentary speaks candidly about the fact that rarely is any business accomplished during formal meetings. Rather, deals get done in the elevator, in the cafeteria, in the parking lot, in the corridor, etc.

There is colossal value inherent in the legendary "meeting after the meeting."

Follow-up
Savvy business professionals know to follow-up in a timely basis after the meeting. Beyond merely addressing technical business issues, *personally* following-up with clients presents another opportunity to *stand apart*.

Thank You Notes by Email
Fine: Send a quick perfunctory email note of thanks some point in time after the meeting to your host.

Fabulous: Send an email note of thanks (the same day or within 24 hours at the most) to:
- Your host.
- Every person at the meeting — even if they were not on the original schedule.
- Any other individual you met where you exchanged cards and had a conversation.
- The person who arranged the meeting.

Thank You Notes by Mail
Follow up the email note of thanks with a PERSONAL handwritten thank you note on your *personalized, quality* stationery. This should be sent within 24 to 48 hours after the event; the longer you wait, the less impact the gesture holds.

Write with blue ink (warmth), and use a postage stamp versus metered mail — they are not one of "bulk" mail (e.g., one of "many").

The timeless traditional thank you note gets noticed, particularly these days, because so few people take the time to actually write one. If people had any idea the explosive impact this one small gesture holds, everyone would be writing personal notes.

Sending a real thank you note is always appreciated, reflects exceedingly well on you and your company brand. Sending the timeless traditional thank you note following the email note of thanks allows you the opportunity to leave another *positive* impression of you and another imprint of the "Judy Jones" *brand*.

> *"Being **fabulous** is writing a 'thank you' note you can mail."*
> **—Matt Schiffman**

Taking Personal Client Notes

Fine: Try to remember personal information shared during the course of the meeting.

Fabulous: Take personal notes about your clients, sometimes *sub rosa* during the meeting, and definitely recap notes as soon as possible thereafter while material is fresh in your mind.

Given that you have this personal information, be sure to mention something *personal* in your email and handwritten thank you note. Express, for example, your hope that their daughter's (name of daughter) team wins the soccer championship, that they have a nice vacation in Alaska, that their wife (name of wife) is on the mend soon, etc.

Taking personal client notes and using this information in future communication is absolutely fundamental in forging relationships. Their perception of you is wholly thoughtful; your attention shows that they have made a positive impression on you — that they are memorable, and that you care.

A "Thank You" for a "Thank You"?

This question is posed frequently: "Is it necessary to send a thank you note for a simple thank you gift or a thank you note?"

No. It is not *necessary* to send a thank you note for a thank you gift or note, unless it is over the top **fabulous**… or you just want to. For example, if you receive something particularly thoughtful, beautiful, clever or costly, you may want to acknowledge this with a note of thanks.

Please know that sending a thank you note is "never wrong" and purely discretionary. If you would like to, do so.

Fabulous: When thanking someone for flowers or a special gift such as a vase or cutlery, take a photograph and send the photo to the giftor, sharing their beauty (flowers) and showing (the vase) displayed. This is a very thoughtful, **fabulous** and unexpected gesture which will be remembered, appreciate and again, reflect exceedingly well on you.

Gifting

Gifting in and of itself should never be merely about the gift. Always accompany the gift with a personal note. Here are some nuances regarding the enclosure card's envelope:

Fine: Seal the envelope.

Fabulous: Do not seal the envelope when the note accompanies a gift.

Fine: Address the envelope with the recipient's full title and honorific.

Fabulous: Do not put business titles on personal notes of enclosure.

(See Chapter 10, *Fabulous @ Business Travel & International Protocol*, for more suggestions on gifting in a professional setting.)

Greeting Cards

Consider sending personalized seasonal, holiday, and special event greeting cards to clients, not only family and friends. Sending a greeting card is a personal, thoughtful gesture which shows you regard them in more than just a business sense. This gesture demonstrates that you care and are genuinely interested in them.

Fine: After learning of a client's birthday, promotion, anniversary, new baby, etc., immediately place this on your "to do" list: go to your favorite card store, find a suitable card, personalize it, and mail it out. How many times does this action item go to the bottom of our "to do" list and the task never gets accomplished? While our intentions are good, the thought is lost.

Fabulous: When your favorite card/stationery store has their 50%-off sale, invest in *plus des* greeting cards to have on hand so you can send this out the same day.

Fine: Buy cards that have a pre-written message and sign "*Best regards, Jack*"

Fabulous:

- Buy blank cards and write your own message, or personalize a pre-written card. Either way, never send a greeting or holiday card without writing a personal note, even if this is one line.

***Rule**: Resist the tendency to sign a card (or letter) "Best regards"* which is over-used and may be seen as insincere or as though you are simply going through the motions.

- Sign the card any way other than "Best regards," i.e., "My best regards," "My best wishes," "Warm regards," "Very sincerely," "Appreciatively yours," … anything other than "Best regards."

CHAPTER 7

Fabulous @ The Presentation

In this chapter, we will delve more deeply into ways to be **fabulous** at another type of communication — *The Presentation*, an event rich with opportunities to be **fabulous**.

We have all conducted and endured countless presentations. Just like *The Meeting* or a conference call, *The Presentation* is a given in the business world. Because presentations are so commonplace, we may have a tendency to gloss over them... which means we would be missing an opportunity, of course, to be **fabulous**. It is precisely because presentations are so ordinary and even lackluster, at times, that the presentation presents another outstanding opportunity to *stand apart*. Take the time to hone, practice, refine and deploy the following **fabulous** tools and tips from your powerful presentation arsenal.

I am not referring to rolling out the red carpet or engaging in theatrics to entrance and lure our audience. Rather, I am suggesting that we focus on a few, very specific nuances which are so subtle even our audience may not be able to detect or even articulate precisely why we were so **fabulous** and engaging, only that we were. We will inspire *trust*, confidence and ultimately be successful in conveying our message as well as relating to and connecting with our audience.

Let's get started.

Advance Preparation

Tailor presentations to this group you will be addressing.

Make sure:

- Material is presented as if it were the first time. Even if you have given this presentation a thousand times previously, *these* people have not been in your audience and this is brand new to them.
- All supporting material (i.e., graphics, handouts, etc.), are impeccable.
- You are mentally prepared to make this your best presentation ever!

Remember, we are performers, and we are only as good as our last performance.

Attire

Remember, 55% of you and your presentation to the world is visual (see Chapter 5, *Fabulous @ Professional Attire*, for more information on the *Mehrabian Rule*). Therefore, what you wear and how you look should be carefully considered. You are being viewed and regarded as the authority in your field. Be aware of the image you project and the opportunity you have to let your professional attire illustrate volumes about you before you utter one word. As one of my esteemed business colleagues puts it, "Dressing professionally for a business presentation is the *Easy A*."

Fine: Dress appropriately for *this* presentation.

Fabulous: Research this company and whatever their dress code, always dress a notch above. Dress as the consummate professional in your field, reflecting the genre of your profession, always with your audience in mind. Remember: *Look the part!* Whenever in doubt of what to wear or how to dress, please be assured that professional attire is "never wrong."

That said, an audience of investment advisors commands one look while an audience of "creatives" from an advertising agency will respond better to another. Be aware of your audience as you selectively draw from your (quality) attire arsenal. And remember, you need to "earn the right" to wear: the confidence colors, the funky jewelry, the tassel loafers, etc., in a professional setting. (See Chapter 5, *Fabulous @ Professional Attire*, for more specific and detailed advice about selecting the appropriate attire for any business setting.)

STORY

Socially, we dress according to how we feel that day. In business, we dress according to whom we plan to meet with that day.

A very senior woman who works for a conservative financial services firm was giving a major presentation to the president of her firm and her colleagues. The previous evening, she set out two suits. One was her quality, classic, "never wrong" professional black suit and the other was pink. That morning, she chose pink. I asked her about the audience's response and she told me the president gave her high marks and never said anything about her pink suit.

My question to her: "Would you have chosen pink if you were giving the same presentation to the president of your firm and clients or prospective clients?" And she said, "No, never."

My question here: do you believe this very savvy, successful senior woman earned her high rank in this very professional conservative financial services firm wearing a lot of pink? No.

Presenting at a Seminar/Workshop

Fine: Show up and present away!

Fabulous: Ask for the list of attendees in advance. Review and practice pronouncing names so that when you meet, greet and address guests, you *stand apart* simply because you say their (perhaps challenging) name — fluidly, perfectly the first time. Something as simple as saying another's name makes them feel special, valued, and reflects well on you.

Once again, this implies that you take the time, make the effort, and go to the trouble to practice and prepare in advance for other things as well. Subliminally, this resonates and the *trust* factor is ignited.

Preparing Your Presentation

Fine: Rely on your strong book knowledge, industry expertise, and business acumen to get you through.

Fabulous: Write, practice, review, rehearse and practice your presentation some more until you own it. Great athletes, dancers and musicians make their craft seem effortless and appear flawless, and we all know how much time, work and preparation goes into a stellar athletic or theatrical performance. Our presentation is no different.

Presentations that stand out are those where the presenter is confident and fully knowledgeable in their subject matter. Presenters who demonstrate that they own their material earn credibility, audience confidence, and *trust*.

Room Preparation

Fine: Arrive on time. You can rely on your host and event coordinators to have prepared the room per your specifications.

Fabulous: Arrive early and participate in room preparation.

When we participate in prepping the room, we are more likely to know where things are and have everything we need. Check lighting, air conditioning and the microphone. Have a glass of water (versus a plastic bottle), and identify the clock in the room. Designate where you want flip charts, audio visual equipment, etc. And have ample support material/handouts available for distribution. Ensure all technical equipment works or ask the AV representative. If not...

Question. What is the perception of failed mechanics?

Answer. A failed presentation. You and your presentation have also fallen.

Therefore, when we walk up to the podium we are not only mentally prepared, but confident that the room is ready and all technical equipment is operational. Arriving in advance provides the opportunity to make adjustments if necessary, and avoid surprises which will help to ensure a seamless presentation.

Beverages

Fine: Arrive with your coffee cup in tow.

Fabulous: This may be a habit, however, do *not* stroll in carrying your coffee!

Fine: Have whatever is available, i.e., soda, coffee, water.

Fabulous: Soda gives you gurgles. Coffee gives you bad breath.

Ask for a *glass* of water, with a napkin. While it may be common to have a bottle of water on stage, when you use a glass, you give your audience a "crystal" clear visual of you. You are not a plastic water bottle presenter or a Styrofoam cup presenter; you are a fine crystal presenter. There is a difference.

Fine: Drink water from your water bottle whenever you are thirsty.

Fabulous: Know that drinking in public — as well as coughing, burping, nose blowing, sneezing, any bodily function — is associated with one word: AWAY!

- Turn *away* (from the audience, the microphone — your audience prefers not to hear gulps, guzzles or bodily sounds!) and *gesture* that you are going to drink.
- Hold the glass (versus plastic bottle) in your first three fingers (thumb, index and third fingers) toward the *bottom*/bowl of the glass — do not use all five fingers clenched in a tight fist — the "death grip" (tacky).

STORY

My brother Stephen ran (unsuccessfully) for U.S. Senate, and I remember him pausing at the podium during a speech to heartily gulp some much-needed water (yes, in a glass).

He held the glass in a tight fist with all five fingers and eagerly guzzled the water. The perception of holding the glass with all five fingers (the "death grip"): A bit too hearty. (So sorry, Stephen!)

Plus, the perception of gulping water at the podium? The microphone amplified the guzzling sounds and the audience heard every one, which presented an awkward moment.

This could have been eliminated had he simply turned away, acknowledged the action to the audience and said, "Please excuse my back," and then taken that much-needed drink of water — away from the audience, podium, microphone.

Your Watch

Always be mindful of time, out of respect for your audience and their time.

Fine: Wear your watch and keep an eye on time.

Fabulous: Remove your watch and place this on your podium or a nearby table for easy reference. This way, you will not have the unenviable "George H. W. Bush" visual where the presidential candidate was caught checking his watch during his televised debate with Bill Clinton. Few remember what was actually said during that debate, however, nearly everyone remembers President Bush looking at his watch. The inference — "Is it time to go, yet? Is this over? Can I get out of here?"

Upon Arrival for your Presentation

When you arrive:

Fine: Arrive on time and go directly to your designated room/area.

Fabulous: Arrive in advance. Meet and briefly chat with your introducer. Take advance of this silent opportunity to arrange a *fabulous* moment with respect to the hand-off.

The Hand-Off

Pre-arrange the handoff. Ask your host to pause for a moment after introducing you in order to shake hands. This is a brief but very important moment. The image of you shaking hands with your host is just a small dose of *fabulous* which:

• Sets the tone for your professional presentation.
• Will be quietly yet positively noticed by your audience.

Your Introduction

Fine: Assume the introducer has your bio (for your introduction).

Fabulous: Bring extras just in case.

Now, you have prepped your props, support materials, mechanics and your host/introducer. You have one more opportunity to distinguish yourself before your presentation begins

Greeting Seminar Participants

Fine: Smile politely as seminar participants enter the room.

Fabulous: *Position yourself* at the door, or just outside your presentation room, to personally meet, greet and welcome each seminar participant and shake hands. Be warm, animated and pleasant. Your (genuine) excitement is contagious. Look at and welcome guests, and give the "sticky eye," e.g., an extra 2-3 seconds like you mean it, as you shake hands. This makes them feel acknowledged, special. (See Chapter 1, *Fabulous @ Networking* for a more detailed description of the "sticky eye.")

Thank seminar participants for coming, just as you would if you were welcoming these guests into your own home. Personally meeting and greeting seminar participants sets the tone, your standards and audience expectations. Your warm, engaging and professional demeanor hits a high note.

Handshaking

Shaking hands in advance instantly distinguishes you as this is unexpected and most presenters do not do this. Handshaking is professional and personal and accomplishes several important objectives:

1. Handshaking affords you, the presenter, the opportunity to learn, use and remember people's names — (refer to name badges and use them!) — and ask how to properly pronounce any difficult or unusual names; repeat the correct pronunciation.

2. Shaking hands gives you volumes of intelligence — you know who prefers to keep you at a distance, who is writhing with anxiety, who warmly embraces you, etc., which ultimately gives you, as the presenter, a higher degree of awareness and greater comfort level to tailor your presentation for this group of individuals.

3. Handshaking also gives your audience a first blush assessment of *you*, which breaks down some barriers and helps place others more at ease. However "warm and fuzzy," touchy-feely — make no mistake, presenters are being judged.

It's all good. (See Chapter 2, *Fabulous @ Handshaking & Business Cards*, for more information about this important business skill.)

Your Bio is Read

Fine: Stand anywhere near the stage. Look pleasant and nod as your bio is read.

Fabulous: Be imperceptibly visible. Position yourself off the stage — in the back or side of room — and gauge audience reaction as your credentials are shared. This time is another opportunity to garner more audience information as you endeavor to connect with this specific group.

Then walk briskly, enthusiastically, purposely onto the stage and extend the prearranged proverbial handshake with your introducer.

Opening Remarks

Fine: Make your entrance and begin.

Fabulous: Pause. Feel the room's energy. Adapt your presentation to *this* audience.

Presenters are performers. In the acting profession it is said, "You are only as good as your last performance." Be assured, there is no such thing as "just another presentation." Every audience is different; therefore, every presentation is different.

Regardless of how many times we have practiced or given our presentation, perhaps the greatest single challenge remains delivering it as if we were saying it for the first time. Therefore, we need to *feel* the energy of the audience. Permit yourself to inhale, respond, adapt and infuse the room with your own energy, to ultimately connect, and allow your message to resonate with *this* audience.

There are obvious differences in generations, for example, and you will vary the way you relate to, i.e., undergraduate students versus M.B.A. candidates, seasoned executives vs. a women's group, visiting international dignitaries vs. your own industry colleagues, and so on. Or, if you are the third presenter at an event that day, this may require that you delve deeper within to conjure up and summon even more energy to reach your delivery octave. Pay attention; look, listen, observe. (And, of course, your presentation content has been tailored to suit *this* group, based on advance research.)

Take the floor and begin your perfunctory yet extremely important "Welcome" remarks, which include many "Thank yous," e.g., thank your host/s for inviting you, thank your audience for attending and for welcoming you, thank any corporate sponsors, etc. Look at each group or individual when saying their name. Do not rush through these thank you's; they are not just a segue into your presentation, they are important unto themselves as they speak of your authenticity and sincerity.

Beginning the Presentation

Studies show the first 60 to 180 seconds is dominated by the visual aspect. You may have begun speaking, however, your audience is not really listening yet as they are still in high *visual* mode. Know that you are being viewed (and assessed) from the top of your head to your shoes; *pause*.

Fine: Begin by telling a joke or story to help break the ice and place your audience at ease.

Fabulous: Assume the *Professional Stance*, have a pleasant facial expression, and let them look! This time presents a real opportunity for them to become accustomed to and comfortable with you, and you with them. (See below for illustrations and variations of the Professional Stance.)

While they regard you, you should also take this time to look out at your audience and make eye contact. Start at the farthest point in the room and work your way IN. Be inclusive. Make each person feel acknowledged — "looked at" — special — so they are not feeling like one of many in a crowded room. Your audience will immediately get the sense you are truly speaking with versus talking to (or worse, at) them. This practice is key and distinguishes you from other presenters and helps connection with your audience.

STORY

I once attended a live performance featuring Jerry Seinfeld and sat in the first row. I stood at the end of his performance and he looked right at me. When someone later asked if I ever met Jerry Seinfeld I said, "No, but he looked at me!"

Feeling I had been "looked at" by Jerry Seinfeld was really something and made me feel special, a feeling which remains with me to this day, even though he was a solo performer onstage in front of a huge audience. (Of course, I also thought Cher, Diana and "Sir Elton" looked at me, too!)

The Stage

The stage is configured to set us apart and is inherently a barrier. If we forever strive to eliminate barriers in order to connect with our audience, why not eliminate the stage?

Fine: Talk to your audience on the stage from behind the podium.

Fabulous: Move away from the podium and get off the stage to eliminate these barriers, in order to better connect with your audience. We want nothing to interfere with the relationship we endeavor to develop between us and our audience.

STORY

Jack Kemp was the Keynote in Boston, and even though he had just undergone knee replacement surgery two weeks prior to this event, after graciously accepting a warm welcome at the podium said, "You know what? I came here to talk to YOU." He dismounted the stage (despite his bad knee) and began to successfully engage, charm and connect with his audience.

Professional Stance

1. Stand with feet approximately shoulder width apart, left or right foot forward one to two inches.
2. Shrug your shoulders up high to touch your ears and then let them drop down to determine your natural posture and not be forced.
3. Relax joints (elbows, wrists and knees). We want to appear relaxed, even though we may be a bit anxious.

Hands

During the presentation, ideally, hands belong at your sides (which is challenging for many). Alternatively, keep hands in any one of the three *Professional Stance* positions:

1. Hands behind your back
2. Hand over wrist

3. Touch the tips of all ten fingers to form a triangle (trinity/trilogy affect) and gesticulate at three different levels — high, mid-way in front of you and low. In general, gesture above your waist and away from your body.

*Avoid the "fig leaf" stance (hands clasped over the lower body area), crossing arms across the chest, fidgeting, excessive use of hands and excessive gesturing, placing hands in pockets or leaning against the wall or desk/podium. (See Chapter 8, *Fabulous @ The Interview*, for reasons to avoid the messages conveyed by this body language.)

Pacing and Gesturing

Fine: Maintain the proper, very correct *Professional Stance* throughout your entire professional presentation.

Fabulous: Be conscious of the opportunity to use your bearing as a way to help break down barriers particularly as you walk and weave among your audience. A stiff, rigid frame and perfectly correct posture may make you appear rigid and off-putting, even aloof. Bend at the waist, ever so slightly and lean IN toward them, as this helps eliminates barriers and is also more conducive to connecting.

How and how much you move and gesture will convey or betray emotion. The simple act of selective movement and gesturing is actually an art, and holds the power to help you *stand apart*.

Fine: Gesture and move as you normally would to make your point. Pacing and gesturing help alleviate nervousness.

Fabulous: Use of artful, selective gesturing is expressive and effective. Certain gestures help illustrate and even emphasize your point. Use hand gestures that match your message. Use a wide gesture with both hands if you refer to something expansive and a small gesture with one hand if you refer to a minor point. Take care: over-gesturing will be distracting and kill your presentation.

Fabulous: Be aware that any movements — particularly those made within the first three minutes or so — will be highlighted and perhaps even cemented in our audience's mind. Pacing will distract them visually from what we are saying; therefore, walk deliberately, purposefully and position yourself solidly; gesture selectively.

Support Materials

Even where you stand during your presentation presents another huge opportunity to *stand apart*.

Fine: Stand where the audience can best view visual support materials.

Fabulous: Position yourself to the *left* of your visual aids as the audience views you. Remember, we read from left to right. We want the primary focus to be us, not our support material, which we respectfully refer to as "Props" because while we want to refer to this information, we really need to *own* it. Refer selectively to support materials... and whatever you do, do *not* choose the moment when you are clearly most anxious or nervous to display a "prop" for all to behold... your trembling hands!

Fabulous: Also, while technical wizardry may be appropriate if you are in a technical field, animated graphics and other fireworks can be downright distracting. Consider going in the opposite direction. While other presenters are using the latest and greatest software, you have pre-printed boards or use a jumbo-sized flip chart and hand-write your points using colorful markers.

Remember, colors have significance. For example, green implies trust and friendship; blue, warmth; red — go! etc. When writing on a flipchart, use symbolic colors with words which hold subliminal messages. Use good penmanship, of course. This is a way to draw from a timeless bygone era and *stand apart.*

PowerPoints

Fine: Read each slide word for word.

Fabulous: We can all read! Plus, remember we *own* our information, yes? Therefore, refer to slides selectively and resist the urge to read word for word, which is insulting to our audience's intelligence and completely diminishes the impact of our powerful presentation.

Rule: No more than three (power) points per slide; less is more.

Voice

Our voice presents yet another opportunity to distinguish ourselves. Tonal quality, diction, pace, inflections, pregnant pauses, the non-words (um, like, you know) all should be considered. Pre-plan where you will start building up to your crescendo. If we aren't passionate about our message, how do we expect audience buy-in?

Fine: Speak as you normally do, knowing the microphone will amplify your voice.

Fabulous: Know what your voice sounds like to others. Record your voice and really listen to how you sound, objectively. A clear, strong voice is so important. However, **fabulous** presenters will also speak with their facial muscles, using facial expressions, body language and selective gesturing. Emphasize key words as you endeavor to make your point.

Articulating and enunciating clearly and even use of pregnant pauses are critical to any successful presentation; mumbling or rushing through the material doesn't make it. Practice developing, cultivating and projecting your voice.

Exercises:

- Use a recorder and listen to how you sound. Listen to what others hear.
- Read a poem or a paragraph from the newspaper. Stand in one room and position a friend in another room. Focus on tonal quality and projection.
- Use a mirror and concentrate on using facial muscles and active body language.
- Over-emphasize everything. Over-articulate, over-enunciate so that the person in other room can hear you clearly.

This way, when you present in real time, you will not only be heard by everyone in the room, you will come across as deliberate, emphatic, passionate, strong, confident. While at first this may feel awkward or even unnatural, ultimately, you will become accustomed to these practices. You will be heard, your message will be conveyed, and you will connect with your audience naturally.

Most importantly, when you deliver your presentation *speak from your heart*. Let your audience hear your conviction and feel your *passion*.

Pausing

1. Pausing and looking down gives us time to formulate and articulate our next thought.
2. Pausing permits us to breathe, sending oxygen to the brain and providing energy for the next sentence.
3. Pausing gives the audience the opportunity to process our message.
4. As noted above, strategic use of pregnant pauses during a presentation can be highly effective, show you as a thoughtful person, e.g., you think before you speak.
5. Silence actually draws people IN and is tantamount to whispering. When we lower our voice, others are by nature drawn to what is being said.

Note: Be judicious, and do not let the pause extend for too long! Dead silences can be "deafening" and may make others anxious.

Fine: "Non-words" (um, er, you know) are good fillers.

Fabulous: Speak deliberately and purposefully; avoid use of the infamous "non-words."

The Eyes

Body language experts tell us what we do with our eyes is telling.

- Looking up: the perception is "heaven help me."
- Looking sideways: suggests we are "shifty."
- Looking down, pausing again, completing the thought while making eye-contact: implies a thoughtful individual, and is an effective technique.

Eye-contact — too much or too little — can help open and invite or close and limit potential connections. Be unmistakably aware of the supreme power eye-contact holds.

Fine: Make eye-contact as you present and look directly at others when speaking.

Fabulous: Eye contact is important; however, know that after we achieve over 80% of eye contact, we then begin to invade the other person's personal space. After 80% eye-contact, refer to the Professional Gaze (or Power Gaze):

<u>Professional (Power) Gaze</u>: Plant an idea in one eye and then plant or punch an idea in the other eye and go back and forth across the bridge of the nose and up to the eyebrows (not the hairline).

<u>Social Gaze</u>: Look from their eyes, down their cheek to their lips — the second third of their face is considered the Social Gaze. This is good — it's a "buy sign." Others are regarding you as a total person, if in an interview situation for example, considering "Will this person fit in with our company's culture?" (Every company has their own culture, just as countries have their own cultures.)

<u>Intimate Gaze</u>: If we give someone the "Up/Down" look from head to toe and this is reciprocated, this suggests something *else* may be developing!

While we may not technically be able to engage our gaze with everyone in the room during a large presentation, make the effort to do so, and use these techniques in the networking session following the event.

(See Chapter 2, *Fabulous @ Handshaking @ Business Cards*, on the importance of being aware that in other parts of the world (i.e., Japan) eye-contact is *not* a desired goal — although most Japanese executives are aware of our customs and traditions and train their business professionals to make eye-contact when meeting U.S. executives. In the meantime, U.S. executives are being trained to focus on the knots of their ties! Hence, research cross-cultural differences and when in doubt, always *ask*.)

Nuances During the Presentation

Turning Your Back on Your Audience
Yes, even something as simple as *turning away* affords the presenter with another opportunity to *stand apart*… Remember, "It's not what you do, it's how you do it!"

Fine: Turn as necessary to write or work on boards, graphs, etc.

Fabulous: *Acknowledge* as you turn and say, "Please excuse my back."

Protocolically speaking, one never turns their back on The Queen. Turning away or turning your back on anyone should be avoided, or if necessary, should be acknowledged, as a gesture of respect.

Pointing
Be aware that *pointing* has some salient points.

Fine: Point with one finger — the index finger. (Actually, this is *not* fine. Perception: threatening or admonishing… and certainly never use the third finger!)

Fabulous: For emphasis, use:
* The first two fingers *together* (index and third fingers),
* The open hand, or
* Thumb over fist.

STORY

At the 2008 Democratic National Convention we saw Sarah Palin speaking as she pointed with the infamous admonishing index finger. Coaches and advisers were quick to respond and we have never again seen the single index finger displayed by Sarah Palin.

George W. Bush is famous for use of the thumb over fist.

President Obama uses the open hand frequently.

Storytelling

Good storytellers are legendary in the speaking arena, and storytelling is a good way to break the ice and warm up the audience. Storytelling facilitates a personal connection, and helps to place the audience at ease so they will be more receptive to US and our message. The way we segue into our story presents another opportunity to *stand apart*.

Fine: Say, "Let me tell you a story!"

Fabulous: *Ask, "*May I share a story with you?"

Earn the right to advance to build trust and connect.

Referring to Others

The way we refer to others presents another opportunity to *stand apart*.

Fine: "He said... xyz."

*Never refer to someone as a pronoun.

Fabulous: Use their name! "Mr./Ms. X brought up the point..." or "Judy Jones suggested... xyz."

When Speaking

Interjecting our own feelings or beliefs is natural and expected, and presents us with yet another opportunity to distinguish ourselves.

Fine: Say, "I *think*," "I *think* that..."

This is weak. And, respectfully, who really cares what we *think?*

Fabulous: Say, "I *believe,"* or "I *feel*," which are stronger and carry more conviction.

Fabulous: Use collaborative language such as "we," "us" and "let's" which is inclusive and helps to foster relationships (versus "I," "me" and "mine.")

Answering Questions

How we respond to anyone who asks a question presents yet another opportunity for us to distinguish ourselves.

Fine: Say, "That's a great question," or "That's a terrific question!"

Question. What if you don't say this to *everyone* who asks a question?

Perception. 1) Theirs is *not* a terrific question. 2) We are rating or grading them/their question in some way.

Fabulous: Say, "Thank you for that question" and then proceed to authoritatively answer the question.

Particularly with a large audience, repeat the question (for all to hear) before answering.

Use the Q&A as an opportunity to reinforce your message.

There is Always One!

At some point during your presentation career you will invariably encounter "that person" — there's always one! You know, that person who comes in with a chip on their shoulder, challenges whatever you say, asks inappropriate questions... or they are just plain difficult. These individuals can rattle some presenters; however, the **fabulous** presenter will not be deterred.

What to do?

Fine: Ignore them; do not engage.

Fabulous: Recognize that this individual provides us with not only a challenge but a terrific opportunity to *stand apart*. Know that you are (consciously or subconsciously) being tested not only by this individual but also by your audience to see how you handle them and the situation.

Embrace this opportunity. Know that this individual is clamoring for attention; therefore, we say, give it to them!

Approach and stand next to or behind the difficult person. Methodically invade their comfort zone and do something unexpected, i.e., place your hand on their shoulder, violating (unspoken) rules of personal space. Remember, we embrace the notion that "the beauty in knowing the rules is knowing when it is okay to break them." When we break the rules and violate personal space, we are able to:

- Get a better sense of their energy, and infuse them with some of our own energy in order to diffuse this potentially volatile situation.
- Look into their eyes, better read facial expression and interpret body language.
- Identify their behavioral mode in order to adapt, engage, *connect*.
- Ask pointed, open-ended questions to get them involved.

Your physical presence and personal overtures will be disarming. You will not only be successful in diffusing and connecting, you will earn their respect as well as the respect of your audience. Remember, **fabulous** endeavors to ingratiate — not nullify.

STORY

Many years ago, two men who had been with my client firm for over 30 years were attending a seminar where I was presenting... and they knew everything — just ask them! They were like frick and frack. If one said one thing, the other countered or echoed the sentiment. They declined to participate and mocked those who did. They were obnoxious, however, I had made the decision not to ask them to leave.

After our seminar presentation, many apologized on their behalf. I later learned both were terminated because they had been disrespectful not only toward me but also to their company, which was clearly invested in our message.

The Lesson: Even though we may not particularly care to attend any given company-hosted program, do show courtesy and respect to the presenter. Your company is making an investment — in YOU. Even if we do not feel like attending the program or feel it would be beneficial to us, sit respectfully. Be attentive and *contribute*. Disrupting the event or randomly leaving the room will reflect poorly on you.

Running Tight on Time

Fine: Apologize and say, "I am sorry, we are running over-time." Acknowledging and apologizing is appropriate; do your best to wrap-up quickly.

Fabulous: Revise your presentation so that you finish within the allotted time. In doing so, we demonstrate respect for our audience and their time while further advancing the *trust* factor.

Fine is apologizing and minimizing the problem. **Fabulous** is ensuring this does not even occur.

Concluding

The way we conclude presents another opportunity to *stand apart*.

Fine: Stand at the podium and thank everyone for their time. Quickly collect your belongings and exit stage left.

Fabulous:

- You have honored the allotted time. As you conclude, return to the focal point of the stage, unearth all the graciousness and sincerity displayed at the opening of the presentation, make eye contact with those in the audience and connect with them once again.

- Restate your purpose and give your audience a one-sentence capsule of your key message. In so doing, you end as strong as when you began, and now bring it all together. You make your ending the beginning of what is next for your audience. Give them the action step they need to take it to the next level.

- As you extended your "Thank yous," in the beginning, do so again now. Thank your host, audience and sponsors, and make eye-contact with each.

Bowing

Bowing (in and of itself) presents another opportunity to *stand apart*.

Fine: Bowing? Really?

Fabulous: Yes, bow. So few people do these days that bowing is an easy and elegant way to demonstrate respect toward your audience, show you as a professional and *stand apart*.

Please consider these three levels of bow:

- 15% angle
- 35% angle
- The 50% angle is the lowest bow. When we bow at a 50% angle, we demonstrate the highest respect for our audience; used more with an international audience.

*Graciously accept applause or even a standing ovation!

Handling Individuals Standing In Line

There may be those standing in line to meet you, to thank you, or to ask a question that they may not have felt comfortable asking during your presentation for whatever reason.

Fine: Do your best to get to each person and answer their questions.

Fabulous: Use your peripheral vision and be aware others are standing in line. Acknowledge them using very brief eye-contact and the two-finger wave (subtly gesture towards them; do not flap your entire hand). Be very aware of not slighting the person with whom you are speaking, and return your full attention to them immediately. *Be fully present in the moment.*

STORY

My friend Richard Whiteley, co-founder and vice-chairman of The Forum Group, and a noted speaker and leadership expert, shares a story about Bill Clinton, regarding the importance of "being fully present."

Last summer, Richard was in Aspen, Colorado to deliver a keynote presentation. As he approached the elevators in his hotel he noticed there were several gentlemen in dark suits hovering around the alcove where the elevators were located. The small shiny lapel pins and telltale earplugs suggested that these were security personnel.

Sure enough, as he rounded the corner there was none other than Bill Clinton, in conversation with a family who appeared to be guests in the same hotel. The woman was letting her feelings be known on some political issue which sounded trivial to him but obviously was not to her.

As Richard waited for the elevator, he studied Clinton closely. He was only ten feet or so from him and, after a cursory nod to acknowledge Richard, Clinton returned his absolute full and undivided attention to the woman speaking to him. He appeared to be rapt, hanging on her every word.

Clinton is legendary for this kind of attentiveness, and having seen it close-up and in action, Richard was thoroughly impressed. President Clinton could give us all lessons in being fully present.

*More **Fabulous** Ways to Handle Those In Line:*

- Ask facilitators in advance for permission to have a sign-up sheet to collect attendee name/contact information for the purpose of follow-up (to send your/company updates, industry tips, e-newsletters, etc.). As we forever endeavor to expand our databases with qualified individuals, this method is effective.
- Have your business cards at the ready. Ask for their card, and ask if you may offer them your card.
- Remember to ask before writing on (the back of) their cards. (See Chapter 2, *Fabulous @ Handshaking & Business Cards* for more details.)
- Follow up with those who have given you business cards, and use personal information you noted down discreetly to personalize the conversation when following up.

Accepting Compliments

Unfortunately, some feel awkward accepting compliments and others simply do not know how to accept a compliment graciously. To belittle the compliment is to belittle the person offering the gesture.

Fine: "I could have done better, but thanks anyway."

Fabulous: Accept compliments graciously! Simply say, "Thank you!"

Fabulous: Never accept a compliment without returning one. For example: "Thank you, I am sure I could learn a lot from you, too!"

The Final Act

Fine*:* Quickly collect your belongings and leave.

Fabulous: Time permitting, or if you are the last presenter, *return to the door* to once again shake hands and remember to use names. Make reference to their specific questions and contributions if possible. Above all, make this time personal; make it count. And, just as if they were guests in your own home, thank them for coming and for their participation.

After the Presentation

Fine: Thank your host for inviting you and leave.

Fabulous:

- Thank your host/s personally for inviting you, and shake their hand, of course.
- Send a quick email note of thanks within 24 to 48 hours.
- Write a personal note of thanks on your personal, quality stationery. (Be sure the thank you note arrives before your invoice for the event!)
- Write a personal note of thanks to each relevant person who helped coordinate and facilitate your presentation, including the senior person who engaged your services, as well as the special events coordinator, the administrative assistant, and

even possibly the AV person, if appropriate. Write an accolade letter to the Hotel GM or whoever hosted the presentation, if appropriate.

- Follow-up soon with those whom you exchanged business cards, or add them to your mailing list if you had a list at the event for people to sign up.

CHAPTER 8

Fabulous @ the Interview

Whether you are entering, re-entering, or transitioning in the job market today... or just want to get ahead in your current position... being **fabulous** can help. All the book knowledge and technical expertise aside, the fact is that people hire people and people do business with people they like and *trust*. Regardless of business discipline, we are all people, dealing with and interacting with people. Anything we can do to *stand apart* is critical, and interpersonal communication skills are absolutely key. As always... *Nuances* matter!

In this chapter we will examine fundamental issues to consider for those who are actively job hunting or even quietly grazing. We not only refer to Gen X and Gen Y and Future Generation Graduates (ages 13-33), but also the many seasoned adults at various stages of their business careers who find themselves in flux.

Networking
Fine: Let those in your inner circle know you are actively looking for a new job or business opportunity.
Fabulous:
- Make your intentions known to everyone you know and meet.
- Share your passion, particularly if this is different from your profession.

- Reconnect with college, high school and even childhood friends.
- Access the social media network.
- Reconnect with those you have met at social occasions, business networking events and even randomly.

STORY

Dr. Sanjiv Chopra, Dean of Continuing Education at the Harvard Medical School, told me the story of how he met a fellow at Starbucks one day many years ago. These two distinguished gentlemen, from two different professional disciplines — medicine and business — struck up a random conversation, and became fast friends and respected colleagues. Ever since, for the past 18 years, they meet at the same Starbucks every morning at 6:30 A.M. for coffee, unless one or the other is out of town. They continue to make referrals (including myself) to each other in their respective fields of expertise to help expand business connections.

- Make it your practice to extend yourself to new people.
- Attend *plus des* networking events. Get out there and let your brand be known. You never know who you may meet and if they may guide you to an opportunity as yet not considered.
- Consider taking a position which may not be your *ideal* position, as this situation could serve as a career launch.

Educational and technical qualifications are important — however, today, so many are well-educated, even over-qualified and more than capable of performing position specifications. Yes, it is true that landing your dream job involves a bit of luck, a bit of being in the right place at the right time, and a bit of having respectable connections. The other big "bit" is all about the one and only *you*.

Self-Presentation

The reason *you* will get hired over the myriad of other equally qualified noble competitors is because of *who you are*. The inner confidence you exude when you walk through that door is impressive and sought-after by interviewers! You are that individual who possesses the "X" factor, that *je ne sais quoi…* it's *you*.

Therefore, the way you carry yourself, the way you dress, your positive energy and enthusiasm, your contagious positive "can do" attitude and your personal *style*… must be compelling. *Be mentally prepared to embrace the Interview Challenge and take advantage of the opportunity to stand apart!*

STORY

My esteemed Human Resource insiders rectified a common misconception with respect to positions in the Sciences, Pharma and Biotech fields... industries which are renowned for attracting brilliant individuals with exceptional technical expertise... and perhaps not as exceptional interpersonal communication skills.

Our sources wholeheartedly assert that possessing "people skills" is as important if not more important in these fields, because interviewers have become accustomed to not expecting that *"je ne sais quoi"* factor from these candidates. Therefore, when someone engaging and energetic walks through the door exuding confidence and personality — they get noticed! These are highly prized individuals, because even in the laboratories employees must be able to communicate and interact effectively if they are going to advance.

Many PhDs, for example, generally speaking, have decent people skills because they must defend their dissertation as part of the process in obtaining their doctoral degree. However, PhDs are accustomed to presenting to other academicians, etc., and not those in the private sector which is essentially a different "culture." Hence, it is important to know your audience; collaboration and communication are key! Similarly, accountant types, those who work in back offices or those who may not interface directly with clients, must also interact with colleagues internally. They, too, need to be team players and possess effective interpersonal communication skills in order to advance.

When candidates arrive at the interview displaying their highest level of their "people skills" set, this suggests that they are also prepared for and capable of achieving at the highest levels. People skills and the ability to effectively communicate is crucial in any industry.

Interviewing Skills

Advance Preparation for the Interview

Do your homework. Research this firm and the individual/s with whom you are meeting and learn proper name pronunciation. Visit the company's website, and perhaps those of their top competitors as well. Read recent news stories to be well-informed regarding current activities pertaining to their business, the competition and industry trends.

Prepare questions to ask the interviewer, i.e., what they consider some of the firm's greatest accomplishments, future challenges and direction, how long they have worked for the firm, why they work for this company, etc. Remember, the interview is an opportunity for you to evaluate *each other*. Phrase your questions as if you are already their first choice for the job. Ask the interviewer how they view you and your expertise benefiting them and their company. Let them articulate this. Then bring this answer full circle in your closing remarks.

Attire for the Interview

The way we dress for the interview is to be considered. Project a professional image and remember that 55% of your presentation to the world is visual (Ref. *The Mehrabian Rule*). Therefore, the way you look and what you wear is important. Wear appropriate business attire to your interview. Think: quality, conservative and investment dressing... and consider dark colors, for men and women.

Fine: Show up for your interview in casual clothes. (You don't have the job, yet.)

You want to project the visual that you are a viable contender therefore:

Fabulous: Dress for the position you seek. Remember, professional attire is "never wrong." (See Chapter 5, *Fabulous @ Business Attire* for more details.)

Travel lightly. You have researched the company and dressed appropriately; travel lightly. Do not carry your largest briefcase unless everything in it is intended for this interview. Perception: they are one of MANY you are meeting with that morning or that day, rather than making them feel as though they are highly valued, most sought-after prospective employer. Un-encumber — leave overcoats and ladies, (large, brand-name) pocketbooks in the car. Quality calling cards are in your *quality* portfolio — (everything about you speaks of quality... including pens.) Ladies — lip gloss, comb may be placed in your jacket pocket or your briefcase. (See Chapter 5, *Fabulous @ Professional Attire*, Chapter 6, *Fabulous @ the Business Meeting*, and Chapter 9, *Fabulous @ Dining @ Social Situations* for more information about coats and other accoutrements.)

STORY

I learned many useful business skills while working as a Headhunter for Norman Matté of Matté & Company many years ago. Mr. Matté invited me to join him at a meeting labeled "sub rosa" with the president of a major Boston bank. The meeting was scheduled for late afternoon at a beautiful Boston hotel in one of their lovely private lounge areas. I was extremely nervous because it was the first time I had actually been invited to attend a meeting; up until this point, I just scheduled them.

Attending was an opportunity and I knew this was a test and that I was being evaluated. I dressed in my classic navy blue suit, fine cotton white blouse and silk Brooks Brothers tie, classic pumps, small purse and of course, my Etienne Aigner briefcase (which I still have today). I had to act totally professional. I had to be perfect.

We all met and were seated. I placed my briefcase down on the floor, however, neglected to close the clasp. At one point during the intense meeting, I moved in my chair. My briefcase tipped over and out came rolling a huge can of hair spray (they did not make small cans in those days!). The big obtrusive can rolled out and right into the middle of the meeting room floor. I was mortified!

Ladies, please learn from my embarrassing experience and do not carry personal effects or hygiene products of any kind in your briefcase unless they are under "lock and key," so to speak.

Arriving at Your Interview

Remember the *15-Minute Rule!* Arrive early for the interview, but no more than 15 minutes early. As soon as you arrive at your destination, cell phones and other devices: *off.* Stand in the reception area. (You have already been to the restroom and checked everything — dandruff, stray hairs, etc. and, popped a breath mint. You have washed your hands thoroughly with warm water and soap and dried them thoroughly, which helps eliminate body oils that cause clammy hands... the "kiss of death!") Stand "at the ready" and wait to confidently meet your host. Keep your right hand free, lean in and offer a firm, dry handshake. (See Chapter 6, *Fabulous @ The Meeting* for more reasons why it is important to remain standing while waiting for your host.)

STORY
(A TIP FOR HELICOPTER PARENTS)

I know a young woman whose mother often accompanies her on job interviews and waits in the lobby. This is a lovely example of mother/daughter bonding; however, it does not bode well in the professional world. The young woman needs to fly out of the nest and call Mother after the interview.

Moreover, if mother is waiting in the lobby, this may undermine their young adult's credibility as a viable candidate. As a potential candidate, you want to come across as independent, confident with a "can do," "take charge" persona and Mom can't do that for you, with all due respect to loving, caring, doting, interested mothers.

*Do not tell the interviewer your Mother is in the reception area (although word may get out).

*Do not tell the job interviewer you need to consult with your parents before making a decision!

Forms of Address

Never assume the familiar, i.e., "Hi, Jack," or "Hey, Dude... how ya doin'?" Rather: "Hello" — and use the honorific/title (i.e. Mr./Ms./Dr.) + last name of the interviewer, "How are you this morning?" Remember to close the "-ings" ("morning" not "mornin'"). Always ask, "How do you prefer to be addressed?" before assuming the "Jack" and "Judy" stage. Remember, we are "earning the right" to advance.

Attitude

"Assume the Sale!" Attitude is key. Whether you are speaking on the telephone or entering their building for the interview, act as if you already work there, with this person, in this building. Project positive energy, enthusiasm, sincerity, style. People are attracted to

positive, upbeat people! Be well-rested, well-prepared, and well-dressed to perform at your personal best.

Remember to Connect

Make good eye contact, and be "chameleon-like." When they sit back, you sit back. When they sit forward, you sit forward. When they pick up a pen to write, you do the same... not within the same second, however within seconds. This lets them know you are "with" them, you are "connecting."

Initiate small talk; anything *visible* in the office, or even *outdoors*, is fair game for conversation topics: photos, plaques, artwork, books, office décor — or the weather, sports, travel directions, etc. Share personal information, however, not too much personal information.

Leading the Way to the Interview Room

Regardless of gender, permit your host to lead the way to the interview room. *Reason*: there are no gender rules in business — and, they know the way!

Decline Offers of Hospitality

Graciously decline offers of coffee, croissants, etc., and have your coffee before you go to your interview (and do not walk in carrying your cup of coffee). *Reason*: you do not want to risk crumbs landing on your lapel, food getting stuck in your teeth and above all, we certainly do not want to have "coffee breath!" However, whatever you do, *Don't Take the Last Donut!* (I couldn't resist!)

Also, given that 94.7% of all of us are a bit nervous or anxious, the "spillage factor" is real and you do not want to be the person remembered for spilling coffee on your résumé, your tie, their desk, etc. There are exceptions, of course, especially in certain parts of the world. Even here in the U.S., if a porcelain or silver coffee or tea service appears, it would be rude to refuse such an offer. (See Chapter 6, *Fabulous @ The Meeting*, for more on accepting/declining offers of hospitality.)

Sitting and Seating

Think of sitting and seating as another opportunity (!) to *stand apart*.

Rule: *Always permit your host, the interviewer, to be seated first.* Think: a courtroom; the judge enters, all rise; judge is seated, first.

The person of honor is always seated to the host's right. The second most important person is seated to the host's left, etc. (See Chapter 6, *Fabulous @ The Meeting*, about how Carolyn Kepcher acquired and kept the "power" seat to the right of Donald Trump.)

If you have the option of sitting across the desk from or angular to your interviewer, choose angular, eliminating the desk "barrier" because you want nothing to interfere with the relationship you are endeavoring to forge. (See Chapter 6, *Fabulous @ The Meeting*, for more information on selecting the ideal seat.)

If given a choice between sitting in the least comfortable chair or most comfortable chair, choose the least comfortable chair. Large, over-stuffed chairs tend to encourage slouching, compromise posture, make you appear much too comfortable, plus getting in and out is more difficult.

Take Notes

Even though it is presumed we will be taking notes, *ask* first, "Would you mind, Mr./Ms. X, if I took a few notes?" Asking shows that we assume nothing, as we endeavor to build trust, grow the relationship. Take *personal* notes about the interviewer and use this information in follow-up communication.

Informational Interviews

Informational interviews are very different from formal job interviews. The fundamental differences: purpose and approach. Informational interviews suggest you are asking a favor from a mentor (official or unofficial), trusted friend, or acquaintance, for the purpose of obtaining background and/or counsel about work in your chosen field, or at a particular firm.

An informational interview holds no expectations relative to a job, only appreciation for the interviewer's time and help as you endeavor to discover your purpose, find your way, and learn more about their industry in general, or their firm specifically. This individual *may* offer to reach out to one of their contacts to provide further counsel, learn of opportunities or create connections; however, this would be a gift and is *not* the purpose of an informational interview.

Fine: Arrange to meet at their office unless they suggest otherwise.

Fabulous:

- Invite them to meet you outside their office.
- Suggest a venue which you have pre-determined they would prefer.
- Ask them to join you for coffee or lunch (not to interfere with their office time)
- Be sure to pick up the check.
- Have specific questions prepared.
- Be open to new ideas.

STORY

When I started my career, there were very few women in business. A good friend, Jackie, owned a travel agency, which she bought (was not gifted) from her father. We all referred to Jackie as a "girl's girl" because whenever one of us needed advice, a really good laugh, a shoulder, or even a job, Jackie was always there — for all of us. I think we all worked for Jackie at some point in our budding careers! Jackie was and remains a gift.

At the time, I wanted to get into the corporate travel incentive award business and was lucky enough to have landed an interview with the president of the oldest travel company in the United States! In advance of the interview, I called Jackie and asked her if she would coach and help prepare me for this interview in this industry (about which I knew nothing) because, of course, I wanted to come across as knowledgeable in the Corporate Travel & Incentive Award business. Jackie gave me the right questions to ask, words to use, word tracks specific to the industry, etc. (I needed to talk the talk, yes?). Jackie role-played with me, told me how to dress, what accessories to wear and carry, reminded me to ask before I took notes, told me to be sure to pick up the check, reminded me about writing a thank you note that same day (!) etc.

Mr. X was apparently so impressed that he asked me on the spot when I could start and actually created a new position in his company (pour moi). I was responsible for bringing new corporate business in-bound — into Boston as a destination — a concept way ahead of its time.

The point is, my informational interview with Jackie prepared me for my real interview with the company president and helped me to obtain the position I sought, in the industry I wanted, with the company I targeted.

Today, more than ever, we need more "Jacks" and "Jackies."

Interaction
- Acknowledge their accomplishments, and be sure to ask about any challenges they encountered along the way, how they met them and what they learned.
- Ask what motivates them.
- Ask for their thoughts and welcome advice.
- *Listen* and learn.

Fabulous:
- Permit them to be seated first.
- Be candid… however, not too candid (!).
- Be open to ideas and constructive criticism.
- Shake hands before and after your time together.
- Bring extra résumés and calling cards.
- *Ask* before taking notes.
- Honor designated time together.
- Handle the check (in advance).
- Ask if you may keep them posted on your journey.
- Always send an email thank you (only after you have determined they are an e-person) and a personal thank you note the same day.

Formal Job Interview

Formal job interviews are very different from informational interviews. While an informational interview suggests we are asking for a favor and looking for guidance, a formal interview casts us as a viable new hire. We meet face-to-face to corroborate our credentials with who we are and take the time to evaluate *each other*. Formal interviewing provides us with the opportunity to persuade and positively convince interviewers that we — our education, background, experience/expertise AND our interpersonal communication skills, energy and personal style — will benefit *them*.

The Interviewee's Perspective

The moment you drive onto their company property, be as close to 100% "at the ready" as possible because you never know, especially these days, who is watching or listening when or from where.

As you approach the building, harness a (deliberate) mental attitude adjustment. Walk through the doors as if this is your building, as if you already work there, as if the person with whom you are meeting is already your boss or manager.

The confidence you exude is fundamental to casting a professional image and creating a positive *First Impression*. You want to be viewed positively, professionally and come across as a viable candidate. Your qualifications, generally speaking, are a given. The personal one-on-one interview provides you and them the opportunity to evaluate each other in terms of "fit" and to show your mettle. Know that you are being judged, of course. Our all-embracing goal is to be a person "well-met," and *stand apart*. Our presence, energy, flexibility and passion, personality and leadership values are all being evaluated.

The Interviewer's Perspective

Candidates, you should expect that interviewers will:

- Approach the interview knowing specifically what they want to learn about you.
- Endeavor to avoid negatives when speaking about the competition or other companies; you should do the same.
- Be prepared to tell you what they like about the company, and invite you to share your views.
- Endeavor to develop a synergy. Interviewers are trained to build on your questions and answers and to encourage genuine dialogue.
- Take notes. (Interviewers should acknowledge this act with candidates.)
- Use affirming gestures such as nodding, verbal feedback and re-phrasing techniques.

Cultural Fit and Diversity

Given that Gen X, Gen Y and Future Gen grads (those ages 13-33) will be CEOs in 10-15 years, companies today value diversity. Where being compatible with a company's "culture" has traditionally been and continues to be important, companies today who thrive must have cultural diversity. Therefore, more value is placed on diversity as well as collaboration and being team-oriented today than ever before. Ergo, while candidates should endeavor to highlight common ground, know that what you bring is *different* and valuable. Embrace the ways that you are different and show your rare, unique, one-of-a kind authentic self.

Leadership and Behavioral Interviewing

Behavioral interviewing is a style which espouses the notion that the best indicator of future behavior is past behavior. The practice of "Behavioral Interviewing" is common today. For example, if the only credential a candidate has is (i.e.) a B.A. from Boston College, the interviewer will look at the candidate's activities at Boston College in terms of leadership interests.

Interviewers are not necessarily looking to see if you were president of your class or captain of the swim team; however, they do look to what you did in college to exhibit leadership interests. The interviewer endeavors to ascertain on some level how you view the world and evaluate if/how you would be a leader in their organization. Interviewers also look at non-conformist ways of leading.

There may be six senior individuals in leadership positions at any random company and these leaders want to know that those coming in and going up through the ranks have leadership potential. They want to know that you are motivated and will therefore be productive and contribute to the company's successes. Hence, an interviewer will regard candidates and consider if they might be future management material. Even with administrative positions, interviewers want to know if you would be that person others look to under stressful or unusual conditions, if you exhibit maturity, and would manifest (our *mantra*): *Grace Under Pressure.*

Candidates

Passion

Having a passion for what you do is tantamount to exceeding and excelling. So, how might an interviewer be able to determine your passion?

Fine: Ask if you have a passion for X.

Fabulous: Ask questions pertaining to why you like to do X or Y or what stimulates your adrenaline. Interviewers may look for your "story" or ask you to share an "aha" moment. For example, you realized how (naturally) proficient you were at X when you would become enraptured and found that time had passed but you hadn't even realized it...

Candidates: Be prepared to share how you feel your passion for X could help make a difference in the company or even change the world, in some small (or large!) way.

Flexibility and Adaptability

We find ourselves immersed in an ever-changing global business environment where more executives are coming out of their corner offices. Knowing that you are flexible and adaptable is very important to the interviewer.

Fine: Everyone does their own work and is responsible for their own area.

Fabulous: Everyone contributes to whatever needs attention.

- Interviewers also evaluate whether or not the candidate is able to manage relationships and if they are team-oriented players. As we become more global, characteristics more traditionally recognized as part of High Context cultures are quickly becoming highly prized and part of our own Low Context culture.
- Interviewers want to know if you are a "roll up the sleeves"-type of individual, "no job too small," etc., and not a *prima donna*.

Professional Presence

Possessing overall *Professional Presence* is tantamount to making a positive First Impression. Exhibiting self-confidence (versus displaying a little *too much* confidence!) is noticed.

Fine: There is no such thing as having too much confidence. Demonstrating maximum self-confidence is always the goal.

Fabulous: There is a fine line between possessing confidence and exhibiting *Professional Presence* versus being seen as self-important, over-confident and maybe even labeled a know-it-all. You want to show you are receptive to learning from (and working with) others and possess an element *de humilité*.

Interviewers are also discerning as to your self-awareness as well as awareness of your surroundings. Do you seem glad to be there, do you look them in the eye and ultimately, "Are you a person they really want to get to know *better?*"

Remember: People hire and people do business with people they like and *trust. They need to get to know you, before they can like and trust you.*

Length of Interview

The standard length of a typical interview is 30–45 minutes. Most candidate decisions these days are made during the first interview (unless the position is very senior, in which case multiple interviews are the norm).

Interviewing today is more likened to *speed dating*. The difference: interviewing is 45 minutes versus *speed dating*, which is eight (minutes).

Communication

Seventy-five percent of actual "talking time" should come from the candidate, however, be prompted by the interviewer; the candidate must be deferential.

Expect the interviewer to ask broad-based questions at the outset.

Fine: "Why are you interested in this position?"

Fabulous: "Would you be able to give me a succinct verbal autobiography, focusing on the choices you made, why you made them, and how they have led to the next level which has brought you here today?"

Asking this broad-based question:

- Enables the interviewer to assess your communication skills and thought processes.

- Encourages candidates to tell their story.
- Helps create a genuine connection.
- Helps the interviewer ascertain what is really important to you.

Grammar, Diction, Articulation, Vocabulary

Virtually every first interview is conducted via telephone because, in approximately 90% of cases, the way people present themselves on the telephone is, indeed, how they present themselves in person. Telephone interviews provide interviewers with invaluable information relative to communication skills, grammar, diction, energy, etc., and anyone with poor communication skills or projecting low energy may be subject to immediate elimination.

*When English is a second language, interviewers expect to hear accents, different dialects, a few imperfections; there is certainly some leeway here. *Nonetheless, the importance of grammar, diction, articulation, vocabulary, energy cannot be overstated.*

Skype

Skype is used in the interviewing process typically with candidates situated in another part of the country or world and, of course, there are different time zone considerations. A Skype interview may be conducted at hours which are very early or very late (for the candidate). While Skype does provide the opportunity to help ascertain a candidate's verbal communication skills and enables facial recognition as well as the opportunity to get an idea of the candidate's persona and energy, Skype is a bit stilted and still imperfect.

Fine: Present yourself less formally on Skype, and it is fine to dress down (because it is Skype and) because it may be 3:00 A.M. your time! (Certainly, you are not going to *dress* at this hour.)

Fabulous: Candidates should treat every interview — yes, even those conducted via Skype, even at 3:00 A.M. — as an opportunity to *stand apart*. Present yourself with the same level of professionalism and energy that you would at a personal, one-on-one, face-to-face interview — yes, even as it pertains to attire. Interviewers definitely take note of the extra effort made in this regard.

References

The expectation is to have candidates provide interviewers with three to four business references from former direct supervisors. References are particularly helpful if there is an issue which has surfaced during the interviewing process.

Fine: Candidates should give interviewers more references than they ask for.

(Please allow me to repeat the story from Chapter 6, *Fabulous @ The Meeting*, about the dangers of providing references who may not speak well of you.)

STORY

I had been interviewing for a new Administrative Assistant and finally met my ideal candidate whom I wanted to hire. I asked for three references and she gave me six. Only one out of the six references spoke well of my choice candidate. Of course, I was not at liberty to divulge why I did not offer her the position; however, the point is, the candidate merely asked these individuals if she could use them as references. She never asked them if they were willing to speak well on her behalf.

Be aware that if more than one reference does not check out, from the interviewer's perspective, there is a problem.
   Fabulous:
   - Always ask, in advance, if you may use someone as a reference.
   - Always ask references if they are willing to speak *well* on your behalf.
   - References should be outstanding.

Interviewers will often ask references to rate candidates on a scale of 1 to 10, and ideally they would like to hear all 10's — however, if ratings are not at least an 8, that candidate most likely will be eliminated.
   Informal references are common… someone who used to work there and knew them when, etc. Hence, candidates please be reminded: never burn bridges!

Social Media Presence

Interviewers will frequently Google a candidate to gain more insight, and LinkedIn is considered to be the most business/professional social media network. Anyone actively interviewing (or already in the world of business, for that matter) should ensure that whatever is "out there" about them in the social media world (Facebook, Google Plus, LinkedIn, Twitter, YouTube, etc.) should not be inappropriate, knowing that anyone, anywhere in the world can view this material.
   Fine: "This is who you are" — so you may have a wild side — post it!
   Fabulous: Make sure you have nothing out there about which you would not want a perspective employer to view or know. Use a photo on LinkedIn which shows you as professional. Photos of us on the beach catching a few rays, going crazy with friends, (ladies) in a cocktail dress trying to look sultry and seductive are not advised. None of these are considered professional; do not try to look sexy.

Compensation

Compensation is clearly important, however, it is certainly a delicate topic. The way we approach this topic is to be considered.
   Fine: We do not want to waste anyone's time. Ask up front about remuneration and benefits.
   Fabulous: Wait for the interviewer to initiate this topic.
   Actually, a good interviewer should initiate this topic during the first telephone contact. The interviewer should crystallize understanding and expectations on both sides in advance before things progress too far. Doing so is respectful and professional and helps avoid any misunderstandings.

Expect interviewers to ask your current salary or desired salary/package.

Fine: It is okay to stretch the truth a bit — you feel your value is more than your current compensation suggests.

Fabulous: Tell the interviewer your current salary or let your desired salary/package be known. However, suggest that this does not reflect your true value because (i.e.) the company has not given any raises due to the economy in a number of years, etc.

Be prepared for this discussion.

*When discussing an internship position or very entry level situation:

Fine: Give them your bottom-line $$ number.

Fabulous: While the financial piece is important, of course, let them know that you are more interested in the opportunity to work with and learn from them, and you are confident they will be fair in this regard. Remember that many internships are unpaid, and any salary demand may remove you from consideration.

Offers and Negotiation

A good interviewer will try to pre-close candidates on offers early on. For example, "We are looking to render an acceptable offer of $X by Z date. Does this sound reasonable to you?"

Fine: Candidates should take whatever compensation the interviewer offers, especially in this economy, with the mindset that once you get hired your work will be noticed. You can always advocate on your own behalf and negotiate further once you are onboard.

Fabulous: *Now* is the time to advocate on your own behalf and negotiate. Interviewers usually have some financial leeway. Candidates should be prepared to negotiate; interviewers are!

(See Chapter 6, *Fabulous @ The Meeting*, for more information about compensation issues in the Mika Brzezinski story.)

Asking for the Job

If you are interested in this position, ASK for it.

Fine: Say, "Can you give me an idea of when I can expect to hear back from you regarding my candidacy?"

Fabulous: Say, "Are you able to provide me with the internal time-frame and criteria for this *position?*"

*Make this question about the time frame relative to the *position* — not you and your candidacy.

Companies may have other candidates and candidates may have other opportunities. Asking this question is not inappropriate, rather it is wise, and will be respected.

Accepting a Job Offer

Fine: "When do I start?"

Fabulous: "Thank you for your interest in me and I appreciate this offer. Based on my XYZ together with my ABC, as well as my EFG... not to mention the fact I would love the opportunity to work with and learn from YOU (and your colleagues), I welcome the opportunity to bring my expertise to bear in this situation. I am confident in my ability to make a significant contribution to your organization — your short-term and long-term goals and objectives."

Body Language

Endeavor to communicate excellent body language and exercise strong body control. A candidate's overall professionalism and "executive presence" includes voice, facial expression, energy, posture, and confidence. A good interviewer will assess non-verbal communication as well as the actual words we use.

Fine: Slouching, twitching, use of the non-words (er, um, uh, y'know, etc.), are fine because interviewers realize candidates are usually nervous.

Fabulous: The way you sit, gesture, gaze about, your verbal tics, etc., are all noticed. Be aware that you are communicating *plus de* non-verbal information and being evaluated.

Body language sends volumes of information you can use to your advantage. Pay close attention to non-verbal signals being sent and received through body language. For example:

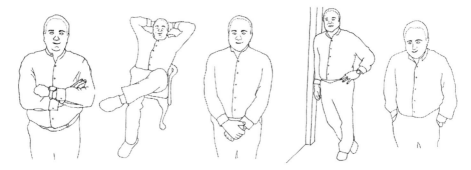

- Standing, arms crossed: Body Language 101 — "All defenses are up."
- Hands on hips OR hands behind head AND/OR feet on desk: the "Know-it-all"
- Hands crossed in front of lower body: "The fig leaf" (I am protecting myself)
- Leaning (against anything): Suggests boredom… "Is it time to leave yet?"
- Hands in pockets: Unprofessional and a bit too casual. This position also compromises your posture.
- Fidgeting: Betrays nervousness.
- Talking with hands (too much): Although acceptable in certain cultures, the interviewer is looking at your hands rather than focusing on *you*!

Clammy Hands

Clammy hands are often referred to as "the kiss of death!" … however …

STORY

My highly respected "interview expert" friend shared with me her views in this regard which I would like to share. When a candidate presents themselves well in terms of appearance, communication skills, knowledge AND exhibits confidence, despite the nerves and yes, even "clammy hands," she is impressed. In fact, she will even have an elevated view of this candidate because they have demonstrated that they are able to overcome the stress and still present themselves well. "This candidate has fought through it and that is impressive."

Ultimately, we are all just people meeting other people with compassion and kindness and we all have human frailties. Know that underneath, we all have vulnerabilities. We can only be us and do our best to present ourselves well and project our professional and personal best.

Your Résumé

Fine: They already have your résumé; it is not necessary to bring another copy.

Fabulous: Bring extra copies just in case.

While this book focuses primarily on interpersonal relations and subtle nuances of etiquette, we also want to be seen as *fabulous* on paper and in print. Our résumé often precedes us and serves as our introduction. Therefore, it is important that this document be as professional in presentation as our physical presence. What else do we take the time, make the effort, pay attention to detail, and ensure is letter-perfect? Our résumé matters.

Fine: Write up your own résumé, following a model you find online or in a book, and proof it for any typos.

Fabulous: Hire a professional résumé writer to create a résumé that really highlights your skills and accomplishments. Have them write up a brief profile section at the top that can also serve as your LinkedIn or professional Facebook profile, to maintain consistent branding across all media.

You want your résumé to be easy to read (bullet points), custom-designed to suit you, utilize industry-specific terms, and demonstrate results in your field. An experienced writer can make you stand out from the crowd and let your strong track record shine (or build up one that may need a little support). Professional résumé writers also know the importance of double- and triple-checking to prevent any simple errors, and how to format résumés optimally for print vs. online submission. They can often help you to craft effective professional cover letters as well. Be sure to print on quality (cotton bond or linen weave) paper.

Discussing Your Accomplishments

Fine: It is fine and now is the time to boast about your accomplishments: "I got the Sarsfield J. O'Connor Scholarship and I spent a year in Argentina! I was also voted 'Top Dog' of the Year!"… "I was xzy of my ABC," and "I did this" and "I did that" and "I" "I" "Me" "Me" "I" — etc.

Fabulous: Describe and summarize your background, credentials, experience and goals *avec humilité* — in a non-boasting way.

STORY:

My nephew Sarsfield was fortunate enough to have spent time in Argentina for several months and he said it truly changed his life. Here are some examples of how he described the impact of this experience:

- "I was humbled that my teammates felt me worthy of… (i.e.) electing me to be team leader."
- "I was honored to have been awarded (i.e.) the Sarsfield J. O'Connor Scholarship."
- "I was fortunate to have had the opportunity to… (i.e.) live in Argentina for several months."
- "We had the chance to experience first-hand (i.e.) a completely different culture."
- "We were able to help (those extremely disadvantaged)."
- "As a result of this amazing experience, I have (grown exponentially as a person)."
- "My objective is to build on everything gleaned from this (raw yet incredibly rich and rewarding) experience."
- "I look forward to helping others here, in a different way."
- "Witnessing the results of my hard work motivates me."
- "Recognizing how my humble efforts directly affect others inspires me."
- "My goal is to make a difference here and perhaps even, ultimately, in the world."

Interestingly enough, Sarsfield's younger sister, my niece Honor, recently won the Distinguished Senior award at her high school, C.B.A., emphasizing excellence in character. Her younger brother, Cormac, commented to my mother that "It was the interview that clinched the award for her."

This is a talented family: Cormac himself was just nine years old when he earned his first black belt. When I asked how did could possibly break through a one-inch board with his bare hands, my little nephew responded, "Auntie Judy, you tell yourself you can do it, and you just do it." Thank you, Master Cormac!

Answering Questions
Fine: Be prepared to answer questions.
Fabulous: Interview the interviewer, as well!

Yes, certainly be very prepared to answer questions, however, you have thoroughly researched them and the company. Interview them as well.

Remember, never ask a question to which you do not know the answer or at least have an idea of the answer.

Calling Cards and Business Cards

Invest in quality personal calling cards which reflect *you*. Carry and use your personal calling card at a business interview, even if you are presently gainfully employed by another firm; you are there representing *yourself*, not marketing your current employer. Handing the interviewer your (current) business card when discussing a business opportunity with another firm is wholly unprofessional (and even tacky).

Fine: Clip calling cards to your résumé.

Fabulous: Personally present your card and accept theirs if offered.

Do not ask a very senior executive, i.e., the Executive Director of Global Staffing, for their business card!

Acknowledge their card should they present this to you. Keep their card *with* you vs. "discarding" their "life." (Ref. Japanese; see Chapter 2, *Fabulous @ Handshaking & Business Cards*.)

Responding to Job Postings

When applying for a position, follow instructions, however, look for ways to *stand apart*.

Fine: If instructions say "Reply via email," do so.

Fabulous: Yes, do so however, follow the *"Call-Send-Call"* rule:

- *Call* (to introduce yourself and express an interest in the position).
- *Send* (your application/résumé as instructed by email).
- *Call* (follow up to ensure receipt).

If instructions say "send hard copy:"

Fine: Send hard copy via U.S. Postal Service or Pony Express (kidding!).

Fabulous: When applying via hard copy, send your materials via Fed Ex. For a few extra dollars you will *stand apart*. You may also consider having materials sent by messenger or personally hand-delivered by *you!*

Hand-delivering

Hand-delivering credentials yourself can work exceptionally well for you. Should you decide to access this approach, be sure to dress professionally. You never know who may just step out of their office just as you step in, upon which occurs "the viewing." You may even have the unexpected opportunity to sit down with your target for an informal or preliminary chat! Actually, you should dress expecting such an encounter. In addition, you never know who *else* may notice you (make positive judgments) and want to connect with you as long as you are there.

The personal drop-off will:

- Help you *stand apart* because so few do this these days.
- Demonstrate your keen level of interest in this opportunity.
- Show you as a pro-active, "get it done" person.
- Help leave a positive First Impression.
- Dispense a small taste of **fabulous**. Be sure to leave having them want to know more about you and want you back!

Be respectful and personable to everyone you encounter from security to receptionists and admins to anyone passing in the hall. Offer sincere thanks to those who have agreed to pass your information along to the appropriate individual/s there internally. Make even brief encounters *personal;* be *fully present.* Endeavor to be memorable and to let them know you have been there!

Temping

Fine: Take a temp job, collect a check and go home.

Fabulous: A temp job presents *plus des* opportunities, as more often than not talent is promoted from within. You may find yourself in a dull temp job, however, if you perform well, you may be offered a permanent position and even promoted once inside. Or, they may like you and your work so much that they create a position for you, which occurs more often than one might think. Always look for ways to contribute.

STORY

Remember the story in Chapter 3, *Fabulous @ Telephone Skills* about Karen Kaplan Sands of Hill Holiday, and how she advanced from receptionist to CEO of the company. When we view ourselves as the CEO of our position — even CEO of our temp job — we may follow the same path.

A temp job facilitates a personal entrée to those in the company's inner sanctum which may include key decision makers and gives you an opportunity to:

- Display your **fabulous** work and work ethic.
- Show you as a team player and high-energy.
- Demonstrate that you are a "roll up your sleeves" business individual.
- Show you as flexible and willing to do whatever it takes to get the job done.

Ultimately, you and your work and business/personal style are noticed.

STORY

That said, I would be remiss not sharing the following story about a temporary position I held many moons ago: At one point in my budding career a friend suggested temping, and for all the reasons outlined above, I thought, "But of course!"

I was thrilled to be offered a temp job the very next day working for a company that needed thousands of letters signed (stamped), folded, put into envelopes, labeled, and run through a postage meter. The position was presented as a ten-day project, at a good hourly wage.

Anyone who knows me knows that when I work, I give 1000%. Well, I finished the entire project — not in ten days, or seven, or even five — but in three and one-half days! I not only felt confident that they would pay me for the ten-day project as budgeted, I even entertained the idea that they might offer me a permanent position, yes?

Wrong! They paid me for exactly three and a half days. They did not even round it up to four days, and that was that. If I had taken my time and drawn out the process I would have saved a lot of (my) energy and received full compensation.

The lesson: Alas, "life is not always fair" and this was my lesson here — however, I still never give less than 1000%, ever.

After the Interview

Thank You Notes

It *is* acceptable to send a quick email note of thanks first, if you have ascertained they are an e-culture individual/company, and then follow up with the timeless, traditional thank you note on your quality personal stationery. You have taken *personal* notes during (or immediately following) the interview; mention something personal in your handwritten note afterwards. So few people these days even bother to follow up with an email or call that anyone today who takes the time and goes to the trouble to send a handwritten personalized thank you note gets noticed, big-time.

Top Tips for being **Fabulous** @ The Interview

1. Research the company in advance and prepare detailed questions for the interviewer. Ask questions as if you were already first choice for the job.
2. Dress for the position you want, not the one you presently hold.
3. Remember the *15-Minute Rule*: on time means arriving 15 minutes early, but no more than 15 minutes early.
4. STAND in the reception area and wait for the interviewer to arrive.
5. Do not assume the familiar form of address. Always *ask* how they prefer to be addressed.
6. Initiate the handshake (always be the initiator!) — regardless of gender.
7. Make good eye-contact.
8. Initiate small talk; share personal information (but not too much).
9. Decline offers of hospitality.

10. Permit the interviewer to lead the way to the room and allow them to be seated FIRST.

11. If given a choice, choose the *least* comfortable chair.

12. Select the chair angular or next to them should your goal be to eliminate barriers (e.g., the desk) and establish a connection.

13. *Ask* before taking notes.

14. Accentuate your uniqueness and highlight your cultural fit as it pertains to leadership qualities, passion, and flexibility.

15. Demonstrate your professional presence and excellent communication skills.

16. Project professionalism and a positive attitude, even on a telephone or Skype interview.

17. Provide solid references (those who have agreed — in advance — to speak well on your behalf).

18. Ensure that your social media profile (Facebook, Twitter, LinkedIn, etc.) enhances your professional presence.

10. Defer to *them* to initiate the topic of compensation.

20. If you want the position, let this be known, however, frame your question in terms of their timing for the *position,* not you and your candidacy.

21. Read their body language and endeavor to exhibit excellent body language and body control.

22. Take precautionary measures to prevent "Clammy Hands" (the "kiss of death").

23. Bring extra copies of your résumé, and invest in a professional résumé writer to highlight your skills and experience.

24. Do not be shy about highlighting your accomplishments (different from boasting).

25. Use your quality *calling* cards — not your business card from your current employer.

26. Follow their instructions when responding to job postings. Find ways to *stand apart* including accessing the *Call-Send-Call* Rule, and consider hand-delivering a hard copy of your résumé and cover letter.

27. Remember, temp jobs, internships and entry-level jobs can lead to permanent positions.

28. Send a brief email note of thanks the same day and a personal handwritten thank you note on your quality personal stationery within 24 hours after the interview.

Above all, be yourself. Your attitude during the interview is key. Project a positive attitude and you will evoke positive recognition, reaction and results, whether you want the job or not!

CHAPTER 9

Fabulous @ Dining & Social Situations

The Business Meal

With all due respect, no one suggests lunch because they think we look hungry and need to be fed! Lunch or any other business meal — from a quick cup of coffee to a formal dinner — presents another terrific opportunity to *stand apart* and be **fabulous**.

We may think our table manners are just fine, and they probably are. Many business transactions are either strengthened or shattered as a result of something we may or may not have done right at lunch. Therefore, this chapter will visit the many nuances to consider, as host or guest, to ensure a seamless, most productive and enjoyable business repast. And remember, all the rules governing casual and formal dining are in place to help make business dining and the entertaining experience easier — not more challenging.

The fact is, the little things orchestrated pre-, during and post-business meals are not small at all and do not "just happen." These nuances are specific and, once deployed, powerful. However, they need to be practiced in order to become automatic.

FIRST PERSON

I thought that because I attended a good college, I would know how to conduct myself during an interview or presentation. When I did not land my dream job with the company of my choice, I know this did not happen due to my lack of any book knowledge or technical expertise. As so many of my peers, I have been accustomed to communicating via social media networking channels, and although extremely adept and proficient with high-tech anything, my one-on-one people skills were not stellar. When it came to interpersonal communication skills, I lacked self-confidence and was not sure what to say or do in many situations. After not getting the job I wanted, I learned how important people skills really are in the business world. With respect to the nuances related to building trust and growing relationships, I can only share the analogy: it's like upgrading from dial-up to high-speed.

—**K. Johnson**, Financial Services, Purchase, NY

Never even *think* about attending a business meal as a chance to scarf down all the free shrimp you can eat or beer you can drink. There is plenty of time to eat and drink later. Because what you say and do are noticed, even scrutinized and actually judged, be particularly aware that others especially notice when what you are doing is NOT right. Therefore, conducting yourself at the business meal presents a great opportunity to distinguish yourself at the highest level of your skill set.

STORY

Many employers use the interview lunch to test a job candidate's mettle. Microsoft founder Bill Gates is known for this. In his writing, he has described his interviewing technique which includes identifying several equally qualified candidates, with equally impressive credentials, and conducting the final interview over dinner. Bill Gates tells us that he will make sure things are amiss such as their steak, which they may have ordered medium rare, arrives char-broiled, or something that is supposed to be served chilled arrives warm and soupy, or some other culinary "miss."

Mr. Gates will then observe how the various candidates handle the challenge. How do they (if at all) interrupt Bill Gates, the wealthiest man in the world? Do they complain, or ignore the predicament? Do they say anything? ... How do they treat the wait staff? Do they show them respect? Are the candidates authoritative or apologetic? Complicit? Rude? Direct?

There are no right or wrong answers here. Mr. Gates believes this rite of passage provides insight into the candidates as to how they might conduct themselves under similar subtle pressures on the job, dealing and interacting with clients, management and co-workers.

Be mindful that the reason we are invited to any business or dining-related function is not for the sole purpose of being fed. It's not about the food. We are invited to have others become better acquainted with us and grow and cultivate critical business relationships outside the office setting. Demonstrating finesse and orchestrated nuances will help propel you to the next leadership level.

The social nuances of which we speak in this chapter suggest a direct business tie-in, which begs the question: what else do you take the time, go to the trouble, make the effort to learn about in advance, prepare for, practice, master, and execute well? This is the bottom line and our premise: when you demonstrate attention to detail at the business lunch you indicate how you will perform in business matters. Your conduct at the table has the potential to engender trust and actually inspire dining companions to want to do business with you. Even when it's portrayed as "just lunch," embrace the business meal as a terrific opportunity to deploy these very specific nuances, be dining savvy, build *trust,* grow critical relationships, *stand apart* in all the most positive ways and advance your career.

STORY

A corporate client hosted a staff dinner at an upscale Boston restaurant. One young rising star with tremendous potential was being groomed to be promoted and go on the road to represent the company. The rising star made the fatal mistake of picking up his lobster bisque and drinking from the bowl. That single cup of soup cost the rising star his advancement opportunity; it was decided he was not yet ready!

Be mindful that everything said and done during a business meal is noticed and judged. And remember, others notice especially when something is not done properly!

Restaurant Business Meals

Choosing the Restaurant
You invite me to lunch.

Question. Who decides where we go? You (host) or your guest?

Fine: The host permits their guest to select the restaurant which should be moderately priced and proximate to both parties.

Fabulous: The host selects the restaurant, based on knowing the guest's preference.

Question. How do you learn your guest's preferred restaurant?

Hint: How did you meet this person to begin with?

Answer. Most often, through a "mutually respected third party." Therefore, ask the mutually respected third party, or the gatekeeper, "Where does Mr./Ms. X prefers to dine?" How impressed am I, Ms. Guest, when you suggest we meet, or better yet, you pick me up and bring me to my *favorite* restaurant? How did you *know*, for example, that Brasserie Joe was my favorite restaurant?

Taking this initiative honors your guest and by extension, reflects well on you. This is the *nuance*; once again, the business tie-in: what *else* do you, Mr./Ms. Host (Prospective new vendor/service provider) take the time, go to the trouble to investigate, practice in advance, master, execute well. The bottom-line result: your dining companion feels "I *trust* you, and I want to do business with you."

Consider how, when, where, why and what else you can do to go above and beyond!

STORY

A reporter from a major magazine was flying into Providence to take me to lunch and interview me for a story. I was very excited and we identified the best restaurant in Providence. I was new to the area at the time and was unfamiliar with the roads (actually, I still am). I offered to pick Ms. X up at the airport (gracious!) and she accepted. I did not want to drive — I wanted to focus on my guest and the interview, not on driving, directions or parking. I needed a car. I had a black car; I needed a driver.

"Oh, Honey! ... may I ask you a big favor?" My husband very generously agreed, however, good-naturedly said he would not wear a chauffeur's cap. Jay drove, dutifully held doors, I was "Ms. Bowman," etc., and this lovely reporter and I were able to chat away in the back seat *sans* distraction. This freed me to give my full attention to my guest. After lunch, we drove my guest back to the airport and I returned to the back seat of my car — where I remained — (and with good humor enjoyed the ride) all the way home, much to my husband's chagrin!

We do what we have to do! Thank you, Jay!

Getting to the Restaurant

Fabulous: *Offer* to personally pick up and return guests — with or without a driver.

Note: Given daily pressures and time constraints, we all need "down time." Therefore, be mindful that although this gesture to collect and drop off guests may not always be accepted, it will be positively noticed and most definitely appreciated. The nuance here is *offering*.

Meeting at the Restaurant

Situation. You agree to meet at the restaurant and you arrive first.

Fine: Secure the table and be seated.

Fabulous: Stand in the waiting area, at the ready, to personally meet, greet and receive your guests.

Rule: *Never be seated until guests arrive.*

Many restaurants will not even seat you until/unless your entire party has assembled. *STAND*, either outside (weather permitting) or in the reception area, keeping your right hand free to shake hands upon your guests' arrival.

FIRST PERSON

I used to think standing and waiting was overkill. I felt awkward and thought it made me look too eager. But once, when I decided to sit and wait, I learned the hard way. I was meeting a potential client for lunch. I was early and so I sat down in the waiting area on a low, leather couch, and began to flip through some paperwork I'd brought along.

When my party arrived, he called my name and I jumped up — papers went flying and I spent the first few minutes on my knees, trying to gather my papers, apologizing to my guest who was also pressed into service helping me. Not a good start. Whenever I feel like sitting to wait, I always remember that moment. Now, I always stand.

—**P. Law**, Sales Executive, Entertainment Industry, Los Angeles, CA

Fine: Establish the agreed-upon date/time/location and be on time.

Fabulous: "On time" is late. Follow the "15-minute rule." Arrive (at least) 15 minutes early… you have much advance work to do! Plus, you always want to be there *first*. Email or call the day before to re-confirm. Exchange cell phone numbers in advance, in the event of the unexpected, and leave your phone on until everyone has arrived.

Fine: Have a drink at the bar and use this wait time to check mail, make calls, etc. (It is actually *not fine* to check messages or make calls while you wait.)

General Device Rule: *As soon as you arrive at your destination, all devices OFF.*

Exceptions to the General Device Rule

As noted above, leave cell phones ON until everyone has actually arrived, as they could be trying to reach you (or you them) in the event of the unexpected. Therefore, keep cell phones on and close at hand until everyone has arrived safely, and then turn off.

*If you are expecting an important call or message during the course of your meal, there is no need to share details. Alert your dining partner *in advance* that you may be receiving an important call and leave your device on the vibrate option. If/when the call comes through, excuse yourself from the table (you do not need to give a reason) and take the call outside the restaurant, in the restroom — any place other than in the presence of your dining companion, so as not to suggest that someone/something else is more important than the reason you are here, e.g., to share quality time and get to know this individual outside the office environment. Smartphones and other IT devices never belong on a (dining) table without mutual consent.

STORY

Kathy Lee Gifford tells the story of how she actually cast off a friendship because of this breach. A friend whom she had not seen in a very long time had been nagging her to get together and told her how much she missed her and wanted to see her and catch-up, etc. They finally sat down to a meal together, and the friend had her Blackberry out on the table and used it to read and send texts to other random people throughout the entire course of their dinner together. Kathy Lee just sat there, looking around. These actions cost them both their special friendship.

Why bother getting together if you are not going to enjoy and interact with each other? (This story is repeated from Chapter 4, *Fabulous @ Electronic Communication,* for it is worth repeating.)

At The Restaurant

Pre-planning Arrangements
*You will have made a reservation in advance.
Fabulous: ARRIVE EARLY to:
- Select your table.
- Introduce yourself to wait staff and learn their names.
- Review seating arrangements with wait staff.
- Review the order of ordering.
- Arrange for the check in advance.
- Familiarize yourself with everything in the restaurant, including location of restrooms, because you never want to be placed in the position of having anyone ask you anything to which you must reply "I don't know."

Doors and Revolving Doors
Question. Who always goes first through a door? Men or women?
Answer. The woman. (The man should open and hold the door.)
However, a revolving door requires some forethought.
An automatic revolving door: The woman precedes the man, as with a regular door.
A manual revolving door is typically heavy, and the gentleman should:
Fabulous: Precede, however acknowledge this and say, "Let me go ahead and push the door," or
Fabulous: Some men prefer to push the door and have the woman precede them; they will follow from behind.
Either way, acknowledge the door.

Greeting Your Guests

STAND in the foyer and wait for your guest/s; do not be seated (see <u>Meeting at the Restaurant</u> above).

Fine: When your party arrives, alert the *maitre d'* and ask to be seated.

Fabulous: Embrace the "welcome moment" as another *opportunity* to extend a genuine warm and enthusiastic greeting. Welcome guests as you would a guest in your own home. Greet them by name (lean in) and shake hands, setting the tone. Positive energy emanates from your voice, eyes, facial expression and body language. Draw from your **fabulous** arsenal and use your finely honed "small talk" skills to help place guests at ease.

Remember, your guests have extended themselves to be with you. Gracious hosts will *acknowledge* this effort, thank guests for coming and signal the *maitre d'* who should be standing by, that your guest has arrived and you are ready to be seated.

The Procession to the Table

Fine: Follow the *maitre d'* to the table in the order of however you are aligned.

Fabulous: Permit guests, by order of rank/status to directly follow the *maitre d'*. You, gracious host, will always be <u>last</u> in the procession to the table, regardless of gender.

Note: In the **United States**, you honor the most important person by having them directly follow the *maitre d'*. Social situations are different: if a man and women meet for dinner socially, the woman will always follow the *maitre d'*.

*In **Europe**, the host, e.g., the gentleman, will <u>always</u> lead, permitting him to check-out and secure the restaurant for *safety*.

Please know: There are no gender rules in business. Women hosts should defer to their guests — men and women — allowing the guest/s to precede the host and follow the *maitre d'*. This said, fortunately, most of our male colleagues are traditional gentlemen and will usually defer to the woman (host), allowing her to precede them and follow the *maitre d'*. And, at the risk of engaging in "the dance," the rule here holds that after one gesture, women hosts should graciously accept and precede.

Seating

Guest Seating

Guest seating presents another opportunity for hosts to distinguish themselves and show they know "the difference" while quietly acknowledging and even honoring guests.

Fine: Suggest guests be seated anywhere they'd like.

Fabulous: Designate seating arrangements in advance and review with wait staff. Guest seating order should be strategic and hold significance.

Host Seating

Fine: Hosts may sit anywhere they would like.

Fabulous: The host is seated at the "head of the table." The head of the table is based on where the *doors* of the room are located because nearly everyone watches the entrance. Sitting facing the doors permits the host… (who forever endeavors) to be in *control*… of their table and the room, the opportunity to know who is coming, going, approaching, etc.

Order of Seating

You honor the most important person by seating them to the host's *right*.

The second most important person is seated to host's *left*. Co-hosts are seated directly across from the host so that together, they can *control* their table through eye-contact, silent signals, body language.

Seating When a Co-Host is Present:

- The most important person remains seated to the host's right.
- The second most important person is seated to *co-host's* right.
- The third most important person is seated to host's left.
- The fourth most important person is seated to *co-host's* left.
- Other guests are filtered throughout either side of the table.

*Exception: Always offer guests the better view/most comfortable seat/banquette.

STORY

"Thomas Jefferson… brought democracy into international etiquette. Until then, seating at state dinners was rigidly controlled, with great attention given to who sat where. Foreign dignitaries were given the place of honor at the right hand of the ruler of the country they were in. Jefferson declared this undemocratic, and said that seating would be 'pell-mell' — sit where you want, without regard to rank. Some were insulted." (p. 174, Cuisine and Culture; a history of food and people, 3rd ed., Linda Civitello, NY: Wiley, 2011.)

Clearly, the White House has changed a lot since then, and the Office of the Chief of Protocol, under the Department of State, provides guidance for state affairs (although different administrations adhere to these guidelines to varying degrees).

Like the White House ceremonials division that maintains timeless traditions, we all have the responsibility and the opportunity to adhere to every possible detail, including cultural considerations, to ensure that guests feel welcomed and special. We never know when any one of us may be dining at the White House or even with the Queen of England. Truly!

STORY

Once when I was traveling to Half Moon Bay, Jamaica, the Queen happened to be staying at our resort. (She may have owned it!) One day, word spread in no uncertain terms that the Queen was "off property" and so we did not even think about trying to get a "Royal sighting."

I was at the pool when someone gave the alarm: "She'll be coming out of her residence in 10 minutes!" I tied a cover-up around me and dashed over to see the Queen. I immediately zeroed in on her Chief of Protocol and, after a bit of conversation, asked if he would introduce me (the mutually respected third party, yes?). He said he would be happy to do so, however, I was wearing a two-piece bathing suit and was only half covered. He explained that if I were fully covered, he could have introduced me. (Alas, I did not have time to run back to my room to change.) I was so close to meeting the Queen!

As a direct result of this chance meeting, however, my new friend, the Chief of Protocol, invited us to Buckingham Palace where we had a private tour of all the magnificent Royal carriages, and more! This was all very exciting, and very special.

SEATING TIPS... AT A GLANCE

The host is seated at the head of the table (the seat facing the entrance). Follow seating by order of importance (most important to host's right, next most important to host's left, etc.) with these exceptions:

- Offer your guest (of honor) the seat at the table with the best view, or the most comfortable seat.
- Should you have a choice between sitting across the table from your guest or angular to them, you are encouraged to sit angular to your guest, eliminating the table as a barrier and encouraging a more personal rapport.
- Gentlemen help ladies on their right be seated.
- Enter and exit from the chair's right.

Note: Socially, couples should be separated unless they are newlyweds or newly engaged. The idea is to *share* this couple.

Being Seated

Fine: Verbally suggest guests be seated anywhere they would like.

Fabulous: A *fabulous* host has not only pre-arranged seating by order of importance but also placed (framed) calligraphied place cards and menu cards (which may serve as a keepsake) at each setting.

Fabulous: Host or *maitre d'* will personally escort guests to pre-designated seats and assist with seating.

Fabulous: Enter and exit from the chair's RIGHT.

*Note: The person of honor/host will <u>not</u> have a place card (nor wear a name badge) as others know who they are. The Queen, for example, would never have a place card. Rather, she is shown to her seat. (An exception may be made for this rule at a large function, out of consideration for those who may not know the person of honor.)

Coats, Purses, Jackets (and more)

Coats, jackets, briefcases, ladies' purses, computer cases, umbrellas, backpacks, gym bags, travel luggage… yes, it's better not to have these when you attend a business meal, but often this cannot be avoided.

Fine: Bring these items with you to the restaurant.

Fabulous: Generally speaking, leave travel bags, gym bags, backpacks at the hotel or office. However, should this be unavoidable, leave belongings with the coat check, restaurant manager or even bartender. These items should not be in public view, subject to scrutiny; toting them may pull you off balance — literally and figuratively.

STORY

I have resorted to asking the doorman at a nearby hotel to valet my encumbrances which is very helpful. (Remember to collect these after the dinner!)

Fabulous: Briefcases, computer cases and purses should be placed under the table during the meal, available if needed, to support a presentation or provide handouts (see <u>Distributing Support Material</u> below).

Coats and the Coat Check

Fine: Each person is responsible for checking their own coat with the coat check.

Fabulous: Host will personally assist checking guests' coats, or will have prearranged a designated coat check person. Hosts should tip on behalf of all guests.

When There is No Coat Check

Fine: Rest your overcoat over another chair at your table.

Fabulous: Unbutton coats (from the bottom up) and be seated. Once seated, remove your coat and let it drape over the back of your chair. Sit on your coat for the duration of the meal.

Coats After the Meal

Fine: Put on your coat, as usual.

Fabulous: Regardless of gender, hosts assist women and gentlemen guests with their overcoats.

Fabulous: Once on, the host should extend the proverbial "shoulder squeeze" which is both reassuring and endearing.

Ladies' Purses

Ladies' purses at the table present another quiet opportunity to *stand apart*.

Fine: Place your handbag on the table or hang the strap over the back of your chair.

Fabulous: Small purses should be placed behind your back on the seat of the chair, or on the floor under the table by your feet for security reasons. Slinging a hand bag over the back of a chair is tacky (and not fine).

STORY

There is a story about the Feng Shui saying: "Purse on the floor is money out the door" (or variations such as "Purse on the floor means you'll always be poor"). This has led to people not wanting to leave their purses on the floor in restaurants or at meetings, in fear of bad luck. There is a wonderful device called a "purse hook," a weighted disk with a flexible hook allowing you to hang your purse below the table which is **fabulous**! (Look for one in your local Chinatown or order online.)

Suit Jackets

Fine: It is fine to remove your suit jacket at the table if you would like, based on warmth/comfort.

Fabulous: Men and women should keep suit jackets ON and BUTTONED at the dining room and boardroom tables. The top two buttons should be buttoned and the third button should be left open as a sort of vent.

Exception: If/when your host removes their jacket, consider this a silent signal that it is permissible to remove yours. Mirroring your dining companion helps this individual experience a greater comfort level and suggests you are together, connected, always the goal.

That said, if the reason you would like to remove your coat is because you are extremely warm and may be perspiring, you may care to rethink this option for obvious reasons!

Fabulous: To unbutton jackets: start from the bottom and work your way up.

Immediately After Being Seated

After being seated, there lies an instantaneous opportunity to *stand apart* in two important ways:

Time Check

Fine: Chat away and let dialogue take its natural course, so to speak.

Fabulous: Once seated, before you even think about opening the menu, do a time check and ask guests, "How are we set for time today?" and honor this. Doing so demonstrates thoughtfulness and respect. Share this important information with your server and pace yourself accordingly, during the course of your meal. This gesture will be noticed and appreciated and you will be remembered well when your guest is on schedule for subsequent obligations.

Often times, a guest may *say* they have only one hour, however, it would not be unusual to ultimately enjoy much more time together, a nice situation indeed! Either way, it is courteous and thoughtful to ask. The *gesture* of asking is welcomed, positively noticed and appreciated.

As in the rest of this book, the guidelines presented in this chapter are generally in the chronological order of the meal or dining event. Generally, a wine steward or waiter will ask if you would like a cocktail before taking your food order; therefore, the following section precedes the reference for ordering food, eating, concluding, *et autre* activities.

Ordering

The time when you first sit down presents another opportunity to take *control* of your dining situation, substantiate your role as host and *stand apart.*

Fine: Order after you and your guests have had a chance to chat and catch-up.

Fabulous: Immediately after the executing the time-check, make the suggestion that everyone look at menus to get ordering out of the way in order to share quality time together. If not, you risk losing this precious time you finally have together. This shows you as efficient, foresighted, respectful and in *control* of the business lunch.

(See below for <u>More About Ordering</u>, including *The Order of Ordering, Ordering Whatever You Like, Ordering Course for Course* and *How to Order.*)

Ordering Alcoholic Beverages

Situation. Your guest orders a glass of wine. However, you do not care for a cocktail, or do not drink (for whatever reason).

Question. Should you order a glass of wine or a cocktail so that your guest does not drink alone?

Fine: Yes, order something to drink.

Fabulous: When it comes to alcoholic beverages, many people do not drink for a number of different reasons — religious, health, fitness, taste, effects, desire to keep a clear head at a business meal, etc. There is no reason to call attention or explain why you are not ordering an alcoholic drink.

Order a non-alcoholic beverage instead. Consider cranberry juice, mineral water, or a citrus drink such as an Arnold Palmer (half iced tea, half lemonade), or something with bubbles, i.e., sparkling water or ginger ale. Order anything other than plain tap water.

Wine Ordering

Ordering wine presents yet another opportunity to stand tall or fall short of the vine, so to speak, if you know nothing of the art.

Fine: Permit guests to order their wine of choice by the glass.

Fabulous: **Fabulous** hosts will anticipate that wine will likely be served particularly during dinner and it remains the host's responsibility to order wine for the table.

While it remains the responsibility of the host to order wine for the table, if the host knows that one of their guests is a wine *connoisseur*, it is gracious to "defer the honor" to that individual.

*Ascertain if guests will be having one or more glasses to decide if it makes sense to order by the bottle.

*Hosts should provide one red and one white bottle for their table as the old rules of white with chicken/fish and red with meat no longer apply.

Situation. You are the host and know nothing about ordering wine, and you don't know what to order.

Fine: Confess to guests and ask if anyone would like to help you out.

Fabulous: You, unsophisticated host, will learn about how to order wine at another time. However, in the meantime, you will have had a private word in advance, with the wait staff or *sommelier* (there are fewer, these days!) to let them know your needs. State your price range, and let them select the wine that will complement your meal.

Situation. Your wine *connoisseur* guest to whom you have "deferred the honor" gets a bit carried away and mentions the $500 bottle of, i.e., Château Lafitte-Rothschild, which you know you are going to have trouble getting approved on your expense report.

Fine: Bite the bullet. This is a good customer. If they want the $500 bottle of Rothschild, so be it.

Fabulous: Make the call whether to allow this or not. If not, subtly, yet authoritatively, take *control* the situation and prevent yourself from being taken advantage of.

- Make a pointed reference to those wines in your "price points."
- Ensure they understand the $500 bottle is "out of bounds."

*Others should always be sensitive to and respectful of price, particularly these days.

FIRST PERSON

I was given the task of taking one of our clients and his team to lunch as a thank you. We were seated and menus were distributed. I knew that one member of the client team was a wine aficionado and asked him to order. I quickly realized this was a mistake as I could hear him discussing various choices — all of which were the priciest bottles on the menu. What should I do? Obviously, I couldn't start a price debate with my client over a bottle of wine.

I went with humor. When the client mentioned a very expensive bottle, I said "Oh, we should all have stock in that company!" Everyone laughed and the hint was taken. He selected a more moderately priced bottle.

—**J. Chamberlain**, District Sales Manager, Credit Union, Upstate New York

In a sticky situation, humor often holds an element of truth and may be highly effective.

Refusing Wine

Many people choose not to drink at business meals (or at all). Please know that it is appropriate to permit the server to set the table with glasses and even accept the wine and (go through the motions) of toasting, etc., so as not to stand out. Or, should you personally prefer not to have the glass/wine in front of you for whatever reason, politely decline a wineglass when the waiter or wine steward is setting them. Should you have the glass at your place setting and you are offered wine, the way we decline presents another opportunity to *stand apart*:

Fine: Politely say, "No thank you… I have had enough!" (Or "None for me, thanks.")

Fabulous: The two-finger wave: tilt and wave your first two fingers (index and third finger) over your glass to signal that you pass on wine.

Note: When attending a dinner where a networking event precedes the dinner, resist the impulse to bring your beer, wine or cocktail glass with you into the dining room. *Reason*: your host has presumably gone to significant time, trouble and thought with respect to wine selections and wine pairing during dinner. Leave all beverages *behind* as you prepare your palette for the *total dining experience*.

Filling Wine Glasses

Fine: Fill glasses to the top.

Fabulous: Fill so that there is room at the top of the glass, no larger than two fingers horizontally together.

How to Hold Glasses

How to hold a glass presents another opportunity to *stand apart*.

Fine: Use all five fingers clutched around the glass. (The *"death grip"* — NOT FINE!)

Fabulous: Hold a glass with the first three fingers: the thumb, index and third fingers.

Even world leaders can be reminded — hold glasses by the stem, not the glass!

Stemmed glasses should be held by the stem, as close to the bowl or base as possible.

Cocktail glasses should be held with the same first three fingers, also as close to the bowl or base of the glass as possible… and always, always, always with a cocktail napkin!

Host Duties

A host has many responsibilities, all of which serve as opportunities to *stand apart*.

Fine: Guests have everything they need. Hosts, be sure you get the check.

__Rule__: No one at the table does anything unless / until the host initiates the action, which includes:

Fabulous Host Duties Include:

- Being seated (person of honor is always seated first; enter and exit from the chair's *right*).
- Saying grace (see below).
- Removing napkins from the table to lap.
- Toasting — both types of toasts (see <u>Types and Levels of Toasting</u> below) including elevating glasses to propose a toast.
- Initiating conversation and being inclusive.
- Opening menus.
- Lifting utensils before each course (signaling guests may begin).
- Bringing the meal to conclusion.
- Handling the check (in advance).
- Monitoring and ensuring wait staff does not clear anyone's plate unless/until everyone *at their table* has finished eating.

STORY

Here is a real story of what happens when hosts forget their host responsibility and leadership role. The president of one of my banking clients was hosting guests at his luncheon table. Apparently, the president became so engrossed in conversation with his person of honor that he completely neglected host duties towards his other guests, never offered a toast, never began eating — hence, no one else at his table ate, either!

Grace

Many individuals these days in business offer grace before the meal. Here are some "grace" guidelines:

Fabulous:

- No napkin is touched, no water sipped, no toast is proposed until after grace has been said.
- One should always be asked in advance in order to be prepared with something appropriate to say.
- Grace should be geared to those at *this* table.

Setting a Table

Silverware

The placement of silverware, including how to hold silverware and which utensil to use and when, can be confusing; demonstrating that you know speaks volumes.

Fine: Use silverware randomly as you dine.

Fabulous: A place setting is like a map. You know what course to expect next, based on the way the table is set.

Rule: *Start from the outside and work your way IN.*

Setting a Formal Table

Number of glasses:

>   **Fine**: Any random number
>   **Fabulous**: Six.

DINING BASICS... AT A GLANCE:

- Forks on the Left — Always.
- Knives and spoons on the Right — Always.
- If you forget: "fork" and "left" have four letters, "knife," "spoon" and "right" have five letters.

FURTHER BASICS

- Solids on the Left — Always. (Solids: salad, bread, butter, soup, etc.)
- Beverages on the Right — Always. (Beverages: water, wine, coffee, tea, etc.)
- If you forget: Form a "b" with the thumb and index finger of your left hand and a "d" with the thumb and index finger of your right hand — as in <u>b</u>read and <u>d</u>rink. Alternatively, consider the : "B M W" as in <u>B</u> — <u>B</u>read, <u>M</u> — <u>M</u>ain Course, <u>W</u> — <u>W</u>ater. Use whatever works for you.

Folding Napkins

There are many fun, "foofy" creative napkin folds such as tents, birds, fans, and more. However, there is only one "classic fold." Think: opposite a book, with the fold or *binding* (of the book) if you will, on the right and the flaps or pages (of the book) on the upper left.

Where to Place Napkins

Napkins: napkins are placed to the left of your plate, or on your dinner/place plate — not under your forks.

>   *You may wish to provide black napkins when guests are wearing black (to reduce the lint factor). Upscale restaurants and caterers are doing this more often these days (see <u>Napkin Etiquette</u> below).

Dessert Forks and Spoons
Dessert forks and spoons are positioned horizontally above your dinner/place plate.

Place-Plates (or Charger Plates)
There are no hard and fast rules regarding place plate or charger plate etiquette. This is entirely up to the host's discretion. However, generally speaking, place plates should be removed for the main course and certainly for dessert.

Candles
Fine: Hosts should have all brand-new candles placed in candle holders on the table (and on other surfaces, if entertaining at home).

Fabulous: Please consider the practice of lighting candles immediately after you place them in the candle holder, if even for a minute, to burn the wick. Candle wicks should always be burnt, reflecting the warmth of the home; a brand-new waxy wick is tacky.

More About Ordering

The Order of Ordering
The order of ordering is important. The astute host knows this and will review the order of ordering in advance with the wait staff.

Fine: Wait staff will randomly take orders or begin with the host and go around the table, especially with large groups for efficiency.

Fabulous: The host has pre-arranged the order of ordering as follows:
- The person of honor (seated to the host's right) always orders first.
- Next: ladies at the table order.
- Next: gentlemen order.
- Lastly: the host orders.

Ordering Whatever You Would Like
Hosts have the responsibility of making their guests feel they may order whatever they would like, regardless of price.

Fine: Say, "Order whatever you'd like… it's on the company!"

Fabulous: Hosts recommend specific items on the menu in various food categories in various price ranges so it is clear that guests may indeed feel free to order whatever they like.

You might say, "I understand the salmon is excellent here," or "I have tried the filet and it is terrific." Be sure to mention specific entrees in a full price range from the light salad or soup to pasta dishes to the surf 'n turf.

THAT SAID —

***Guest Rule**: Do not order the most expensive nor least expensive item/s on the menu. Order in the middle price range, even when your host tells you to "Feel free to order whatever you might like." Show moderation and order a reasonably priced meal.*

Ordering Course for Course

Situation. Your guest orders an appetizer, soup, a salad, and a hot entrée. You (host) prefer a simple salad.

Fine: Guests should feel free to order whatever they would like and you (host) should feel free to order whatever you would like.

Fabulous: Despite personal preferences, a *fabulous* host will match their dining companion course for course so guests are not placed in the uncomfortable position of being *watched* (while they eat!). And, as opposed to what many of us may have been taught growing up, when you order obligatorily, it is fine to "play with your food."

Remember your goal: to place guests at ease and create a connection. Therefore, do order course for course with your dining companion.

How to Order

The way you place your order (with the wait staff) presents another opportunity to *stand apart*. After you learn the chef's signature dishes, specials *du jour* and what menu items may no longer be available:

Fine: Say, "Could I get the ...ABC...?" or, "May I have the ...XYZ...?"

Fabulous: Say three decisive words: "I would like... (i.e., the ABC)" and then, "I would like the DEF," and then, "I would like some XYZ ."

The phrase, "Can I get" or "Could I have" is often said when ordering, however, it is inappropriate because you are, in essence, asking permission. The answer to such a question: *Of course you can! You are the paying customer!* Using a weak phrase such as "Can I get...?" suggests subservience. Demonstrate authority when ordering food at the dining table, just as in any other business situation.

Eating

History

Even in the beginning, a time when people ate with their hands, there were right and wrong ways of doing things. A less cultured person would grab food with both hands using all ten fingers while a person of breeding would use only three fingers — the thumb, index and third fingers. Thus evolved the raised pinkie as a sign of elitism, which is an affectation today unless this comes naturally to you.

When you think about it, eating is a fairly cumbersome process. We are trying to somehow delicately cut and dissect food and get bite-sized pieces into our mouths; chew, swallow, digest and — the real reason we are even there — conduct ourselves in table-talk conversation.

American vs. Continental Dining

How to Hold Utensils

Note: Forks come from the left side and knives come from the right side of your place setting.

Lift utensils and align the length of the fork in the left hand palm and the length of the knife in your right hand palm. Grasp the utensils and turn hands and utensils over so that your index finger rests along the neck of the fork and the neck of the knife. You will need to hold this positioning for leverage as you cut.

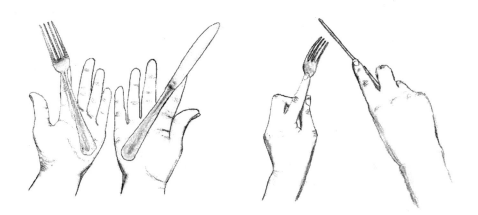

Please note: this is the only way to hold a fork and knife and it is appropriate for both the American and Continental Styles of dining.

How to Eat American Style
- Secure food with fork and use your knife to cut (only one to two small pieces at one time).
- Then rest your knife across the top of your plate — serrated edges facing IN — toward you, NOT towards your glass(es).
- SWITCH your fork from your left to your right hand, and lift the food to your mouth using your right hand.
- Bring food into mouth using lips, not teeth.
- To cut another piece: switch your fork back to your left hand and pick up your knife with your right hand to cut one to two more small pieces.
- Rest your knife again on your plate and switch your fork again back to your right hand to eat, etc. (*Note*: Delicately *swoop* versus stabbing your food with the fork.)

The upper classes in England thought this was much too much work (!) and they simply stopped switching their utensils, leading to the Continental Style of Dining.

How to Eat Continental (European) Style
- Hold fork and knife exactly in the same way and secure food exactly as noted above. However, after you cut (just one to two small pieces), DO NOT switch utensils and do not rest your knife on the plate; rather, continue to hold your knife in your right hand

- Continue to hold the fork in your left hand; fork tines are always DOWN.
- Rest *forearms* — not elbows — on the edge of the table.
- Stab food with the fork tines or fold food on top of the fork tines (fork still in your left hand); remember, fork tines are always facing *downward*.
- Use your knife to help maneuver and balance small amounts of food onto the back of the tines.
- Again, bring food into your mouth with your *lips,* not your teeth, with your fork still in your left hand, tines facing *downward.*

Fine: If you are dining in the U.S., you should use the American Style of dining. If you are eating in Europe, use the Continental Style of dining.

Fabulous: Today, we are global. Americans eat Continental Style and others in Europe and elsewhere eat American style.

Please understand clearly: there is no right or wrong, no better or worse. Regardless of where you are in the world, it is perfectly acceptable and even considered *chic (!)* to eat using a combination of both the American and Continental styles of dining when eating.

Cutting and Eating Food

Fine: Cut all your food at once.

Fabulous: As noted above, whichever style you use (American or Continental), cut only one to two small, bite-size pieces at a time so that when you are asked an open-ended question, you are able to easily respond. *Pre-cutting an entire entree is a practice reserved for young children.*

How to Hold the Fish Knife

The fish knife itself presents another opportunity to *stand apart* simply by knowing how to properly *hold* it!

Fine: Hold as you would any other knife.

Fabulous: Hold the fish knife like a *pencil.*

The very nature of fish prompts using the Continental Style of eating because fish is very delicate; therefore, we need not "saw" fish like a steak. Rather, *fold* fish over the <u>back</u> of the fork tines. Remember to keep fork tines facing DOWNward in your left hand.

The Dessert Spoon

Treat the dessert spoon like the knife and hold this exactly the same way as you would a knife. You will be provided with a dessert fork and spoon if you need to use both to eat dessert, or use one or the

other, as appropriate — i.e., with apple crisp a la mode, use only the dessert spoon when eating the ice cream, use only the fork when eating only the pie and use both the dessert fork and spoon when eating both, i.e., place ice cream over the cut bit of pie with your spoon and eat with your fork in your left hand, tines down.

The Silent Service Code

You Are Resting
Fine: Randomly place utensils any which-way on your plate.

Fabulous: The *Silent Service Code* is the silent signal which indicates that you are either "resting" or have indeed "finished."

You Are Finished
Fine: Push your plate away from you once you are finished eating. (Actually this is not fine; touching your plate is considered taboo.)

Fabulous: Use the *Silent Service Code* in either the American or Continental Style (see below), according to how you are eating at present time, to indicate that you have either finished or that you are resting.

American Style — "I Am Resting"

Fork: Imagine your plate as a clock. Position your fork in the 10:20 o'clock "I am resting" position. This is the silent signal to the wait staff that you are just "resting," e.g., "Please do not clear my plate."

Knife: Rest knife along the top edge of the plate, parallel to the fork, serrated edges facing inward TOWARD you, not away from you.

Fork tines are always UP when eating American style.

Continental Style — "I Am Resting"
Think: a coat of arms, or the letter "V". Place fork over the knife, serrated edges of the knife are facing toward YOU and tines face DOWNward. This is the Silent Signal, Continental Style that you are "resting," e.g., "Please do not clear my plate."

"I Am Finished"
To signal that you have "finished," bring utensils together and position them in a 10:20 o'clock or, 10/4 — "Over and out" — "I am finished" — "Take it away" position.

American Style — **Fork tines are UP**.

Continental Style — **Fork tines are DOWN**.

Note:
- Fork tines are always UP when eating "American Style."
- Fork tines are always DOWN when eating "European Style."
- The cutting edge of the knife should always face inward toward you, not out toward the glasses.
- The fork is always closest to you; your knife belongs on the right side of the fork.

Left- vs. Right-handed People

The fork comes from the LEFT side of the plate and stays in your left hand. The knife and spoon come from the RIGHT side of the plate and remain in your right hand, regardless if you are left- or right- handed.

Rule: *Never touch your plate*

The only time that protocol permits us to touch or move our plate in any way, shape or form, is if our entrée is served and this does not face the waistline. Then and only then, is it permissible to touch and turn your plate around to properly re-position.

As noted above, pushing your plate away when you are finished is not fine and should be avoided. The *Silent Service Code* more properly suggests that "you have finished."

More on Eating

When to Begin

Fine: Begin eating as soon as your food arrives especially if it is hot.

Fabulous*:* Begin eating only after everyone at your table is served, and after the host initiates this.

Hint: If you are the host, be aware that others are waiting for you to begin. It is your responsibility to signal when to begin eating. Others are waiting for you to pick up your utensils to begin. Make eye-contact with all those present and say, for example, "*Bon appétit*!" or "Enjoy!" as you raise your utensils.

Pacing Yourself

Fine: Eat quickly if you are hungry or slowly if not.

Fabulous: Diners should pace themselves with other diners and should not be the first or last to finish eating.

When to Refrain from Eating

Rule: *Do not eat while your dining partner is disclosing important, personal or emotional information until/unless they do*.

Focus on the speaker, not your food. Follow their lead. Maintain good eye-contact and demonstrate active listening skills and attentive body language to convey genuine interest and be an active dining participant; eat when they eat. Use common sense and display common courtesy here.

Remember, we are not here to EAT. Our shared purpose is to become better acquainted in an office-neutral environment. This we cannot do if we are more focused on our food than on our dining companion.

Discussing Business at the Table

If, when, and how to bring up business topics at the table can be delicate and presents another opportunity to *stand apart*.

Fine: Discuss business topics at hand during the course of the meal.

Fine: Sprinkle business topics throughout the business meal.

Fabulous: Remember, this dining occasion presents the opportunity to get to know others <u>outside</u> the office setting. Unless there is mutual agreement or an understanding otherwise, business discussions during the meal should not be on the menu, so to speak. Business discussions, if at all, should take place <u>after</u> the main course has been cleared, over dessert and coffee.

This cannot be overstated. Making this segue to business discussions is the host's responsibility — unless their guest initiates otherwise, of course.

That said, given our current economic climate, more luncheons are focused on cutting T&E (travel and entertainment) costs, and luncheons are arranged specifically for the objective of accomplishing goals or sales in certain industries. In this instance, this would be an altogether different type of business luncheon. Consider accountability and be sure to set and meet established objectives. Clarify this in advance with all participants, unless it is generally understood that business topics will be discussed over the meal.

Situation. Many dining establishments and private clubs do not permit use of cell phones, lap-tops and other business tools at the table while dining and if seen, diners will be asked to put them away. However, you will need to use these tools to communicate with your client effectively during or after the business meal.

Alternative: Reserve a private dining room in the restaurant/club.

(See more on <u>When to Make a Presentation During the Meal</u> below.)

Napkin Etiquette

Knowing how and when to properly bring the napkin from the table to your lap, what to do with your napkin when you are excusing yourself from the table, and what to do with your napkin when you are finished, are small things and simple and yet present opportunities to *stand apart*.

Fine: Once seated, remove your napkin from the table and place on your lap.

Fabulous: Be seated. Wait for your host to signal when to remove your napkin from the table to your lap; always follow the host's lead.

- Holding the upper left corner, remove napkin from the table and bring to your lap.
- Once it is on your lap, begin to unfold the napkin, so that the crease faces your waistline.

- Luncheon napkins (usually smaller) are unfolded in their entirety. Dinner napkins (typically larger) are left folded in half.
- Black napkins are thoughtfully provided more these days, to reduce the lint factor!

Napkins: "Excusing Yourself"

What to do with your napkin when you are "excusing" yourself from the table and when you are "finished" is very specific.

Fine: When excusing yourself from the table, napkins may be left in the chair or on the table.

Fabulous: When excusing yourself from the table, gently dab each corner of your mouth and perhaps the middle if necessary (versus smearing your lips) and leave your napkin loosely folded in your *chair*. Wait staff will usually re-fold the napkin and place this on your chair's arm, on the back of the chair or replace your napkin entirely.

Napkins: "You are Finished"

Fine: Once you have finished eating, remove your napkin from your lap and place it anywhere on the table.

Fabulous: Watch for the silent signal from your host. When everyone else at the table is finished eating, your host will dab their lips and leave the napkin loosely folded to the LEFT of the (dessert) plate from where it came; diners follow host's lead.

The Breadbasket

Knowing how to take, break, offer and pass bread is important and presents another opportunity to *stand apart*.

Passing the Breadbasket

Fine: Help yourself to various types of bread and rolls.

Fabulous: The person closest to the breadbasket is responsible for taking the basket and helping themselves first. Then, this individual should hold the basket and offer this to person on their left, then hold and offer to the person on their right, passing *counterclockwise*.

Remember: Once you touch it, you own it!

Eating Rolls

- Take only one roll at a time.
- Break off one *thumbnail* bite-size piece at a time.

Take small bites so you are not placed in the awkward situation of being asked an open-ended question to which you must respond just as you popped a (large) piece into your mouth. You must now chew, swallow, and… attempt to answer the question. Small, bite-size pieces eliminate any such potentially awkward situation.

- Butter the bite-size piece over your bread-and-butter plate and pop this into your mouth.

(Serrated butter knife edges always face IN, e.g., toward you.)

*Do not dunk bread in soup.

Buttering Rolls

Fine: Randomly take butter and slather over rolls.

Fabulous:

- Use the central butter *serving fork* or *knife* to remove a pat (personal portion) of butter from the butter dish and place onto your individual bread-and-butter plate.
- Use your own *individual* butter knife to butter the thumbnail size piece over your bread-and-butter dish.

(Again, rest your butter knife along the top of the butter dish, serrated edge facing INWARD, toward you.)

Foiled Butter

Butter wrapped in foil should be scraped off the foil. Fold foil once and place the folded foil wrapper *under* your butter plate.

Seasoning Food

Yes, even seasoning your food presents another opportunity show you know "the difference" and *stand apart*.

Fine: If you know you enjoy *plus de* salt or pepper, apply liberally, as you normally would.

Fabulous: Always taste food before seasoning anything.

Some view seasoning without first tasting as insulting to the chef, which is true, especially socially. However, more importantly, in business, this holds an even greater significance: one is viewed as rushing to judgment... making the big decision before evaluating the many details, e.g., "Does this require something else (i.e., more salt/pepper)?"

STORY

As a former member of NEHRA (Northeast Human Resources Association), esteemed H.R. directors shared with me the following:

"If a candidate makes it to the third interview, the one usually conducted over the table — breakfast, lunch or dinner (potential new employers want to evaluate your manners) and if a candidate is seen doing something as seemingly innocent as seasoning their food before tasting it,

"FACT: they will <u>not get the job</u>.

"Reason: they are rushing to judgment, making the big decision before evaluating the many details, e.g., does this require (seasoning)."

The business tie-in: what else does this person take the time, go to the trouble to learn about in advance, assess, evaluate, execute? The bottom line: I *trust* you, I like the way you consider things and conduct yourself, I want you to represent my firm.

Exception: the "Grande Pepper Mill." Wait staff at the finest restaurants are still trained to ask diners if they would like to try (whatever) first — before offering pepper from *le grande* pepper mill.

Passing Salt and Pepper

Yes, there is a *way* to pass salt and pepper, and showing you know how is significant.

Situation. Someone asks you to pass the salt or hand them the pepper.

Fine: Pass them the salt or hand them the pepper shaker.

Fabulous: When asked for one or the other, always pass *both*. Hold them with the first three fingers (thumb, index and third fingers) and place the salt and pepper shakers on the table by the person who requested them.

Asking to Pass Food

As always, it's not what we say, but how we say it. And, it's not what we ask, but *how* we ask.

Fine: Say, "Salt please?" or "Can I have the salt?"

Fabulous: Say, "Could I trouble you for the salt?"

Passing and Serving

- Serve on the left; clear from the right.
- Pass *counterclockwise,* left to right.

*Servers: no stacking and no scraping dishes at the table. (Guests should not do this either.) (See the section on <u>Clearing</u>, below.)

Passing Items with Handles

When passing anything with handles, pass so that the handle of the water pitcher, gravy boat, creamer, etc., faces the other person to whom you are extending the item.

Serving Platters and Placement of Serving Utensils

Think: Spoon bowl UP and fork tines DOWN.

After helping yourself:

- Reposition utensils in this form.
- Offer to hold the serving platter for the person on your right.
- Remember to pass *counterclockwise.*

- When offering to refill someone's glass from a water pitcher, wine bottle or coffee/tea pot at the table, ask "May I freshen your glass?" (rather than "refill... give you some more... top you off... heat you up..." etc.)

Soup

Soup is a food that can be tricky. For example, soup with large pieces of meat and potatoes presents questions and can be a challenge for some and an opportunity for others to *stand apart* because they know how to eat food from a soup bowl. Yes, there is a *way* to properly eat soup.

Question. Is it ever acceptable to use your fork and knife when eating soup?

Answer. *Jamais!* (Never)

Fine: Use a spoon.

Fabulous: Use the pointed end of your oval spoon to pierce the potatoes, large vegetables, pieces of meat, etc.

*Rule: *Never use a fork and knife to eat any kind of soup.*

Types of Soup Spoons

There are two types of soup spoons — oval and round. Oval spoons have a point and are used when a point can help cut through, i.e., the thick cheese of French onion soup *au gratin*, potatoes, vegetables or meat.

How to Hold a Soup Spoon

Fine: Hold like an oar.

Fabulous: Hold the soup spoon like a *pencil.*

How to Eat Soup

Fine: Bring the soup spoon to your mouth and blow on this if it is too hot; slurping is okay. (Only in China is this ever fine!)

Fabulous:

1. Spoon *away*, then lightly tap excess on top of the outer edge of your soup bowl.

2. Bring the spoon from the soup bowl UP, vertically, and then IN, horizontally, to your lips (no teeth).

3. Keep your neck straight, head up and check your good posture.
4. Then: Sip the Soup from the Side of the Spoon (not the tip of the spoon with soup).
5. NO slurping or blowing (unless you're in China)... and no dunking (bread) either!

Situation. You want that last bit of soup:

Fine: Drink it from the bowl.

Fabulous: Tip the soup bowl *away* from you and spoon *away* to get the last drop of soup.

"I am Resting" and "I am Finished" Position (For Soup)

(This is not correct)   *(This is correct)*

Fine: Randomly rest the spoon in the cup or bowl when you are resting or finished.

Fabulous: The "I am resting" and "I am finished" position are exactly the same for soup: rest your spoon in the 10:20 o'clock position.

When the soup is in a cup and "high," rest the spoon on the soup <u>plate</u>; when the soup is in a bowl and is "low"/ flat, rest the spoon on the low soup <u>bowl</u> itself.

Keeping Dining Utensils

When only one of each utensil is provided (i.e., one fork and one knife) and there are multiple courses, while this presents a challenge, it also presents an opportunity to *stand apart*.

Fine: Hold onto your silverware while courses are changed.

(This: ONLY if you are a guest in someone's home.)

Fabulous: Let wait staff take utensils and politely ask them to replace silverware for the next course.

Saying "Please" and "Thank You"

Fine: Say "Thank you" for every service performed.

Fabulous: It is NOT necessary to thank wait staff for every single service performed. Let your verbal expression, or head nod of thanks acknowledge the service. For example, saying "thank you" for clearing your every plate is not necessary, however, thanking the wait staff for bringing you something unexpected is gracious.

More Food Tips

Sharing/Sampling Food

Sharing food is delicate and also presents an *opportunity* for the savvy diner to *stand apart*.

Fine: Sharing or sampling food is acceptable. Go for it.

Fabulous: Sharing food is fairly intimate and so, with those you know well or feel comfortable *socially*, this is fine. However, if a *client* asks to taste your (i.e.) Dover sole, please know there is a *way* to share/sample food:

Ask them to pass you their bread and butter dish and, before you taste anything, cut off a small portion and place this on their bread and butter dish.

Finishing the Last Bit of Food?

Taking the last bite of anything is taboo and virtually instilled in most of us: *Don't Take the Last Donut*! (Sorry, I couldn't resist!) We never need to be reminded, we just somehow instinctively know enough not to. However, guidelines evolve and are even redefined. Knowing yea or nay is empowering and presents another opportunity to *stand apart*.

Fine: Leave something on your plate. You don't want to appear ill-bred or underfed.

Fabulous: It *used* to be that eating everything on your plate was considered gauche. However, these days especially, due to the *très cher* cost of entrées (and perhaps a more healthy respect for food), if we want to finish everything on our plate, we should feel free to do so. *Bon Appétit!*

Finishing the Last Bit of Sauce/Gravy

There are many amazing chefs who prepare the most delicious foods, scrumptious sauces and gravies that everyone wants to get the very last drop. Well, there is a way to do so:

Fine: Take a piece of bread in your hand and swab it up.

Fabulous: Break off a bite-size piece of bread and pierce this with your fork which you will use to absorb remnants of the fine sauce/gravy. (But remember, DO NOT do this with your soup!)

*Note: If you want the escargot (garlic and wine), pierce bread with the escargot fork. If you would like a gravy accompanying your entrée, pierce bread with the entrée fork, etc.

Excusing Yourself from the Table

Yes, there is a *way* to excuse yourself politely from the table and return! Doing so shows you know "the difference" and will help you *stand apart*.

Fine: Announce your departure to all those at your table and say, "Excuse me. I have to go to the bathroom."

Fabulous: Quietly excuse yourself with persons on either side of you, and/or those with whom you have been speaking. <u>There is no need to say where you are going or why</u>. "Excuse me" is sufficient. If you feel compelled to say something, the word "restroom" is a step up from "bathroom," or simply say, "Excuse me while I *freshen*."

Fabulous: A woman is never seen without her purse when going to freshen. Should she visit the restroom without her purse it is obvious she is going to use a stall, which is no one's business.

Remember napkin etiquette here: dab both sides of your lips and leave your napkin loosely folded in your *chair*. Exit and re-enter from the chair's RIGHT.

Ladies Excusing Themselves from the Table

*Rule: *Whenever a lady excuses herself from the dining table and returns, gentlemen STAND.*

Situation. A woman at your table stands to excuse herself and no one else stands, not her spouse/significant other, nor even the gentleman host. You, gentleman guest, know enough to stand when a woman is excusing herself from and returning to the table. *Question*: Should you stand — showing respect for the woman and upholding your high standards, at the risk of possibly upstaging spouse/significant-other and your host, or not?

Fine: Do not stand.

Fabulous: This potentially awkward situation presents a terrific opportunity to shine and be **fabulous**. When a lady excuses herself from the table and returns, gentlemen should rise, of course, out of respect.

The Half-Stand

The answer in this situation: the common practice known as the *half-stand* is appropriate. Arise halfway from your chair as the woman leaves, and again as she returns to the table. In so doing, you show respect for the woman and maintain your (high) standards without disparaging or possibly upstaging her spouse/significant other or your host in any way, while still demonstrating you know "the difference."

> *"Being **fabulous** is rising when a woman arrives or departs from a table."*
> **—Matt Schiffman**

Applying Lipstick / Makeup at the Table

Fine: Apply lipstick or makeup at the table as long as it is done quickly.

Fabulous: Do NOT apply makeup or lipstick at the table, ladies (or gentlemen, chapstick). This is considered part of personal hygiene and should be done in the privacy of the restroom.

Making Conversation with Low-Key Individuals

Situation. You are in a spirited discussion with the person on your left. However, the person on your right is not responding and appears bored or uninterested.

Fine: Try to make conversation by sharing things about yourself and keep the conversation going as best you can.

Fabulous: It is the responsibility of all diners to contribute to table-talk conversation. This includes speaking with those seated on either side, despite challenges with low-key individuals. Try summarizing and asking open-ended questions specifically directed to that individual to encourage their participation.

Yes, share things about yourself; however, endeavor to make the conversation about *them*. Initiate open-ended questions using the five W's (and an H): Who, What, Where, When, Why and How. Use their names. People automatically perk up when they hear the sound of their name. Our responsibility as guest or host is to *contribute* to table-talk conversation and to be inclusive.

People like to feel valued and included. Ask their thoughts and opinions, inquire about their spouse, family, hobbies, vacation, interests, etc. Asking about family members and loved ones by name demonstrates thoughtfulness and makes others feel they must be special to you. This line of questioning reflects well on you… except in some countries, where it may be seen as intrusive or meddling. Do your research here.

Note: Remember, do not eat while another is revealing information or sharing a story. Listen to and focus on them, not your food. Be attentive and use active listening skills and body language to convey genuine interest.

STORY

When Tim Russert (*Meet the Press*) passed away, every person who spoke on his behalf mentioned they never had a conversation with Mr. Russert when he did NOT ask (by name) about their son, daughter, spouse, etc., which deeply endeared Tim Russert to many people.

Conversation Topics

Avoid off-color jokes and vulgar language. Safe topics include books, authors, plays, movies, television shows, etc. Topics of religion, politics, sex and personal health or finance issues remain taboo today… particularly politics. Even though politics is current events, it is dangerous territory and could cost you the relationship as well as a business opportunity. It is wise to stay away from these topics.

Personal Information

Be sure to write down personal information gleaned or topics discussed while fresh in your mind, shortly after your time together. Use this information in subsequent communication. Doing so shows others they are important to you (you remembered!) and will help advance the relationship.

Difficult Situations

Sending Food Back

Situation. Your food arrives and is not cooked to your specifications.

Fine: Tell the wait staff to send it back.

Fabulous: Keep the entrée to avoid any awkwardness or undue attention. Never send anything back and never complain about your food in business, in front of a client. Eat what you can of the entrée and focus on vegetables, potatoes, etc.

FIRST PERSON

I once attended a business dinner where one of the participants sent back their filet because it was undercooked. By the time the steak was re-cooked and re-presented at the table, the rest of the guests were beginning their dessert course. This guest's steak may have ultimately been cooked to specification, however, at what price? This guest was not in sync with the rest of the diners and the absence of their entrée was conspicuous, not to mention distracting.

Remember, none of us is invited anywhere because someone thinks we need to be fed! People and other guests should be the primary focus, not the food.

Gristle, Pits, etc.
Situation. You are eating and come to gristle. What to do?

    Fine: Place gristle in your napkin or swallow quickly!

    Rule: *The way it goes in (to your mouth) is the way it comes out.*

    Fabulous: Therefore, if you used your fork to take this uncertain bite, discreetly place the gristle on your fork and then place the gristle on the side of your plate *sans* comment. If you used a spoon to eat a date and come to the pit of the date, place the pit on your spoon and place the pit on the side of your plate. If you used your fingers to pop an olive into your mouth, put the olive pit in your fingers and then place the pit on your plate. Do not call attention to this maneuver.

Dropping Utensils
Situation. You drop a utensil.

    Fine: Immediately pick it up off the floor.

    Fabulous: Pick the utensil up off the floor ONLY if you are a guest in someone's home. Otherwise, in a restaurant, ask your wait staff to have the utensil replaced.

Handling Accidents
The less said and the less fuss over any *faux pas* or accidents at the table by fellow diners, the better. The wait staff are fully trained in handling accidents.

The Disappearing Wait Staff
Waiters seem to frustratingly disappear (and we feel abandoned) at the most inopportune times. How to get their attention:

    Fine: Snap your fingers or shout out, "Hey! Garcon!"

    Fine: Wave your arms in the air to get their attention.

    Fine: Leave your table and search for your wait staff.

    Fabulous: You know your wait staff's name; therefore *use* it to get their attention while subtly extending the wrist to make the proverbial "two-finger wave," or, if they are completely out of view, signal the *maitre d'*, host or another member of the restaurant staff in a similar fashion and ask them to summon your wait staff.

    *Always treat staff with the utmost respect.

Coffee, Tea, Dessert
Dessert presents another opportunity to show your adventurous, even playful side, share personal preferences (and learn theirs), open a more intimate dialogue, and have some fun. After all dinner food has been cleared, "coffee/tea/dessert" time is when we tend to let down our guard and "real talk" usually begins.

Situation. Everyone at your table orders coffee, tea, dessert, and you do not care for anything.

Fine: Say, "No thank you."

Fabulous: As with the meal, order "course for course" or coffee/tea/dessert to their coffee/tea/dessert.

Elbows on the Table?

*Rule: *Once food has been removed, this is the only time, technically speaking, when it is protocolically permissible to rest elbows on the table.* After dessert, for example, it is acceptable to sit and chat over coffee or an after-dinner cordial with elbows ON the table.

After-Dinner Cordials

As always, when it comes to alcoholic beverages, many people do not drink for many reasons and there is no pressure — ever — to order an after-dinner cordial if you do not care for one. Feel free to continue drinking your tea or coffee while they have the beverage they prefer.

If others have ordered an after-dinner drink and you care to have one as well, order one so you stay on the same time frame. Similarly, if no one else is ordering, you should not be the only person to order an after-dinner cordial as you will stand apart (not in a positive way). This will also be awkward and affect time.

Coffee/Cream/Sugar:

Fine: Add cream and sugar as you normally would.

Fabulous: Pour a little cream into the coffee cup before the coffee is poured, as this absorbs any bitterness from the coffee. Add more cream if needed.

STORY: APPROACHING ANOTHER AT THEIR TABLE

I am frequently asked, "How should hosts conduct themselves when a perfect stranger approaches them at the table where they are hosting a full table of guests?"

By way of answering the question I enjoy sharing this story:

President George Bush (41) was coming to Boston (!) where he was offering the keynote address for the World Affairs Council, of which I was a member. I bought a table. As I entered the ballroom filled with tables, I was trying to identify my table when I noticed that one of my invited guests was speaking with the President! I saw them disengage and I said to my guest, "Do you know him?" to which he replied, "Yes!"

Question. How do we meet the highly sought after individual?

Answer. Through the mutually respected third party.

Moi: "Will you introduce me?"

Him: "But of course!"

As we began to walk over to the President, several things happened almost simultaneously:

- The Secret Service were instantly on high alert (i.e., "Woman approaching at 10 o'clock").
- The President noticed his friend approaching his table, me in tow.
- The friend nodded to the President, referring to me.
- The President gave a silent signal to the friend and the Secret Service that this was fine.
- The friend gestured and turned back to our table.

Then President Bush graciously excused himself from his guests and stood, as I approached. I extended my hand and introduced myself. I would like to tell you that President Bush and I "had the best conversation" — when in fact this wasn't really a "conversation." President Bush expertly asked me all open-ended questions about me — my company, my business, my work... making me feel incredibly special! (See Conversation Skills above.) We then exchanged pleasantries, once again shook hands and President Bush returned to his guests and assumed his host duties.

If the President of the United States can do this — for a perfect stranger — let this be an example to all of us from which we can take a cue!

Sugar Packets
Empty the sugar and fold the empty sugar packet in half and place UNDER your cup and saucer (not ON the saucer).

Refusing Coffee
Fine: Turn your coffee cup over. (Actually, this is not fine, except perhaps at a low-end chain restaurant!)

Fabulous: The two-finger wave: tilt and wave your first two fingers (index and third finger) over your *upright* coffee cup to signal that you pass on coffee.

Refusing Champagne/Dessert Drinks
Fine: Politely say, "No, thank you... I have had enough!" (Or "None for me, thank you.")

Fabulous: Again, the two-finger wave.

You Are Finished
Use the *Silent Service Code* to signal you are finished. Pace yourself with other diners and do not be the first or last to finish eating.

Dab lips with your napkin and place napkin to the LEFT of your dessert plate.

(See above regarding American and Continental *Silent Service Code* on how to position your silverware to let staff that you are finished eating, and for *Napkins* and *Soup*.)

General Rule: Allow the host to lead.

When to Make a Presentation During the Meal

As noted in the section above regarding <u>Discussing Business at the Table</u>, often a business meal is scheduled to include a brief pitch or product presentation. When to make a presentation presents a quandary for some and an opportunity for others, and we should consider the timing of delivery.

Fine: Make the pitch whenever you see an opening.

Fabulous: There are no hard and fast rules governing when a presentation should take place. However, please consider the following:

- If you decide to wait until *after* the meal, you risk running out of time and losing people.
- If you present mid-course, *during* the meal, you risk interrupting conversation flow and dining.

Therefore, we suggest making the presentation *before* you eat so that you do not run over time and are able to address any unanswered questions during the course of the meal. Making the presentation before the repast also ensures you do not run over time or conclude with unanswered questions. This helps control the course of the luncheon to help ensure the most productive use of your time together.

Luncheon presentations should be especially brief and concise.

Distributing Support Material

Distributing support material presents another opportunity to *stand apart* while reinforcing the company brand and reflecting well on you. How, when and where to distribute support material should be considered.

Fine: Bring handouts neatly clipped together and make available on a credenza (in a private dining room) for those to take as they depart.

Fabulous: Present well-put together handouts in a personalized quality case, folder or other attractive covering.

How, when and where to distribute is entirely subjective and ultimately depends upon whether guests will require handouts during the course of your luncheon presentation, or if they are intended as a take-away.

Handouts should not be overwhelming or cumbersome.

Toasting

The Number One Rule: When the toast is being proposed to you in your honor, never drink to yourself!

Toasting — who toasts, when to toast and how, present several more opportunities to *stand apart* as you welcome guests, honor your person of honor, thank those at your table for attending, rise to speak… and more than just the wine will sparkle!

Hosts:

Fine: Anyone may offer a toast.

Fabulous: Proposing a toast is one of many host responsibilities and toasting (and roasting) takes practice. It is wise to have something prepared in advance of any occasion where you believe there may be the most remote chance you will be either be proposing or accepting a toast.

Guests:

In the event that your host does not step up, anyone may and should take the lead as proposing a toast is gracious, civilized and appreciated. Taking this initiative reflects exceedingly well on that individual.

FIRST PERSON

A client once shared with me the story that when, after a long day with the president of his company and their team, the president suggested they all go out to dinner and celebrate a successful day in the trenches. Cocktails were served as a prelude to dinner and the president made no attempt to propose a toast. My client gallantly took the lead and began to propose a toast to their successful day when the president abruptly cut him off and told him he would propose the toast.

A **fabulous** host knows how and when to toast… and will do so!

Types and Levels of Toasting

There are two *types* of toasts and four *levels* of toasting.

1. The first type of toast is less formal and is offered at the start of the meal. The host may sit or stand, hold (a stemmed) glass by the stem with the first three fingers (thumb, index and third) — never use "the death grip" to hold the glass — make eye-contact with everyone at your table, welcome and thank guests for coming, say "Cheers!" or "*Salute!*"

2. The second type of toast is more formal and offered at the beginning of dessert when champagne is typically served:
   - The host will rise.
   - Stand behind their chair (enter and exit the chair's right).
   - Assume the *Presidential Pose* (left arm behind back).
   - Hold the champagne flute with the first three fingers on the stem, near to the base of the flute. (See above, How to Hold Glasses.)
   - Make excellent eye-contact with everyone at the table.

- Demonstrate respectful body language with particular focus toward the person of honor being toasted.
- Propose this, the formal toast to the *person of honor* (seated to the host's right).

When you are being toasted, after your host has finished speaking, wait and do NOT DRINK. It is then your responsibility to graciously *accept* the toast:

Accepting a Formal Toast
- Exit/enter the chair's right and stand *behind* your chair.
- Assume the *Presidential Pose* (left arm behind back).
- Hold a stemmed glass with the first three fingers on the stem, near to the base of the flute. (See above, <u>How to Hold Glasses</u>.)
- Graciously accept the toast. Lean in and make good eye-contact with your host/s as well as everyone at your table; speak confidently.
- Be seated, and then, and only then, may you finally…
- Drink!

Four Levels of Toasting
1. The most formal toasting etiquette suggests that one NOT *touch* glasses at all! Rather, strong eye-contact is absolutely essential here.
2. The second, less formal toasting etiquette suggests you *touch* glasses only with persons on either side of you.
3. That said, if everyone at your table is doing a "skol!" and crashing glasses at the center of the table with a big soccer cheer, by all means, go along. Remember, we embrace the notion: "the beauty in knowing the rules is knowing when it is okay to break them!" Break the rules and skol-away!
4. The "kiss-kiss" has three steps:
   - One, touch.
   - Two, touch and kiss UP.
   - Three, make eye-contact!

The "kiss-kiss" is very special. This can be done cross-gender, at any time and is **fabulous***!* (*Note*: There is no actual "kiss" here. This is merely an endearing term describing how the glasses "kiss-kiss" as you gently touch first the rims together, then the base of the toaster's glass to the rim of the person receiving the toast.)

Take the initiative to propose a toast. So few people do so these days that the sheer act of proposing a toast is gracious and enables you to *stand apart* in all the most positive ways.

Practice and have a generic toast at the ready which you can use anywhere with anyone. Consider something such as, "I would like to propose a toast to old friends and new! Cheers!" Or, "Reach for the farthest end of the branch, for this is where you will find the sweetest fruit."

Note: These days it is acceptable these days to toast with water, juice, milk, etc. as opposed to formerly, when only alcohol was considered proper.

Voice Volume

Conversation tones, loud laughter, etc., should be considered at restaurants and clubs.

Fine: Speak as you normally would (at the table), even if you happen to be loud.

Fabulous: Show respect and exercise consideration of nearby diners. Speak in lower voice volumes, especially when discussing sensitive business or personal issues.

Clearing

Yes, there are guidelines here, as well. Clearing dishes and debris is very specific.

Rule: *Never clear a table unless/until everyone at the table has finished eating.*

Situation. An ambitious wait staff begins to clear plates before everyone at the table has finished eating.

Fine: Wait staff will politely ask diners if they are finished and then clear, stack and scrape plates at the table.

Fabulous: A **fabulous** host has the responsibility to ensure everyone at the table has finished eating before their table is cleared.

Avoid this common *faux pas* and take *control* of your table by simply respectfully suggesting to your wait staff (using their name/s) that they wait until everyone at the table has finished eating.

It is important to demonstrate respect for the wait staff, maintain control of your table and ultimately help ensure your guests' positive dining experience.

*Stacking/scraping at the table is never permissible (unless you are in a private home). You are not helping the wait staff by stacking your plates; they should not stack plates, either.

Exception: A large banquet, where it would clearly make more sense to clear plates as soon as the wait staff notices guests are finished. In this case, the host should *acknowledge* this breach.

Being Remembered

Fine: A thoughtful host will ask to be remembered to those who wait (for your guest) at home.

Fabulous: Actions speak louder than words. A *fabulous* host will automatically send an entrée home to (name of) person waiting. Do not ask. Ascertain their entrée preference and just do it. This costs nothing other than the price of the entrée and goes a long way in terms of building good will and having positive name recognition at home!

Doggie Bags

Question. Is it appropriate to ask for a "doggie bag?"

Answer. The term "doggie bag" is a bit archaic, however, please note the following:

Fine: Ask for a "doggie bag."

Fabulous: Socially, it is fine to ask to have something *wrapped*. In business, *Jamais!* Never ask. However, should your *client* like to take the remnants of their dinner home, tell your wait staff you would like the item "*Wrapped*, please." These days, many restaurants have beautiful wrappings and containers.

Handling the Check... Skillfully

The check arrives, and it is always a bit… awkward! How you handle the check and avert this potentially awkward situation presents yet another stellar opportunity for hosts to *stand apart*.

Fine: The host is responsible for the check. When the check arrives at the table be sure this is presented to you.

Fabulous: A *fabulous* host will eliminate any remote chance of an awkward moment at their table. Even though it is presumed that the host will take care of the check, a *fabulous* host will handle the check in advance as follows:

Please note: Upon arrival, the *fabulous* host will have presented their credit card to the restaurant host or *maitre d'* and say: "Under no circumstances should the check be presented to the table." Instruct them to have the standard service charge (20–22 percent) added to your bill.

After all the dessert, coffee, after-dinner cordials, etc. have been ordered, quietly excuse yourself from the table (as stated previously, there is no need to say where you are going).

Find wait staff and sign the check, add the gratuity if this has not already been included, and sign the check.

The check is never presented at the table. Gracious and attentive wait staff will thank guests for coming and express hopes of a return visit soon.

*Those in the hospitality industry are trained to respond extremely graciously and even extend VIP treatment to those who make this their practice which makes guests feel even more special, another positive reflection on you, their *fabulous* host.

The Check — When You Are the Guest

Guests are "invited" and of course it is expected that the host will handle the check.

Fine: Sit politely and take comfort in knowing the bill is not your concern, the host will handle the check and this is solely their responsibility.

Fabulous: The check is clearly the responsibility of the host and the host alone. However, a **fabulous** guest will *acknowledge* the check and make the *gesture* of offering to pay their share. Of course the host will never entertain this offer, however, the gesture is unexpected and a positive reflection on you, gracious guest.

Table Manners

Question. Is it necessary to use my formal table manners when eating with someone who has no manners, or if I am eating at a low-end chain restaurant versus an upscale restaurant?

Fine: Observe and match table manners of your dining companion in order to be on the same "level."

Fabulous: We are talking about your manners here — not casual Friday and dressing down. Your manners are part of who you *are*. Always maintain your standards and good dining manners wherever and with whomever you dine — including your own kitchen, every day.

Global Dining

Recognize the inherent role that food plays in the business culture. In some countries meals and banquets may be part of the celebration, the negotiation process, even the gift. In still other countries, food is consumed only after terms of the agreement/negotiation have been set. Be aware that "good manners" are relative: in some cultures, burping and slurping is polite, complimentary and shows appreciation; resting elbows on the table is acceptable in other countries.

Understanding what is expected and acceptable as you sit down prior to any business meal in your target country reflects well on you. Research your target country and when in doubt, follow your host's lead, and never hesitate to consult with your mutually respected third party. When in doubt, ask. Asking is a sign of respect, not ignorance, and it will endear you to your host(s) as they recognize your sincere effort to learn and practice their customs.

What to Eat

Fine: Eat only that which appeals to you.

Fabulous: Understand that different cultures present the opportunity to appreciate different foods. Be aware that not eating foods in certain cultures is considered insulting. Again, follow your host's lead, and generally speaking, try everything presented. There may be times when you must swallow quickly!

STORY

On my first international assignment in China, I recall one of the many incredibly lavish luncheons hosted in our honor. My gentleman colleague was seated as the guest of honor to our host's right (women are still working hard to achieve equal status in China).

Course after course was served to the entire table, when one particularly rare and exotic delicacy was presented to my gentleman colleague exclusively as the person of honor. Much whispering then ensued between my colleague and the service staff, whereupon the service staff removed the delicacy and re-presented this to our esteemed host.

I leaned over and quietly asked my colleague what was going on. He explained, "Judy, I may be Chinese, but there are certain things even I cannot eat." He said, "I deferred the honor to our host." It was then that I discovered the gracious art of "deferring the honor"!

Difficult-to-Eat Foods

Fine: Most people know to avoid ordering difficult-to-eat foods such as spaghetti, lobster, pizza while dining with business clients for obvious reasons.

Fabulous: This is a given. A **fabulous** host is further aware of any guest food restrictions, diets, allergies, etc., and makes special plans to accommodate, accordingly.

How to Eat Difficult Foods

First, please know that ordering anything challenging, such as ribs, finger food, lobster and even pizza, can be a potential dining hazard. Remember, we are not there to eat. Order easy-to-eat items during the business meal.

More tips:

- *Hamburger (like a sandwich)*: Cut in half, and using a fork and knife is "never wrong."
- *Pizza*: Once again, using a fork and knife is "never wrong" and easier to manage, particularly if pizza has multiple toppings or is *deep dish* or *Chicago style*. Authentic *Italian style* suggests a thin crust pizza, to be eaten by folding the triangular piece in half and eating beginning from the smallest point up to the crust.
- *Soup*: Hold the soup spoon like a pencil. Spoon away from your body and lightly tap excess soup from the spoon onto the outer edge of your soup bowl. Sip the soup from the side (not the point) of the spoon; no slurping or blowing.

- *Fish Knife*: Hold this like a pencil and fold the delicate fish onto the back tines of the fork; there is no need to use a sharp serrated edge to cut delicate fish.
- *Napkin Bib*: Placing a napkin as a bib around your neck applies only to small children; adults should refrain from such a practice.
- *Lobsters*: Bib or no bib? Yes, for lobsters using a bib is acceptable. In fact, many restaurants will go to great lengths to ritually place the bib on their guest and make every effort to help prevent potential disasters which typically occur when eating lobster, unless you are very adept.
- *Donuts*: Dunking donuts in coffee is reserved only for the privacy of your own home. *Soup*: No dunking bread in public.
- *Sauces*: It is permissible to soak up sauces with your bread, however, as always, there is a *way* to do so:
  - Break off a small, thumb-nail size bite from your roll.
  - Pierce this with your fork.
  - Using the bread on your fork, soak up the **fabulous** sauce.
- *Condiments*: Ideally, condiments should be served in a separate container with a small spoon. Use the spoon to place condiments on your plate, and dip your food into the condiments on your *plate*, not in the service container.
- *Salad*: Ideally, salad should be prepared so that lettuce pieces need not be cut, however, if not, it is acceptable to use your salad knife. *Bread and Butter*: Break the role into a thumb-nail, bite-size piece and butter one piece at a time, over the bread and butter plate, using your individual butter spreader.
- *Foiled Butter*: Use your individual butter spreader to scrape butter off the foil. Empty, then fold the foil in half and insert UNDER (not on) your bread and butter plate.
- *Grapefruit Half*: Ideally, sections should be pre-cut and served with a regular spoon. If not, a serrated spoon should be provided.

Tea vs. High Tea

"Tea" is one of those age-old, lovely, very civilized traditions that remains not only alive but thriving, both as a social tradition and an alternative business forum. Afternoon Tea has experienced renewed popularity today.

Fabulous: Suggest you meet for "Afternoon Tea," a chic, less expensive form of business entertaining.

The timing of "Tea meetings," e.g., 3:00 P.M. to 5:00 P.M., is such that most people can get away for an hour in the late afternoon and does not cut into private or family time. Tea is also a less expensive form of entertaining. Regardless of what the dining establishment calls it — "Tea" or "High Tea" — know there are two types of tea and two ways to serve tea.

First, A Bit of History:

Correct behavior dictated that ladies not eat much at regular meals in the 1800's and so the Duchess of Bedford, England felt the need for a "little something" in between lunch (served at 12:00 noon) and dinner (not served until 8:30 or 9:00 P.M.). At first, she would sneak cookies but then decided to invite her friends and make it fashionable.

Interestingly, "High Tea" is the *less* formal of teas, and was actually the dinner meal for the common people. Much more substantial food is served on a *high* table, hence the term "High Tea." While tea was always served, in addition there would also be meats, fish or eggs, cheese, bread and butter, and cake.

Today, "tea" is typically served with scones, dainty finger sandwiches, sweet cakes, and pastries, on small *low* tables. (Clearly, due to class connotations, the term "low tea" did not catch on!) A silver tea service, porcelain china, tea leaves from around the world are all part of the wonderful "tea" tradition which remains quite fashionable today.

The Wenham Tea House in Wenham, Massachusetts is the oldest tea house in this country and one of my favorite places to visit and revisit this tradition, which they continue to uphold so beautifully today.

Making Tea

Offer a selection of tea leaves from around the world. Use a tea leaf strainer or tea ball. Steep the tea well! If using a tea ball, remove once tea is brewed to prevent bitterness.

Tea Bags

Fine: Let tea bags stay in the tea cup and brew. (Not fine; tea will become bitter.)

Fabulous: Remove tea bags by lifting the tab of the tea bag so the tea bag rests on the front of the teaspoon. Wrap the string around the tea bag and spoon thrice. Then, using your thumb and index finger, guide the paper tab/tea bag off the spoon. Detach and rest the tea bag onto the saucer (or a tea bag holder if available).

Serving Tea

Fine: Serve tea in Styrofoam or paper cups.

Fine*:* Serve tea in a large coffee mug.

Fabulous: Use porcelain or a silver tea service with teacups and saucers.

Serve with scones, dainty finger sandwiches, sweet cakes, pastries on small lower tables.

STORY

It has been said that when Jacqueline Bouvier surprised then-Senator John F. Kennedy with lunch service on a cart with a silver tea service — that was the clincher — he proposed!

Ending the Meal

Gathering Overcoats

Fine: Guests should attend to their own coats and outerwear.

Fabulous: A **fabulous** host will take care of tipping the coat check on behalf of all guests, and assist guests on and off with their overcoats, or they will have designated someone to assist.

Leaving

How you bid *adieu* presents yet another opportunity to distinguish yourself.

Fine: Thank guests for coming and part company.

Fabulous: A **fabulous** host will personally walk guests to the restaurant door, and on to their cars (or a pre-arranged car service or taxi). Take advantage of this time and use it as an opportunity to engage in "real talk" to help advance the relationship.

Thank You Notes

Sending thank you notes facilitates another positive impression of you and your brand and, of course, "repetition is reputation!"

Fine: Send an email note of thanks.

Fabulous: Send a quick email note of thanks (only if you know this individual represents an e-culture person) and then:

- Follow-up with the timeless, traditional, handwritten note using your personal stationery.
- Use blue ink for social correspondence and black ink for business correspondence.
- Use a postage stamp versus meter; they are not "bulk" (mail).
- Personalize the note with something personal.
- Send notes the same day or within 48 hours; the longer you delay, the less impact the gesture holds.

Dining with Disabled ("Differently Abled") Persons

We are all conscious of not wanting to offend our guests who may arrive in a wheelchair, use a cane, or have issues with limited sight, hearing, etc. It is never wrong to inquire politely if there is anything you can do to make your guest more comfortable. Equally, if you (the host) are in a wheelchair, have a cane, are blind, deaf, etc. — make your preferences known upfront so that your guests feel comfortable and do not "walk on eggshells" for fear of offending you unintentionally.

Wheelchairs

There are no hard and fast rules; be guided by personal preference. While some would rather remain in their wheelchairs, others prefer to sit in chairs. The astute host is aware of this opportunity to show they care, respect their situation and *stand apart*. My brother Peter, past Director of the Spina Bifida Association, State of Washington, who has always been in a wheelchair, offers the following **Fabulous** tips:

Fine: Assume your guest prefers to remain in their wheelchair.

Fabulous:

- *Ask,* "Would you like to sit in a chair?"
- When addressing disabled persons, speak to them directly and not to their attendants (if they are accompanied by them).
- Physically disabled persons are not hard of hearing. We do not have to speak loudly for them to understand us.
- Kneel down or sit on a chair when speaking with them so that you will be on the same (eye) level. This shows respect and that you are not just patronizing or paying them lip service.

Positioning Wheelchairs (at the Table)

Fine: Wherever wheelchair best logistically fits.

Fabulous: Position wheelchairs wherever the person is most *comfortable*; typically, at the head of the table or, near an entrance/exit.

*Most restaurants, movie theatres and churches have designated areas for disabled individuals to provide easy access… it's the law!

Canes, Walkers, Crutches

Fine: Assume people want their walking aids out of the way, and out of sight.

Fabulous: *Ask* — "Would you like me to take your (i.e.) cane or would you prefer to keep this with you?"

Visually Impaired / Blind

Specially trained service dogs are legal, even in restaurants that do not permit dogs.

****Rule**: Do not talk to, pet, feed or distract service dogs; they are on duty.*

When the Menu is Not in Braille:

Fabulous: *Ask* — "Would you like me to read (you) some of the menu items?"

Hearing Impaired / Deaf

Be aware of ambient noise when selecting the dining location. Noisy restaurants make it harder to hear. If your guest has a hearing aid, or indicates that they can hear better from one side or the other, take the seat on that side so that they can better hear you (without having to raise your voice). Remember to *Ask*.

Position yourself so your guest can easily read your lips, or view their sign language interpreter. Remember to speak to your guest, not the interpreter (as with foreign language interpreters).

CHAPTER 10

Fabulous @ Business Travel & International Etiquette

Business Travel

There was a time when travel was exciting and glamorous — when flight attendants were extremely polite, overly attentive, even nurturing, and travelers were excited as they anticipated their trip, dressing fashionably for this special event. The terrorist attacks of September 11th and other very real 21st century events have changed everything. The emphasis at airports and other transportation hubs today is not service but safety; travel clothes focus on functionality (can you quickly remove and replace your shoes and jacket?) and comfort, rather than high style.

The dynamics of air travel, including expectations and the overall travel experience, have shifted. Delays, cancellations and baggage inspections are commonplace, and procedures we could never have imagined a few years ago — such as pat-downs, body screenings and even confiscating toiletries and drinks — are real. As a result, emotions run high, tempers can ignite quickly and we have seen that travel today can bring out the *worst* in human nature. All that said, we assert that business travel is a journey in and of itself which presents many opportunities we urge you to embrace and leverage to expand your horizons (*double entendre*) — *stand apart* and be a **fabulous** business traveler anywhere in the world.

Time Concerns

So much *time* is involved in travel — arriving hours early, waiting in long lines, frequent delays, countless cancelations and menacing security clearances — that many view travel time as lost time. To others, travel time is down time, time to catch-up, re-charge or just time to *veg out*. You are out and among new people... however, remember that it is not uncommon to run into those you know!

STORY

My husband and I went to Italy for our honeymoon and, unbeknownst to us, one of my former roommates from college, her husband and children turned out to be on the same flight!

In any event, we suggest that the **fabulous** traveler consider business travel as a journey unto itself, and use this as an opportunity to fortify one's inner circle. Choose to enjoy the journey and the entire travel experience! This way, whether you are biding your time or frantically dashing to make your next travel connection, you may just end up making an important business or life connection.

Wherever we are — at the airline check-in, the car rental desk or the boarding area, getting a newspaper or a sandwich — we have the opportunity to extend ourselves. Whether this means exchanging a simple "hello" or a smile, offering your assistance or a thoughtful compliment, embrace the opportunity to help make business travel a more pleasant experience for yourself and others, as well as meet and connect with individuals you would never otherwise have the opportunity to meet.

Fine: Expect long lines, delays, rude people and get through it. Grit your teeth and read a magazine, ignoring everything going on around you.

Fabulous: *Attitude adjustment!* Approach business travel with a positive attitude and decide to make this a positive experience. Make a conscious effort to display unexpected courtesies and show respect toward others you encounter anywhere including restaurants, gift shops, restrooms and especially toward overworked airline personnel. At times most challenging, embrace your new mantra: *Grace Under Pressure!*

Nuances Matter

Small things count:

- *Look* at the person who just assisted you.
- *Thank* them, even if it feels awkward thanking someone who just inspected your personal belongings.
- A *smile* goes a long way and is appreciated especially by those behind the counters, because so few people do.

- *Greet* gate agents.
- Extend small gestures of *courtesy* to fellow travelers.

When you extend courtesies and project an upbeat attitude this is not only appreciated but *infectious!* You will truly begin to personally experience the familiar adages, "What goes around comes around," and "You reap what you sow."

Hotel Check-In

After a long journey, you arrive at your hotel anxious to get to your room. The check-in process presents another opportunity to *stand apart*. Your actions and the way you treat front office staff and others will influence many things during your stay — including your assigned room!

Fine: Arrive and routinely check in at the registration desk.

Fabulous: Greet all those with whom you come in contact, from the taxi or shuttle driver, to the doorman, to the bell staff, to the concierge, etc., and tip appropriately. Say "Please" and "Thank you" like you mean it. Make small talk and make it about *them* — their well-being, their job, their day, their beautiful property. Common courtesies and something as seemingly insignificant as extending yourself to make polite chit-chat do not go unnoticed, and the rewards are immeasurable.

Situation. There is an issue checking in. Your room is not ready… they can't find your reservation… the type of room you requested is not available… you were assigned the wrong room… or you don't like your room for whatever reason. After a long journey fraught with hurdles, the last thing you want is to deal with yet another obstacle.

We all expect the room we requested, want our room to be ready when we arrive, and prefer the best room possible (or would appreciate an upgrade). There is a **fabulous** way to go about this, and you have already begun the process, simply by being cordial.

Fine: Complain and be persistent. The squeaky wheel gets greased.

Fabulous: Artfully reach into your **fabulous** arsenal and, as my husband says, "lock and load." The way you handle yourself and treat others will set off a barrage of events, the results of which, frankly, could go either way. Did the staff hear that you cursed at the cabbie, stiffed the doorman, were rude to the bell staff, had an attitude with the concierge? Or does your **fabulous** reputation precede you for being polite, courteous, respectful, appreciative, a good tipper?

Your outcome will be largely determined based on how you have conducted yourself and treated others thus far. Have you made thoughtful requests or imperious demands? Whatever we display will come back to us, therefore it is in our best interests to represent the best in human nature.

Fabulous: Keep your **fabulous** armor on and your kid gloves and continue in **fabulous** mode. Recognize this issue as an opportunity to wield your mantra: *Grace Under Pressure.*

- Display respect and convey gratitude for any consideration, however small. Be courteous, charming, polite, humble.
- Ask for their *help* (!) — a word to which most people, by human nature, innately respond.
- Be positive!
- Connect — on a personal level — so that they will *want* to help you and you will be accommodated. You will get the room change, the better view, the upgrade, and more!

Word spreads like wildfire in the hospitality industry — one way or the other. We have the ability to control our reputation and fate.

Also, the impact of saying the simplest, yet most powerful words in any language, "Please" and "Thank you," "I'm sorry" and "Excuse me," when said with sincerity, is extremely powerful and cannot be overstated (especially in High Context cultures). These, together with a smile, are *passwords* to open any door, in any language, the world over.

Plus, you never know who may be watching or listening. Suppose you "lose it" and are arrogant, rude or demanding with the hotel clerk. You may get the room change; however, at what price? You arrive at your meeting the next morning only to learn that one of your colleagues (or even the CEO) was one of those behind you in line at the hotel. Wouldn't it be better if they had witnessed **fabulous** you easily and respectfully handling a challenging issue rather than boorish, discourteous you?

Treating others with respect extends well beyond the hotel clerk, a potential employer or a prospective client at lunch. Being **fabulous** means treating everyone, every day, everywhere with respect. We need to live it every day. "Walk the walk" and "talk the talk" not only with people in the office but also with the taxi driver, the valet, the cashier, at the bank, the post office... Any interpersonal interaction holds the potential to enable a connection or collision.

Begin to consciously regard routine interpersonal interactions as opportunities to display common courtesies and show respect. Doing so makes others feel **fabulous** while reflecting well on you... and makes you look and feel pretty **fabulous**, too! Impacting another person's morning, day — *world* — in a split second costs nothing and means everything. Simple, seemingly insignificant opportunities present themselves at every turn. Acting upon these everyday situations will ingratiate you with others, strengthen and fortify relationships and reflect well on you.

> *"Being **fabulous** is having a smile for everyone regardless of pay grade."*
> **—Matt Schiffman**

Travel Attire and Luggage

When you travel, should you care about how you look, what you wear or even what luggage you use? Is any of this really important? After all, you are just traveling. You are not in the boardroom or a meeting room (yet). The answer is an emphatic *yes!* We submit that while it is fine to dress comfortably, it is **fabulous** to make the effort to dress well. While selecting travel attire, envision yourself randomly seated next to someone who happens to be a high-powered influential individual whom you would give anything to meet at any business networking event. Well, here they are and here it is — the individual, the opportunity, sitting right next to you. How do you look?

STORY

Growing up, my mother used to caution us about expecting the unexpected, even going to the grocery store. (Actually, at the time, she was referring to the potential of meeting a husband — another story for another time!)

I am acutely aware of how my attire has positively impacted me and my good fortunes in interactions with other people through the years. I am also absolutely certain I never would have had even an opening for a "hello" had I not been presentably attired — at the store, in the gift shop, on a plane, waiting for my luggage — anywhere. No how. No way.

Others do notice what we wear. Remember, 55% of us and our presentation to the world, however subliminal, is visual (Ref. *The Mehrabian Rule*). Do not let a potential business connection elude you because you chose sweats and comfort over style and looking well put-together. Let your travel attire reflect your personal statement and style.

The same can be said about your luggage. Let's say you met a V.I.P. on the plane and had a great conversation. You may have even exchanged cards and the possibility of future business together is out there. You are now both standing at the baggage claim carousel together. Will you be claiming your tattered, taped, antiquated suitcase, or let it continue to circulate? Yes, your luggage is also a reflection of you and speaks volumes.

Fabulous: Invest in quality luggage and keep this in good condition.

STORY

I remember boarding a plane once when a very distinguished gentleman who was sitting beside me made a comment about my luggage overhead. We chatted for a few moments about the particular (name brand) luggage. After making small talk, we had a most enjoyable and substantive business conversation. At the end of the flight, he offered me his business card and, as it turns out, he was a very high-ranking diplomatic official. We mutually chose to change a chance encounter and an innocuous comment into a business opportunity, and an alliance.

Would this have occurred if I had come on board dragging a well-worn backpack, dressed in a wrinkled tee shirt, flip-flops, blue jeans, or in my workout clothes? (Actually, I don't own blue jeans, I don't wear wrinkled anything and while I do have cute workout clothes, I'm sure you get the point.) I don't think so!

Tipping and Travel

You want to tip appropriately and come across as a seasoned traveler, however, it seems that tipping and the rules regarding tipping change all the time. Sometimes gratuities are included and sometimes not. Also in some countries, tipping in cash used to be considered insulting but today, especially among younger generations, not so much. The younger generations (even in High Context cultures) appear to be adopting some of our Low Context cultural ways.

While some travelers are afraid they may not be tipping enough, others are concerned that they are over-tipping. The word "tip" stands for "<u>T</u>o <u>I</u>nsure <u>P</u>romptness." Tipping is a way of saying "thank you" for services rendered in the ways that matter for exemplifying excellent service, attention and attitude. Friendliness, professionalism and efficiency are all-important. Tipping is big business in the service industry and tipping is not only appropriate but expected; however, tipping is not mandatory. When in doubt, ask.

There are some instances where a "daily service charge" is required, such as on a cruise or at a high-end resort hotel with many amenities, and this fee is often added to your daily bill. If such a gratuity is part of the (i.e., cruise) package, and you just experienced exceptional service, giving an extra gratuity is **fabulous** and goes a long way in terms of:

1. Showing your appreciation for the extra effort.
2. Helping to ensure more outstanding service/attention in the future.
3. Making you feel good, too.

(Of course, the "tippee" should always acknowledge the additional tip and be sure to say "Thank you.")

There are no absolutes in terms of who should be tipped. Feel free to offer the gesture to anyone you would like. However, generally speaking, any *service provider* should be tipped. Here are some guidelines to help you know who to tip and how much and those you need not tip:

*Tipping Rules

1. Never tip the owner/proprietor. In fact, it is their professional responsibility to tell you that they do not accept tips.
2. Never tip salaried staff or those on commission.
3. The 10% to 15% tip is dead; 18% to 22% is appropriate today in the 21st century (more for exceptional service; less, accordingly).
4. Tip 10% for a buffet (as you are doing the work of serving).
5. Do not tip on tax.
6. Extend the tip by folding the $$ in your palm and make good eye-contact. Say "Thank you" sincerely and place the $$ in their palm.
7. Service providers should graciously accept the gesture by making good eye-contact, and offer a sincere "Thank you," along with saying the tipper's name. They may

add something to the effect of, "We look forward to your return visit" or, "We look forward to the opportunity to be of service to you again soon."

Tipping at the Hotel

- Sky Cap — $2-$3 per bag, firm. Or, you may never see your bags again. Size, weight and total number of bags should also be considered.
- The Doorman — $2-$3 per bag. This amount is also contingent upon size and even the weight of bags being transferred from car/cab to inside the door.

Note: $1 is not what it used to be and can be considered insulting. This said, the elderly individual on a fixed income, for example, who offers $1 to anyone should be applauded and the service provider should accept the gesture as graciously as they would a $100 gratuity.

- Bell Staff — You are in great shape if your luggage is on wheels, but that said, this is also an opportunity to make yourself known, and to have hotel services and amenities explained. This exchange and the personal connection are as important as the physical assist. Otherwise, $2-$3/bag is appropriate and, if extras are performed such as retrieving ice, making calls on your behalf, etc., tip accordingly.
- The Doorman who hails you a cab — depending on the traffic, level of difficulty and/or your level of need. Inclement weather is also a consideration; $2-$5 to $10 or more. How much is securing a cab at this moment worth to you?
- The Valet shining your shoes — Shoes are typically delivered to your room, leaving you physically unable to tip; make the effort to find the valet in advance, or at a later time, and tip $2-5.
- Dry Cleaning (also delivered to your room) — Delivery charge is typically included in the price; not necessary to tip.
- Room Service — Because tipping room service staff has been abused, many hotels have initiated mandatory "tipping" under the guise of "room service charge" and/or "delivery charge." Your server should inform you that their gratuity has been taken care of. When in doubt ask the room service attendant or hotel manager to know their policy regarding gratuities.
- Valet Storage — Luggage/articles: usually $3-$5. Length of time in storage, number of items, size and space are also to be considered when tipping the valet for storing articles.
- Concierge — The American version of the European concierge suggests an altogether different tipping mentality: European concierges (the "s" is silent; pronounce this word the same way as the singular "concierge") rely almost exclusively on their tips. American concierges are almost always salaried individuals. One would not tip a concierge here in America for doing their job, i.e., making a restaurant reservation, providing directions, etc.

However, if the concierge performs unusual duties for you, above and beyond the norm, such as securing the impossible-to-get theatre tickets, you invariably develop a personal rapport and should tip accordingly, at the end of your stay. This cash amount should be placed in an envelope, along with your personal note of thanks, placed directly in their hand, along with your warm and sincere words of appreciation. Depending on length of stay and services performed, while $5, $10, $20 is never wrong, $50, $100 or more is entirely discretionary.

- Housekeeping — The appropriate tip for housekeeping services is $2-$5 per room per night. The general rule is that the level of tipping for housekeeping personnel would not vary regardless if you are staying at a Four Seasons or a local motel. Clearly, one needs to use common sense when applying this rule. If you were staying in a local motel with a room rate of $30 per night and little in the way of housekeeping services, $2 per night would certainly be acceptable. At the other end of the spectrum, at a Four Seasons where the room rate may exceed $300 per night and housekeeping would render substantially more services such as replenishing amenities, re-arranging toiletries, hanging up clothes, turndown service, one would clearly exceed the $2 per night guideline.

  A cautionary word regarding leaving cash in your room, assuming it will reach the appropriate housekeeping staff member. Too many people have access to your room for you to be assured your tip will indeed reach the intended individual. In fact, it may even end up inadvertently going to a new member of the housekeeping team who just came on duty. The safe course is to personally deliver your tip, placed in an envelope along with a brief note of thanks (hotel stationery is fine) directly to the housekeeper who has been caring for you and your room. In the event that you do not see this individual, you should leave this envelope with their name on it, on a desk or, an obvious location where this will be noticed. Alternatively, you may leave the envelope with the concierge or hotel manager on duty for them to pass along.

  A word here for those hotels that leave an envelope for tips for housekeeping staff: tacky. This practice is unbecoming and reflects poorly on the property.

- Engineering — It is not necessary to tip for engineering services as these are salaried individuals.

- International — Please note that tipping practices vary widely from country to country. It is advised that you research the country you are visiting to learn local practices in advance of your visit.

Restaurant Tipping Etiquette

- *Maitre d'* — There are no hard and fast rules regarding tipping the *maitre d'* and tipping is not expected, rather, discretionary. If the guest feels they have been treated especially well and made to feel special, perhaps even like "family," then a tip would be appropriate and appreciated. Amounts: $5, $10, $20 is appropriate, although in an upscale restaurant/hotel, $50 and $100 is not unusual. How much are you willing to tip to help build a solid relationship? The higher the tip, the better the relationship — and not only with the *maitre d'* — everyone in the restaurant comes to know you as a "good tipper" and will most certainly take good care of you. If you are a "regular" at a restaurant, you are probably a very good tipper.

- *Sommelier/Maitre d'* — A true *sommelier* is rare in a restaurant/hotel these days. As a general guide, tip a percentage (20%) of the bottle. Due to the physical distance of the sommelier making it more difficult to actually tip, restaurants generally pay the sommelier a higher hourly rate; tipping remains discretionary.
- Captain — The captain and wait staff frequently share tips — 18 to 22%.
- Wait Staff — When in doubt, simply write on the check — Gratuity: 22% (split captain and wait staff); more for better service, less, accordingly.

Tipping Faux Pas / Restaurant Tipping

Question. Isn't a lower percentage called for when the bill exceeds a few hundred dollars?

Answer. This notion is completely fallacious. *The size of the bill does not change the percentage of the gratuity.*

Naturally, if service is poor, one would leave a smaller tip; however, one should always communicate the reason for the lower gratuity directly to the manager. Leaving a lower tip without communicating the reason is completely inappropriate and will typically leave the establishment and the server to believe that you are cheap.

Question. How much do you tip on a bottle of wine? Is the percentage different depending on price?

Answer. There is much controversy regarding this; however, generally speaking, one would still tip approximately 20% on a $50 bottle of wine, as one would a $500 bottle. The thinking being, if one can afford the $500 bottle, they can afford to tip on this amount.

However, some restaurants have come to the rescue and addressed the topic by stating a wine tipping policy: i.e. no more than $30 or $50 tip per bottle, regardless of the price of the wine.

The argument here: why isn't the same principle applied when ordering food? Regardless of whether an entrée is priced at $12 or $45, the wait staff is performing the same service: e.g., taking the order, processing the order, making the presentation, clearing the entrée, freshening the table, etc. Yet tipping 18 — 20% of the total amount of the food portion of the bill is not an issue.

So why is there any question regarding the tip when it comes to the price of a bottle of wine? The service here is the same (with the exception of possibly making an appropriate recommendation, if there is no sommelier).

With this premise, I generally agree. However, there is a big difference between $12 vs. $45 and $50 vs. $500. Another argument: if one can afford to order a $500 bottle of wine, one can certainly afford to tip proportionately.

Personally, I feel if one would like to tip proportionally on the expensive bottle, they should do so. However, I do not feel this should be mandatory. For example for the $500 bottle of wine as mentioned above, leaving a healthy $50 to $60 tip is fine.

Question. *If I order a glass of water at the bar and there is no check, obviously, no tip is required, yes?*

Answer. Even though there is no check, you must understand that the bartender has taken as much time and provided to you the same level of service and personal attention as if you had ordered any other beverage. You should also be sensitive to the fact that by taking up a seat at the bar you are potentially costing the bartender revenue. For both of these reasons, a tip is required when ordering even water and sitting at the bar.

Gratuities are based on service, not just whether there is a bill. Take the example of the host who seats you at the best table at the restaurant with an exquisite view. Even though there is no charge specifically for this kindness to you, a tip for him or her is definitely in order. Another example is the wine steward or sommelier who is so considerate and helpful and educated that they recommend an exceptional bottle of wine for half of the price you are prepared to pay. This clearly would suggest an additional gratuity.

- <u>Bartenders</u> — 18-22% of the bill.
- <u>Coat check</u> — $5-10; mink or other fur suggests more $$. TIPS extended early — "To Insure Prompt Service."

The Bottom Line

Those who frequent certain establishments do so for a reason: excellent service and personalized attention. Servers converse among themselves and everyone in the restaurant knows the "good" tippers. These individuals are treated by everyone with the best service and attention and the utmost respect. The servers almost become like "family" and will treat you as such... only they get paid!

Remember, those in the service industry tolerate much from a varied clientele. The service industry is an extremely challenging profession which requires tremendous diplomacy, discretion and patience. It is appropriate to show appreciation for their standards of quality, dedicated service and personalized attention, accordingly.

Top Tips in Travel... More Ways To Be **Fabulous**:

Fine: Tip appropriately.

Fabulous: Leave cash together with personal letters of thanks (as stated) and...

Fabulous: Write an accolade letter to the General Manager or proprietor of the restaurant, the hotel, the cruise line and mention each person by name whose performance exceeded expectations, particularly those in management positions who do not accept tips. Speak to specific ways they enhanced your trip or visit.

In the tour/travel/hotel/hospitality industries, letters from guests are *everything*. Accolade letters, emails and telephone calls help with evaluations, promotions, even raises. Often times, letters are read aloud at staff meetings. Everyone likes compliments and few take the time to write, however, doing so is a **fabulous** gesture which is always **fabulous***ly* well-received, and a **fabulous** reflection on you. Make it a part of your regular business practice to write accolade letters as automatically as you prepare your expense report.

Expense Reports

Fine: List and delineate all expenses incurred through business travel.

Fabulous: It is <u>not</u> fabulous to submit a receipt for every single item you purchased during business travel.

STORY

The Chief of Police in Providence, Rhode Island, who makes $189,000 per year, submitted a receipt for a 39-cent banana. This was broadcast all over the news and in the newspapers.

Use common sense, and know that regardless of the fact that you may be making this trip for business, you will always be eating, i.e., a banana, drinking coffee, buying breath mints, etc. It is categorically <u>not</u> fabulous to submit a receipt for every ice cream cone, pack of gum or magazine you purchase during business travel; it's tacky.

Technology and Travel

Most people today travel with cell phones, laptops, tablets and other ways to stay connected. Let us consider the ramifications of trying to stay connected and being technologically efficient while traveling.

Staying Connected

Fine: Leave an "away" message on your voice mail and automatic reply email to let others know where you are, the nature of your business and when you will return.

Fabulous: Leaving an "away" message on your voice mail/email is unnecessary, counterproductive, and simply draws attention to the fact that you are *away*. Moreover, it is no one's business where you are, nor the nature of your business outside the office.

*Exception: If you plan to be out of your office for an extended period of time, i.e., on sabbatical or maternity leave, for example, then certainly leaving an "away" message is appropriate. When leaving this message, remember to state name of the individual to contact in your absence, including their contact information. However, if you are simply *away* for training or attending a conference, there is no need to explain or even share this information with everyone who calls. Simply be certain on your end that you check your voice and email messages frequently and respond promptly.

Fabulous: Send a brief email or voice mail to those with whom you interact regularly and inform them you will be traveling (specify dates). Be certain to follow-up upon return, accordingly.

In your message, provide the name and contact information that callers may access in your absence. Be sure those taking your messages are aware of who may try to reach you (and why), which depicts them as well-informed and you as **fabulous***!* Those who take your messages should also have your travel itinerary and contact information (not to be given out to random callers).

Being proactive in this regard demonstrates you are engaged, even though you may technically be *away.* This also shows you to be efficient, attentive to detail, respectful, and genuinely interested in growing in the relationship.

Social Networking

It has become commonplace for individuals to use social networking and post updates throughout the day, especially while traveling. A business trip may provide many interesting topics and situations about which to post or tweet. However, be careful and discreet. Do not post anything on the Internet you would not want to read on a billboard or seen on the evening news. This advice extends to Facebook updates and Twitter tweets. Being out of your office, you may tend to let down your guard, which could ultimately undermine and even hurt you professionally. What seems like an innocent or humorous remark can quickly turn into a form of self-sabotage and/or a major public relations disaster.

STORY

Consider the often-told story of the public relations executive who traveled to Memphis to meet with FedEx, which is headquartered in that city. The executive, who was from New York, had a rough morning and a less than pleasant encounter with someone at his hotel as he prepared to leave and attend the meeting. He decided to send a "tweet" about how much he disliked Memphis.

The result: he arrived at his meeting having just publicly insulted every single person there. He had bad-mouthed Memphis and then walked into a meeting full of Memphis residents. This "tweet" may have felt private and personal when he sent it, but it was widely read and distributed, and became a news story by later that afternoon.

(See Chapter 4, *Fabulous @ Electronic Communication* for more regarding social media protocol at home and on the road.)

> *"Being **fabulous** is having a favorite restaurant in every city you travel to."*
> **—Matt Schiffman**

Conclusion

Life is not about where we end up, but how we get there... it's about the journey. Business travel can be stressful and tedious, however, the savvy business traveler knows business travel presents *plus des* opportunities to *stand apart*. I urge you to draw from your extensive **fabulous** travel tool arsenal, expand your connections as you expand your horizons (!) while enriching the lives of others, and your own, along the way, and... enjoy the journey!

International Protocol Awareness

Understanding correct protocols in the global business arena is critical to succeed in today's global environment. Instant global communications and world travel make it commonplace to have business contacts and opportunities around the world. Successful business professionals preparing to conduct business overseas will take time to research and learn their target country's culture and traditions in advance of their visit.

Savvy business professionals understand that researching customs and traditions of one's target country is integral to functioning and thriving in our highly competitive global business climate. Doing so demonstrates respect toward our international business counterparts, and their culture, and will help us *stand apart*.

High Context vs. Low Context Cultures

Interestingly, given all the countries in the world, when it comes right down to it, there are only *two types* of cultures:

I. **High Context** cultures with <u>Polychronic Time</u> — Connected to history and tradition, very ritualistic; relationships based on trust and connections.

II. **Low Context** cultures with <u>Monochronic Time</u> — Here and now, "time is money," very individualistic; relationships based on performance and power.

These two cultures represent very different ways of conceptualizing and communicating including language — verbal and non-verbal communication, customs, perceived values and perceptions regarding time and space.

High Context Cultures (i.e., Asia, Africa, South America and much of the Middle East).

Characteristics:

- Collective group consensus (versus individual achievement).
- Intuition (rather than words, reason).
- Trust is paramount.
- Tradition-oriented, follow historical patterns.
- Emphasis on non-verbal behavioral styles, body language, voice, tone, gestures (sometimes, even the individuals' family status holds greater significance than the situation itself).
- Flowery language, humility and elaborate apologies are expected.

Low Context Cultures (i.e., North America, including U.S. and Canada, and much of Western Europe)

Characteristics:

- Individualism (vs. group opinions and achievements).
- Logical and linear; facts versus intuition.
- Direct and competitive; "time is money."
- More "here and now" oriented; change is good.
- Emphasis on verbal communication (what is said) versus the non-verbal message (what is implied).
- Freedom to openly question and challenge the status quo.

Key Topics to Consider in International Meetings

Most of the following guidelines are covered in the specific chapters relating to handshaking and business card exchange, attire, meeting, dining, etc.; we will not direct you to those chapters after each section, but feel free to refer to them for more in-depth discussions of protocol in these regards. Etiquette and protocol in High Context cultures are not just suggestions, they are tantamount to being hard-and-fast rules... rules which we are urged to follow if we want to establish and grow successful relationships in other parts of the world.

Handshaking

Handshaking is the most common form of greeting in the world today. It is wise to become acquainted in advance with different cultural handshakes around the world. Use their form of greeting from the outset and learn to say "hello" in their language to project a positive First Impression.

STORY

I met with Kerin McKinnon — director of strategic and global sales for Travel & Transport — a savvy, lovely senior executive who travels the world. Ms. McKinnon was preparing a presentation in Rome for client representatives from various parts of the world including Russia, the U.K., Asia, and the Middle East. She asked to review how to meet/greet/shake hands with each individual in the form of greeting to which they are accustomed. Greeting others in this way is gracious, smart, **fabulous**. This single gesture instantly generated high levels of respect and ignited volumes of good will.

Ms. McKinnon's attention to detail — quite literally from the first handshake and "hello" — unequivocally set her apart from the outset, demonstrated her commitment to growing an authentic relationship based on respect, and earned her their trust

Getting the Meeting

The only way we get the meeting, especially overseas, is by enlisting the help of the mutually respected third party.

Meet "level to level." (It is an insult to have an American company send over a lower-ranking individual to meet with the president of a company, for example; your president should be meeting with their president.) Be acutely aware of honoring rank and status — and even age, which is revered in High Context cultures.

Be prepared NOT to conduct business until after two or three initial meetings. During this time, we are basically being sized-up as to whether they even want to do business with us. Given that High Context cultures are very ritualistic in nature, we need to go through the 'evaluation process' in order to earn their *trust*.

Punctuality is respected. Prepare to arrive ten or fifteen minutes early. (More recently in China, however, there is much construction and traffic jams are real; therefore, arriving late for meetings in China these days is the norm and everyone understands. No one considers this an insult in any way.)

Expect to be kept waiting in the reception area, even though we are expected to be on time. Resist the urge to read a newspaper or open your briefcase. Remember we never want to, however inadvertently, suggest that something or someone else is more important than our *raison d'être* (the host). *Stand* in the waiting area, especially in High Context cultures, to show respect and to be prepared to greet your host. Expect to be met and evaluated by trusted business colleagues and even *close family members* during the first meeting.

Meeting Agenda

Fine: Preparing a meeting agenda is optional.

Fabulous: Have an agenda prepared:

- Even if there are only two bullet-points.
- Even if they do not have an agenda prepared, they will be impressed that you do.
- Be sure to put them on your agenda, too.
- Distribute the agenda in advance of the meeting.

This distinguishes you as a professional, shows you are prepared for this meeting, and that you have considered the contribution of everyone who will be at the meeting. This single action will earn you admiration and respect and help to kindle the trust factor.

Translators/Interpreters/Communication

Translators are tricky. We need them — however, we need to make sure we have the *right* one. Words, and their meanings and intentions, are so finely *nuanced,* that not having the *right* interpreter can actually damage the negotiation process. Knowing this presents yet another opportunity to *stand apart.*

Establish a bilingual business contact before arriving. Promotional or negotiating materials should be translated and printed before you leave, and be presented in their native language.

Fine: Use translators provided by your host country. (*Note that translation services in hotels are expensive and not always reliable.*)

Fabulous: Have your own translator.

*Never (physically) position translators between you and your host/s. The translator in this case will be regarded as a barrier and we do not want anyone or anything to literally stand between us and our host, or to interfere with the relationship we are so diligently endeavoring to cultivate.

*Look at your host/s (not the translator) while they are speaking. Make eye contact with your host/s; it is *our hosts'* words we are hearing and we are speaking with *them*.

Advance Research and Pre-planning

Anticipate reactions, objections, exceptions and be prepared to counter, squelch and close (in a culturally appropriate manner); expect your host/s to do the same.

Wherever your business may take you, research the customs and travel issues before you leave and have a person in place with whom you are able to consult during your trip.

Introductions — Know how to execute a formal business introduction. Remember, formality is an integral aspect of High Context cultures.

Honorifics — Addressing others by their first name too soon in the relationship is taboo; do not assume a first-name basis. Always use their honorific until invited to do otherwise. Even then, with senior executives, particularly in the presence of their subordinates, use their honorific as a sign of *respect*. Even if given permission to address this individual by their first name, do so privately, not in a business meeting or during formal negotiations. Titles and honorifics should always be used in professional settings.

Gestures of Hospitality are common — refusal may be misinterpreted. Hosts may offer and guests should accept a shot or a beer. A toast may be offered with an alcoholic beverage and then it is back to business as usual. (However, as noted in Chapter 9, *Fabulous @ Dining & Social Situations*, if you do not drink alcoholic beverages, simply thank your host/s for the kind offer and decline politely and quietly, "No, thank you," no explanation required.)

Hands and Forearms (versus elbows) — belong on the desk in the meeting (and while dining) — not on your lap. This shows you are not hiding anything (ref. sword!) and looks more professional.

Email — Do not mark "urgent" unless it is. We advise not requesting a "reply to sender" as this can be misinterpreted.

Sending Documents Hard Copy — Send via overnight mail or have hand-delivered for maximum impact.

<u>Professional Attire</u> — Conservative and quality are words governing professional attire the world over, regardless of gender. Whether in Europe, Asia, Africa, the Middle East or South America, informality and careless dress will undermine even the most talented executive.

Women: Skirts and dresses versus pants are considered most professional. Pearls and gold, dark colors, classic pumps, hosiery (always), neutral colored hose, closed necklines, hemlines just above the knee or even mid-calf is considered most professional.

<u>Casual Attire</u> — Casual dress, a workplace perk acceptable throughout corporate America, is not as common in other parts of the world. Sloppiness in dress, particularly in other countries, casts a less than positive impression and may even cause others to question our professional credibility.

<u>Business Card Exchange</u> — Remember to present and receive a business card face-up with either 1) Two thumbs on either top corner (most formal) or 2) One thumb on one top corner (the less formal method), and receive "in kind." *Acknowledging* the card is the most important point of business card exchange. After receiving the card, place this someplace *respectful* (refer to Chapter 2, *Fabulous @ Handshaking & Business Cards* for more details). In Japan, we honor the most important person by placing their business card on top of our portfolio.

<u>Vernacular</u> — Colloquialisms, use of slang, telling jokes, and certainly all vulgarity should be avoided.

<u>Gestures</u> — have meaning and hold significance in various countries which may easily be misinterpreted. For instance, the thumb and forefinger "O.K." sign and the "V" for Victory mean completely different things in other cultures, and may be quite negative.

<u>Reversal of the Surname</u> — In many cultures, including China and Japan, introductions are made with the last name first... but also, out of respect for Westerners, the order is often changed to accommodate international visitors. Therefore, when you are introduced to "Wu Shi," you should ascertain that they have not reversed the surname (out of consideration for you) and that this is in fact Mr. Wu, and not Mr. Shi!

In fact, the first name is never used in Japan, even in an informal setting, and a formal bow is always part of the initial introduction.

<u>Religion/Prayer</u> — In many countries, there are often social and religious underpinnings, ceremonies or other activities that carry through to business expectations. Awareness of these shows respect for colleagues' cultural backgrounds.

<u>Language</u> — Endeavor to learn some key words and phrases of their native language, enough to demonstrate you have made the effort — even if your pronunciation is a bit off. This goes a long way in terms of endearing yourself to your hosts in any country around the world.

STORY

On President John F. Kennedy's first state visit to France, which was indeed a storied visit, he was accompanied by his wife, Jacqueline. Mrs. Kennedy spoke fluent French and gave a speech in that language, completely bedazzling not only the audience, but the world. President and Mrs. DeGaulle were charmed as Mrs. Kennedy continued to speak French with them during lunch.

The diplomatic trip to France was a huge success. The French people loved Mrs. Kennedy and everyone was abuzz about the visit... to the point where President Kennedy, opening his first press conference upon his return, famously said, "I am the man who accompanied Jacqueline Kennedy to Paris... and I enjoyed it."

Eating Habits — vary from country to country. Be aware that in other countries such as China, for example, Americans may be struck by the high noise levels while dining. Elbows, which we were always taught did NOT belong on the table here in America, rest comfortably on a Chinese table. Because they come from a history of such extreme poverty, Chinese people let nothing go to waste and eat everything they can including dogs, fish eyes, body organs, fingernails, very rare mushrooms (a great delicacy) and rooster's feet (very bony). Also, there is *beaucoup de* slurping! Bringing soup cup to lips and using chopsticks to literally shovel noodles or rice into one's mouth is the norm. Eating unfamiliar foods considered delicacies in various countries is important; refusal can be highly insulting. Eat, but swallow quickly! Remember, you may always consider "Deferring the honor... to your host!" (See Chapter 9, *Fabulous @ Dining & Social Situations* for the story under Global Dining.)

Entertaining — While it is gracious to serve their foods to help make international guests feel at home when they visit us here in the U.S., bear in mind that they always eat their own foods. Therefore, serving typically American meals, or the chef's signature dish, will give international visitors a taste of our country (pun intended) and tradition, making them feel welcomed and special.

The Presentation — Use table linen, porcelain china or a silver tea service versus paper plates, napkins, or Styrofoam cups. Formality is "never wrong" and a highly valued characteristic of High Context cultures.

Entertainment — is always appreciated and part of the international business landscape, i.e., a harpist, guitarist, pianist, violinist, flautist, or depending on the occasion, a band. Be prepared to reciprocate entertaining as a gift.

A Banquet — is considered an excellent gift to either give or even reciprocate.

STORY

I hosted a banquet my last night in Beijing, inviting all of my hosts and others I had met during my journey. They let me know, emphatically, how much they appreciated this gesture. Hosting a banquet is thoughtful, gracious and smart as this is also a lovely way to create a (another) memory which will linger long after final farewells.

ANOTHER STORY

My brother Stephen and his fiancée just returned from Norway where they were visiting his childhood friend Gunnar and his wife, who is quite ill. As a farewell gift my brother arranged to have a violinist come to their home on the last night of their stay to give a concert of sorts, to the couple, their family and closest friends who had assembled.

Eye Contact — The meaning of direct eye contact with individuals varies from country to country. In some countries looking down or away is seen as being weak, shy, or hiding something; in others, a direct gaze is considered insulting, challenging or presumptuous. Research your target country in advance of the visit.

Restaurant Etiquette — In America, whoever follows the *maitre d'* in a restaurant is the person of honor. Socially, the woman precedes the gentleman; in business, however, the client, regardless of gender, is always the person of honor and should follow the *maitre d'*, trailed by the host/s.

This procedure varies in other countries. In Europe, Latin America and Asia for example, the man always leads his guest/s (men and women) and follows the *maitre d'* first — to check the restaurant out for "safety" — the woman or person of honor and other guests follow.

Tipping — Know who, what, how much, where, when and when *not* to tip. Be aware that throughout most of Europe and Asia tipping ("service") is included in the bill. When in doubt always ask, especially if you are hosting the meal. Remember to take care of the bill in advance, discreetly.

Note: Tipping for buffet is 10% (versus 18 to 22%) here in the U.S.

Limousines

Fine: White or cream limousines are used mostly for weddings and social occasions.

Fabulous: Black, navy or even forest green (rare) are most professional.

Limousine/Car Etiquette — The host is always seated to the rear right of the car or limousine. *Exception*: Japan, where the host sits to the rear left.

It is gracious of the host to defer the position of honor to their person/guest of honor.

*President John Kennedy often gave the honor seat to his wife.

Colors — hold different meanings in various countries, and may even be considered offensive or unlucky. White linen, for example, is almost universally considered the most formal table linen the world over — with the exception of China, where white is considered the symbol of death. Colors such as (i.e.) red and gold are ideal, **fabulous** in China. Research and adhere to colors and customs considered acceptable in your host's country.

<u>Gifting</u> — is a big part of the international business landscape. *"Presentation,"* again, is *everything* — especially in High Context cultures. Be aware of colors used in wrapping gifts which may be potentially offensive in themselves, as well as certain numbers and bows which are considered unlucky. Then, there is the gift itself to consider. Know how, what and when to gift, and be careful not to out-gift!

The gift need not be expensive. Gifts may be useful or completely superfluous items; however, there should be thought and even symbolism in the gift selection. Those in High Context cultures particularly appreciate gifts from name brand stores (don't we all!). The gift may be associated with you, your company, state or country or something specific to them, their country or personal interests. Sports memorabilia, music or books you believe they may enjoy, for example, are almost universally appreciated.

I often bring a signed copy of my own books and say, "I come bearing gifts!" which is unexpected, a (thoughtful) gesture and a **fabulous** way to open the meeting. Bring something personal such as a white paper you wrote or a sample of your blog. Company logo items, coffee table books (remember to personally inscribe the book and remove the price before gifting), a (monogrammed) key chain, a symbolic book marker, mugs, golf shirts, in fact anything personalized or monogrammed is appropriate.

*Some countries regard any sharp item such as a letter opener life-threatening and gifting this may be misinterpreted. Best to stay with "safe" gifts. Think of items they will *use* with special thoughts of *you*.

STORY

You may have heard me share this story, and if you have already heard it, please indulge me. A friend who lived in Boston called to say he had been invited to the home of a prominent CEO for dinner and wanted to discuss some gift ideas.

We decided that since Boston is renowned for the Boston Symphony Orchestra we thought of gifting a CD of the BSO and, for the all-important presentation... we decided that presenting this in a silver or leather monogrammed CD case avec his monogram, was a capital idea. My client preferred the leather case.

We ended up placing his host's first initial to the left, his WIFE's first initial on the right and THEIR last (name) initial in the middle... being inclusive! Mr. and Mrs. "W" will always have this gift of music, the CD and the beautifully monogrammed leather case, and think of their fabulously thoughtful guest, forever.

Another gift idea is one which highlights our particular knowledge or connections. For example, I know a restaurant owner who, when he makes business calls, may bring a box of gourmet cookies saying, "This is a new vendor I've discovered." This not only makes a nice gift, it highlights the special inside knowledge of the giftor while bestowing acknowledgement regarding the new, up-and-coming vendor. This gesture reflects fabulously well on everyone.

If you know someone who enjoys cigars, you may care to consider personalizing the cigar wrapper. My husband and I private label wine and gift this frequently.

Thank You Notes — As always, take the time to send a thank you note to your cross-cultural hosts.

Fine: Send a quick email note of thanks when you get home.

Fabulous: Thank you notes should be hand-delivered, particularly in other countries.

- Send a note to each person you met even if they were not on the original meeting agenda.
- Be sure to *personalize* the note.
- Have your note hand-delivered the next day, especially in High Context cultures.

Keep individual records about those you meet, and be sure to follow up... having details about people you met while traveling can make or break relationships. Send personal notes and thank you notes again when you return from your business trip. "Thank you" can never be said enough in High Context cultures. Make sending these your regular business practice, as automatic as preparing your expense report. Invest in quality personalized stationery to use for these notes.

Personal Space — is to be respected at all costs. Please know that personal space, one's "comfort zone," varies as we travel to various countries.

Examples: North Americans prefer one arm's length of distance, while those in Great Britain prefer more like two arms' length of distance for their comfort zone — and those in Asia prefer closer to *three* arms' length of distance for their comfort zone. Many European nations such as France or Italy have much smaller "comfort zones," and Latin American comfort zones may feel as though they are measured in inches rather than arm lengths! When preparing to conduct business in Latin America, women executives should be particularly aware that Latin American professionals mean no offense when standing very close or touching. This is simply their way.

Sitting — Avoid exposing the soles of the foot. Throughout Europe and Asia, the sole of the foot is the lowest form of being. To display this however inadvertently, may be interpreted as an insult. Ladies' legs should *slope* — either to the right or left. (See Chapter 6, *Fabulous @ The Meeting* for more details about sitting.)

Touching, Hugging, Kissing, Embracing — Customs vary from country to country. When receiving those from other cultures, it is respectful to greet them in the form they are most accustomed, out of respect. (See Chapter 2, *Fabulous @ Handshaking & Business Cards*, for more details on professional greetings in different countries.)

Be aware of *subtleties* in certain cultures, for example, knowing the Japanese will never say "No" because they are a gracious culture and do not wish to offend. Rather, "Perhaps not at this time" or "This may not be possible" are more to be expected. Read between the lines and understand that this subtly really means "No way" ... "Not going to happen."

In Saudi Arabia, for instance, Orthodox Muslim men are supposed to ignore females outside their immediate family. Women, generally speaking, have been taught to know their "place" which is why the Arab Spring is so important. Orthodox Muslim men are not even supposed to inquire about a male friend's female relatives. One should never ask the question "How is your wife?" in this case, even though it is courteous elsewhere to inquire about a colleague's family.

STORY

My friend Catherine recommended our Professional Presence services to the Royal Family of Saudi Arabia during one of their visits to Boston. During one visit, sitting in their elegant suite overlooking the Boston Garden, on one very hot summer day, I asked the ladies, "Boston is beautiful and the view is spectacular, however, would you ever like to get away from the city and visit the country? They replied, "Yes!" and I called my husband right away to say, "Honey, guess who's coming to dinner?"

We scheduled a visit for several weeks from that date and during this time, we were literally preparing to host Royalty — so I had every piece of silver polished, made sure that every crevice in every screen glistened, all of the horses were washed, saddles polished and buffed (the little princesses wanted to ride) and we engaged a caterer who specialized in their culture's food preferences, restrictions, etc.

We live in a sleepy, very rural community. You can imagine the reaction when a caravan of twenty black and navy SUVs journeyed together down our little main street! Upon arrival at our farm, the security staff jumped out of the SUVs and started combing the landscape, checking it out for "safety." There was no way anyone was in those trees, but this was exciting for us to witness royal security "in action!" We were very careful not to take photos, although we did respectfully ask for and received one, which is special.

We enjoyed a lovely afternoon, my husband and the prince puffing away on their cigars, solving the problems of the world together on our front porch, while the princesses, my friend Catherine and I were sipping tea in another area, also solving some of the world's problems — especially those pertaining to women's issues. The security service was in "relax" mode, eating heartily in the kitchen.

Being true to (their) protocol and decorum, the Prince and Princess graciously invited my husband and me, as well as Catherine and her friend Richard, to be their guests for dinner at their hotel to thank us for hosting them. This was another very special and memorable occasion where we all continued to solve many of the world's problems, this time American-style, men and women together.

My husband and I were truly honored to host the Royal Family in our home. This was a privilege and an honor, one we will always treasure and remember fondly.

In *India*, male colleagues automatically shake hands; however, businesswomen may make the decision whether or not to extend their hand together with a vocal greeting. Keep in mind, too, that conflict and aggressive negotiation in certain counties, particularly in India, is to be avoided at all costs.

STORY

My wonderful cousin, Kevin "The Doctor," recently married a beautiful, equally accomplished journalist and television documentary producer from India. Their friends came from all over the world and our entire family assembled to share this special day and experience (my first) very special, exquisitely beautiful authentic Indian wedding ceremony.

At this event, I met Seema's gracious, handsome and charming brother Jay. Being aware of Indian tradition, I wanted to show respect yet it took every ounce of my self-control not to offer my hand or a big hug when we first met. Jay read my body language and, rather than shake hands, we made strong eye-contact, and so it was! We ultimately broke with tradition, and kissed and hugged later, as we left the celebration. The beauty in knowing the rules is knowing when it is okay to break them!

Faux Pas

Finally, if we do commit a *faux pas* (and everyone does), recovery is key. Our honest effort in trying is respected and appreciated.

The one universal action: the SMILE. A smile is used and understood by every culture in every country in the world. A smile can be THE most effective form of communication.

In the final analysis, regardless of how skilled or untutored someone is in matters pertaining to protocol, the greatest compliment one can pay to anyone anywhere in the world is to show we have made the effort to learn their language, their culture and traditions, and demonstrate a sincere and genuine interest in *them*... What else do we take the time, go to the trouble, make the effort, to learn about in advance, practice, master, execute? Bottom line, *trust* is established and business opportunity will abound.

FAREWELL
&
BONNE JOURNÉE

Thank you for joining me on this adventure in business etiquette and protocol, and letting me share some of my life's experiences with you. I hope you have enjoyed our journey together through this book, and perhaps picked up a few pearls along the way.

I believe deeply that it is our responsibility and our honor to perpetuate timeless, traditional American values of pride, freedom, respect, civility. It is important for us to reinforce deferential, respectful behaviors, to help educate our students and business professionals at all levels, and to be aware of the power we each have to make a real difference in each others' lives every day. Our conduct is key because the way we are perceived by others is real — whether face-to-face at an industry function, a business meeting, a client lunch, or on the social media network.

It is my greatest hope that this book will help create awareness that everyday business situations and routine interpersonal interactions present boundless opportunities for us *stand apart* and advance. When we take the time — even a split second — and make the effort to display common courtesies and show respect, we make others feel *acknowledged,* special — while ultimately, reflecting well on us and helping to build *trust* with colleagues and clients alike. Moving from **fine** to **fabulous** costs nothing and means everything.

Remember, life is not about where we end up, but how we get there... enjoy the journey!

ABOUT THE AUTHOR

Judith Bowman is an educator, author, syndicated journalist, and internationally recognized authority on business etiquette and international protocol. Enlightened by twenty years of face-to-face sales and marketing encounters, revelations, and *faux pas* from her work in corporate America, Bowman launched her consulting business in 1992. She counsels Fortune 500 professionals, political leaders, and royalty. Her first book, *Don't Take the Last Donut* (The Career Press) is translated into ten languages, sold in twelve countries, and featured on the recommended reading list of multinational firms, educational institutions, and leading motivational life coaches.

Ms. Bowman has earned and now provides protocol certification including Train the Trainer programs. She is a graduate of Boston College and attended Harvard University. Ms. Bowman authored a weekly etiquette column for the Pulitzer prize-winning Eagle Tribune Publishing Company that was syndicated throughout New England for ten years, and hosted a weekly television segment on New England Cable news for four years. Bowman's views have been sought by *Forbes, CFO, Newsweek, CNN Everyday Money, Business Week, Boston Business Journal, Los Angeles Times, Boston Globe, Boston Herald,* to name a few.

Judith Bowman Enterprises
Protocol Consultants International
400 Putnam Pike, Suite D, #212
Smithfield, RI 02917
Telephone: 401.934.0100
Fax: 401.934.0200
Email: info@howtostandapart.com
www.protocolconsultants.com